FRENCH GRAMMAR

D1293533

*the text of this book is printed
on 100% recycled paper*

COLLEGE OUTLINE SERIES

FRENCH GRAMMAR

FRANCIS M. DU MONT

Late Head of
Department of Romance Languages
The Pennsylvania State College

Second Edition

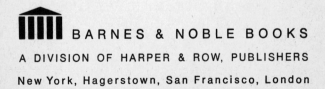
BARNES & NOBLE BOOKS

A DIVISION OF HARPER & ROW, PUBLISHERS

New York, Hagerstown, San Francisco, London

©

Second Edition, 1950

Copyright, 1941, 1950

by BARNES & NOBLE, INC.

Copyright Renewed, 1969

All rights reserved. No part of this book may be reproduced or utilized in any form or by any means, electronic or mechanical, including photocopying or recording, or by any information storage and retrieval system, without written permission from the publisher.

L. C. catalogue card number: 50-7079

SBN 389 00052 3

77 78 79 80   12 11 10 9 8 7

Manufactured in the United States of America

Preface

This Outline of French is essentially a Review Grammar.

It is intended to serve as a textbook in Intermediate French classes. It also may be of considerable help to the student reviewing his French in preparation for the College Entrance or Regents Examinations.

Its purpose is to present systematically the various grammatical elements scattered all over the Beginners' Grammars. Each part of speech is treated separately. The student is supplied with a compact, coherent, and logical picture of each part of speech in itself and of its function in the sentence. New grammar points, not contained in Elementary Grammars, are presented and discussed so as to widen the student's grammatical horizon. Thus, while re-learning or learning more thoroughly what he has already tried to assimilate in his first attempts at the French language, the student will come into contact with new material, new grammatical perspectives. The monotony of reviewing will be broken, and the interest in the study of French will be greatly enhanced thereby.

Each lesson is divided into the following five sections:

1. Grammar Study
2. Verb Review
3. Vocabulary
4. Idiomatic Expressions
5. Exercises

Grammar is presented as concisely and yet as completely as possible in a book of this nature. Every rule stated is elucidated by examples which may be taken by the students as models for sentence construction.

Because of the importance of the verb in the sentence and the neglect of the study of verbs among the students, this second section or *Verb Review* has been deemed essential. It not only furnishes the student with the usual verb forms but offers him as well information about their use in the sentence and about such other

vii

points of grammar as are directly or indirectly connected with the verb.

As the student who uses this Review Grammar is concentrating all his attention upon the constructive work in French, the thumbing of the General Vocabulary would naturally distract him from his task. And yet, an adequate vocabulary is needed. To place a vocabulary at his immediate disposal, a special reference *Vocabulary—French-English* and *English-French*—which contains the immediately needed new words for the *Exercises* is added to each lesson.

Idiomatic Expressions, the fourth section of each lesson, offers to the student's attention the more usual idiomatic expressions entering into the everyday language of the French. These idioms must be used if the student wants to give his constructive work the savor of French.

Finally, a variety of exercises terminate each lesson so as to render the present Outline practical. Most of these exercises should be translated and many of them ought to become a topic for discussions as regards grammatical construction.

An Appendix which contains the verb forms of the auxiliaries *avoir* and *être,* the conjugations of the regular verbs, and the principal parts of irregular verbs together with an alphabetical list of the idiomatic expressions which make up Section 4, and a General Vocabulary—French-English and English-French—conclude this *French Grammar.*

I wish to take advantage of this opportunity to express my sincerest and thankful appreciation to my colleague and friend, Dr. Jean Baptiste Cloppet, of The Pennsylvania State College, for his careful reading of my manuscript and his valuable suggestions; also, to Augusta Barnet (Mrs. M. L. Zaphiropoulos), Licenciée-ès-lettres, University of Paris, of the Barnes & Noble staff, and to Professor André Lévêque, Ph.D., University of Wisconsin.

F. M. du Mont

Table of Contents

	PAGE
Preface	vii
Practical Hints	xiii
French Alphabet	xv
Vowel and Consonant Combinations	xvi
Introduction to French Pronunciation	xvii
Terms Relating to Grammar	xli

LESSON

Preface

I The Definite Article.—Contractions with **de** and **à**—Use of the Definite Article—Verb Review: Present, Imperfect, Past Definite of **avoir** and **être**—Present and Past Participles 1

II Indefinite Article—Its Use—The Partitive Article—Verb Review: Future of **avoir** and **être**—Verbs **porter, finir,** and **vendre** in the Present, Imperfect, Past Definite, and Future Indicative—Irregular Stems of the Future 8

III The Noun—Gender—Number—Verb Review: Compound Tenses—Conditional Present and Perfect 15

IV The Qualifying Adjectives—Formation of the Feminine and the Plural—Position—Comparison—Comparative Sentence—Verb Review: Principal Parts—Present and Principal Parts of **aller, devoir,** and **faire** 25

V The Possessive — Demonstrative — Interrogative Adjectives—Verb Review: Interrogative Form of Verbs—Present and Principal Parts of **pouvoir, vouloir,** and **dire** 37

VI Numeral and Indefinite Adjectives—Verb Review: Negative-Interrogative Form of Verbs—Impersonal Verbs—Present and Principal Parts of **connaître, savoir,** and **mettre** 45

LESSON   PAGE

VII   The Personal Pronouns—Conjunctive Pronouns
      and Their Position—Disjunctive Pronouns and Their
      Use—Verb Review: Orthographic Peculiarities of
      Verbs—Pronominal Form of Verbs—Present and
      Principal Parts of **prendre, partir,** and **venir**   52

VIII Possessive and Demonstrative Pronouns—Verb Re-
      view: Orthographic Peculiarities (continued)—Im-
      perative Mood—Present and Principal Parts of
      voir, rire, and **suivre**   62

 IX   The Relative Pronoun—Simple and Compound Rel-
      ative Pronouns—Verb Review: Idiomatic Uses of
      aller, pouvoir, and **savoir**—Present and Principal
      Parts of **croire, courir,** and **vivre**   70

  X   Interrogative and Indefinite Pronouns—Word Order
      in Interrogative Sentences—Verb Review: Idio-
      matic Uses of **devoir** and **connaître**—Present and
      Principal Parts of **falloir, boire,** and **battre**   79

 IX   The Verb—Conjugations—Voices—Moods—Tenses
      —Verbal Endings—Verb Review: Idiomatic Uses of
      falloir and **faire**—Present and Principal Parts of
      craindre, croître, and **plaire**   89

XII   The Present and Imperfect Indicative—Their Use
      —Intransitive Verbs of Motion—Verb Review:
      Idiomatic Uses of **vouloir** and **plaire**—Present and
      Principal Parts of **mourir** and **naître**   96

XIII The Perfect and Past Definite—Their Use—Verb
      Review: Passive Voice—Present and Principal
      Parts of **mouvoir, vêtir,** and **lire**   107

XIV   The Pluperfect and Past Anterior—Their Use—
      Verb Review: Substitutions for the Passive Voice—
      Idiomatic Use of **valoir** and **penser**—Present and
      Principal Parts of **asseoir, écrire,** and **fuir**   116

 XV   The Future and Future Anterior—Their Use—
      Verb Review: Irregular Model Verbs—Idiomatic

LESSON
                                                                  PAGE

Use of **tenir** and **mettre**—Present and Principal Parts of **recevoir, pourvoir,** and **vaincre**   125

XVI   Present and Perfect Conditional—Their Use—Verb Review: Conditional Sentences—Present and Principal Parts of **luire, maudire,** and **coudre**   133

XVII   The Subjunctive—Why a Subjunctive in French?—Where Should the Subjunctive Be Used? — Verb Review: Formation of the Subjunctive Tenses — Present and Principal Parts of **valoir, acquérir,** and **suffire**   140

XVIII   The Tenses of the Subjunctive—Their Use—Sequence of Subjunctive Tenses—Verb Review: Agreement of Past Participles—Irregular Subjunctive Forms   152

XIX   The Infinitive Mood—Its Use—Verb Review: Verbal Syntax—Present and Principal Parts of **assaillir** and **bouillir**   161

XX   The Imperative and Participial Moods—Their Use—Verb Review: Verbal Syntax—Present and Principal Parts of **conclure, conduire,** and **envoyer**   171

XXI   The Adverb—Its Formation and Position—Comparison of Adverbs—Verb Review: Translation of "how long"—Present and Principal Parts of **traire, moudre,** and **résoudre**   178

XXII   Prepositions and Conjunctions—Verb Review: Use of **ne,** without **pas,** in Verbal Expressions—Present and Principal Parts of **cueillir, tenir,** and **hair**   186

APPENDIX   203

  1. Verb Forms: Conjugations of
     (a) Auxiliaries **avoir** and **être**   203
     (b) Three Regular Conjugations in the Active, Passive, and Pronominal Voices   208
  2. Principal Parts of Irregular Verbs   218
  3. List of Idiomatic Expressions   226

LESSON

PAGE

VOCABULARIES

1. French-English Vocabulary   235
2. English-French Vocabulary   252

INDEX

263

Practical Hints

1. *Plan long periods of study.* Long periods of concentration, such as two or three hours at a sitting, are needed in learning a foreign language, for it takes time to settle down, review preceding lessons, and practice new word forms until they become familiar.

2. *Study each lesson thoroughly in accordance with a systematic plan.* Your plan of work may include the following steps: (a) study the rules of grammar and apply them in thinking, speaking, and writing; (b) read the verb review orally, then write the verb forms and use them in many French sentences; (c) master the vocabulary by making up oral and written sentences based on the new words and idioms; (d) do the exercises orally two or three times before writing them.

3. *Test yourself before and after studying.* Before you begin a new lesson, list the things you know about each rule of grammar and all other topics treated in the lesson. Then concentrate on the doubtful points. For example, if you do not remember a particular verb form, look it up at once, study it carefully, and use it in reading, speaking, and writing. Also write the conjugations of similar verbs and use these verbs in French sentences of your own. Near the end of your study period, close your book and write a summary of what you have studied, checking your summary against the book.

4. *Apply each rule of grammar in speaking, reading, and writing.* Analyze the French example to see how the rule works. Compare the French example with the English translation, noting differences in construction. Restate the rule in your own words and find or construct more examples to illustrate it. As you apply any rule, think in French instead of translating into English. Finally, to test your understanding of the rule, cover the French example and translate from English into French.

5. *In studying verbs, bear in mind their two parts: the stem and the ending.* The stems of regular verbs change in only two instances: (a) in the future and conditional present tenses of verbs

whose infinitives form the tense-stems; (b) in a few first-conjugation verbs which undergo orthographic changes. The endings of irregular verbs are very much alike, though some of them may differ considerably in the present indicative and the past definite. You should review all the principal parts of each verb and analyze the way a particular tense is derived.

6. *Memorize new words and idioms through use.* For this purpose the following are useful suggestions: (a) find each word in its French context or use it in a French sentence, get the meaning from the context and compose your own definition, comparing with that of the text; (b) use each word or phrase in thinking, speaking, and writing original French sentences; (c) examine the words for their English cognates and note any differences in meaning; (d) pronounce each new word distinctly and listen carefully to sound and accent, noting especially the difference in tonality between the French word and its English cognate; (e) study the grammatical construction and the thought of each French idiom and contrast with its English equivalent; (f) do not translate idioms literally; state their meanings in idiomatic English.

7. *Supplement the exercises with additional phrases and sentences.* Express an idea in more than one way in French. This will help you to develop versatility and feeling for the language. Read the French passages again and again, without translating into English, until you grasp the full meaning of each passage. Write in French many facts and ideas which supplement, change, or contradict the statements in the exercises. Check your work by consulting the rules, examples, conjugations, and vocabulary.

8. *Practice conversation.* Try studying with a classmate so that you can check each other's pronunciation and learn to use French in life situations. The section "Introduction to French Pronunciation" will help you to use correctly the thirty-seven French speech-sounds. Note that each phonetic symbol represents only a single sound. Master the speech-sounds and symbols thoroughly. Most of the sounds have English equivalents or near-equivalents. Sounds with no English equivalents you must learn by ear.

9. *Check your work carefully.* Make constant use of the last section of the book, which includes: (a) the three regular conjugations; (b) the conjugations of *avoir* and *être;* (c) the principal parts of irregular verbs; (d) a list of idiomatic expressions; (e) a French-English and an English-French vocabulary.

FRENCH ALPHABET

Character	Name	Phonetic Symbol	Examples
a	a	a, ɑ	la, pas
b	bé	b	bébé
c	cé	k, s	cas, ce
d	dé	d	dos
e	é	e, ɛ, ə	pré, père, le
f	effe	f	fort
g	gé	g, ʒ	gant, géré
h[1]	ache	–	homme
i	i	i	il, île
j	ji	ʒ	joli
k	ka	k	kilo
l	elle	l	lit, lu
m	emme	m	mon, ma
n	enne	n	nous, né
o	o	o, ɔ	mot, note
p	pé	p	par
q	ku	k	que, coq
r	erre	R, r	ri, rue
s	esse	s, z	si, pose
t	té	t	ta, tête
u	u	y	nu, mû
v	vé	v	va, vu
w	double vé	v	wagon
x[2]	iks	ks, gs, s, z	sexe, exact, dix
y	i grec	i, j	cycle, yeux
z	zède	z	zèle

[1] "H" is always silent, even when it is aspirate: le héros [ləero].

[2] "X" in linking or liaison takes the sound of "z": dix amis [dizami]; it is silent before a consonant: dix tables [ditaːbl].

VOWEL AND CONSONANT COMBINATIONS

Combinations	Phonetic Symbol	Approximate English Equivalents	Examples
ai, aî	ɛ	bed	plaine, maître
ay + consonant	ɛ	bed	Raymond
ay + vowel	ɛj, ɛɪj	—	payez, paye
au, eau	o	go	autour, eau
au + r	ɔ	not	aura
ei	ɛ	bed	reine
ey final	ɛ	bed	Jersey
ey + vowel	ɛj	—	asseyez
eu, œu	ø	—	feu, vœu
eu, œu + sounded consonant	œ	bu(r)n	neuf, œuf
oi, oî	wa, wɑ	war	moi, croître
oy	waj, wɑj	—	soyez, croyons
ou + consonant	u	toot	toujours

Semiconsonants:

y, i, ï, il, ill	j	yes	yeux, rien, païen bail, fille
ou + vowel	w	we	oui, ouest, ouate
u + vowel	ɥ	—	lui, fruit, nuée
am, an, em, en	ã	can't [känt]	ample, an, temple, en
im, in, aim, ain, eim, ein, ym, yn	ɛ̃	sang	impie, fin, faim, vain, Reims, sein, thym, synthèse
om, on	ɔ̃	song	nom, ont, non
um, un	œ̃	sung	parfum, humble, un
ch	ʃ	she	chercher
ge, gi, j	ʒ	azure	cage, gilet, je
gn	ɲ	—	digne, gagne

INTRODUCTION
TO
FRENCH PRONUNCIATION

There are two methods of learning to pronounce French correctly: the imitational and the phonetic. By the former method the student imitates the speech-sounds of a competent teacher or native; by the latter method, basically grounded on imitation until the thirty-seven French speech-sounds have been thoroughly mastered, he compares the graphic signs (or spellings) representing a single speech-sound with the phonetic symbol which carries that sound. Then, when speaking, he renders each graphic sign by the sound attached to its phonetic symbol. English counterparts of the French speech-sounds, if carefully chosen, will be helpful in the early stages of the study of French pronunciation.

NOTE. Stress on syllables of a French word of two or more syllables is even, except that there is generally slightly greater stress on the last syllable. If the last vowel of a word of two or more syllables is [ə], the stress is on the next to last syllable.

The following table is set up to illustrate the phonetic method. We take as an example French open **e**, which has as its English counterpart the **e** in **met**.

French open **e** sound is represented:

in phonetics by:	in spelling by:	as in
[ɛ] sounded as **e** in **met**	è	père
	ê	rêve
	ë	Noël
	e + 2 consonants	ferme
	e + silent final t	jet
	e + final sounded consonant	sel
	ai (except in verb endings), aî	plaine, maître
	ay + consonant	Raymond
	ay + vowel	rayon
	ei	peine
	ey + vowel	asseyez
	ey final	jersey
	eil, eill + vowel	réveil, veille

A student of French who wishes to know the correct pronunciation of the word "mettaient" will take the following steps:

1.   He will look up the sound value of **e** and **ai,** represented in the preceding table as being equivalent to that of the phonetic symbol [ɛ].

2.   He will find that the final **-ent,** being a verb ending, is silent.

3.   Examining the sound values of **m** and **t,** he will find them to be counterparts of English **m** and **t,** except for the latter's aspirate character.

Hence he will pronounce "mettaient" as indicated by the phonetic notation [mɛtɛ], which is the correct pronunciation.

This method of procedure is facilitated by the fact that there are many English counterparts—equivalents or near-equivalents —of the French speech-sounds.   By learning the sounds of the French phonetic symbols and their graphic counterparts, the student will increase the rapidity and accuracy with which he can speak French.

In the following pages we shall study—always in connection with the phonetic speech-sound notation—the pronunciation of (1) the vowels and consonants in single words and (2) connected speech in so far as it is affected by the mute **e,** linking or liaison, and intonation.

THE SINGLE WORD

Vowels

French has sixteen vowels, of which twelve are called *oral*, and four, *nasal*.   The twelve oral vowels include eight fundamental vowels, one neuter vowel (mute e), and three mixed vowels.   There are also three semivowels or semiconsonants.

According to their place of articulation, oral vowels are either *front* or *back* vowels; according to the formation of the lips, *unrounded* or *rounded*.   Flattening or protruding of the lips is an essential factor in the formation of French vowel sounds.

As a rule vowels are short in French.   They may, however, become long.   In phonetic sound notation (ː) after a vowel is the sign for length.   A long vowel occurs:

1.   When a vowel is stressed and immediately followed by

consonant sounds [j], [v], [ʒ], [z], or [r] in the final sounded syllable of a word:

fille	cave	cage	vase	avare
[fiːj]	[kaːv]	[kaːʒ]	[vɑːz]	[avaːr]

2. When a circumflexed vowel in the last syllable is followed by a sounded consonant, except in verb endings:

naître	âme	pâtre	maître	tête
[nɛːtr]	[ɑːm]	[pɑːtr]	[mɛːtr]	[tɛːt]

3. When stressed oral vowel [a], [ɑ], [ɛ], [o], or [ø] is followed by a sounded consonant or consonant combination:

oracle	sable	reine	tome	émeute
[ɔraːkl]	[sɑːbl]	[rɛːn]	[toːm]	[emøːt]

4. When a stressed vowel is nasalized and followed by a sounded consonant:

tante	pente	pinte	fonte	défunte
[tɑ̃ːt]	[pɑ̃ːt]	[pɛ̃ːt]	[fɔ̃ːt]	[defœ̃ːt]

French vowels are divided into four categories: fundamental, neutral, mixed, and nasal, to which must be added the semivowels or semiconsonants.

The Fundamental Vowels. There are eight fundamental vowel sounds. Their place of articulation and the position of the lips are indicated in the following phonetic triangle.

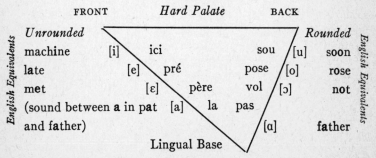

PHONETIC TRIANGLE

English equivalents of French vowel-sounds should be considered approximate, not identical, counterparts.

The fundamental vowel sounds are known as *close* or *open* sounds according to the smaller or greater distance of the tongue from the hard palate at the time when these various sounds are pronounced. Hence the following vowel sound groups:

i =   close [i] si   a = $\begin{cases} \text{close [a] la} \\ \text{open [ɑ] passe} \end{cases}$ o = $\begin{cases} \text{close [o] do} \\ \text{open [ɔ] port} \end{cases}$

e = $\begin{cases} \text{close [e] pré} \\ \text{open [ɛ] père} \end{cases}$ ou   close [u] sou

The tables in this section show the relation between the phonetic speech-sound notation and the various ways in which the respective sound is spelled. By associating these varied spellings with the speech-sounds carried by the phonetic symbols one can learn to pronounce French correctly. We have added to the treatment of every vowel an exercise which should be transcribed into the phonetic script, then read both in the graphic and in. the phonetic transcription.

CLOSE i [i] SOUND. It is represented:

in phonetics by: [i] sounded as i in **machine**	in spelling by: i î ï y	*as in* ri île haïr cycle

Exercise:[1]	ici	vit	gîte	y	mis
ville	haïssant	rigide	mitigé	fini	vite
cynique	illicite	pire	limite	mystique	bicyclette

CLOSE e [e] SOUND. It is represented:

in phonetics by:
[e] sounded as
a in **late**
	in spelling by:
	é
	e + final silent consonant
	e + final silent consonant (not
	   a t) + s of plural
	-**ai** in verb endings
	
	-**ai** in **sais, vais, gai, gaieté,**
	   etc.
		as in
		pr**é**
		che**z**
		cle**fs**, pie**ds**
		
		j'**ai**, je ser**ai**,
		   je port**ai**

---

[1] Exercises should be read horizontally as well as vertically and should be repeated two or three times.

Exercise:	bébé	préféré	célébré	nez
été	clefs	créer	j'ai	sciez
irai	répétai	quai	thé	gai

OPEN e [ɛ] SOUND.   It is represented:

in phonetics by:	in spelling by:	*as in*
[ɛ] sounded as **e** in **met**	è	père
	ê	rêve
	ë	Noël
	e + 2 consonants	ferme
	e + final silent **t**	jet
	e + final sounded consonant	sel
	ai (except in verb endings), **aî**	plaine, maître
	ay + consonant	Raymond
	ay + vowel	rayon
	ei	reine
	ey final	jersey
	e in **ey** + vowel[1]	asseyez
	e in **eil, eill** + vowel[1]	soleil, veille

Exercise:	tête	règle	Raphaël	chêne
vrai	terre	serre	perle	objet
sujet	bel	jette	peine	laine
paie	payez	soleil	réveille	éveil
Raymond	sommeil	mai	sel	jockey

NOTE.   There are three accents in French: the *acute* (´), the *grave* (ˋ), and the *circumflex* (ˆ). They affect the sound of the vowel upon which they are placed. Thus, **e** with an acute accent sounds as **a** in **late** (without the gliding sound), and with a grave accent it takes the sound of **e** in **met**.

Accents do not affect the stress of syllables, but they sometimes distinguish between two words with otherwise identical spellings: la, *fem.*, the; là, there.

The *diaeresis* (¨) separates two vowels which otherwise would be pronounced in one emission of the voice: **Noël [no-ɛl].**

The *cedilla* (¸) changes **c** [k] to **c** [s]: **coq [kɔk], garçon [garsɔ̃].**

---

[1] "Ey" + vowel, "eil," and "eill" + vowel should be pronounced in one emission of the voice even though they are diphthongs: asseyez [asɛje] *not* [asɛ—je], soleil [sɔlɛːj] *not* [sɔlɛː—j].

Close **a** [a] Sound.　It is represented:

in phonetics by:	in spelling by:	as in
[a] sounded as **a** in **pat**[1]	**a** final	sa, ma, la
	a + final silent consonant or consonants	chat, chats, rats
	a in most nonfinal syllables	canalisé, parla
	a in all closed syllables	patte, natte
	a in endings **-ail, -aille**	bail, travaille
	à	là
	â in verb endings	portâmes, donnât
	a in adverbial ending **-amment**	constamment
	e in adverbial ending **-emment**	prudemment
	e in words like **femme, solennel**	
	e, ê in a few words like **couenne, moelle, poêle**	
	i, î, y in **-oi,-oî, -oy**, not preceded by **r, o** being pronounced [w]	moi, boîte, soyons, loi, soi, ployez, croît

Exercise:	la	ta	chat	rat
paragraphe	caractère	rage	flatte	femme
à	dame	tabac	prêtâmes	soif
poêle	moelle	foi	boîte	oie
papa	récemment	constamment	aboi	cloison
travail	taille	soie	noyer	alla

Open **a** [ɑ] Sound.　It is represented:

in phonetics by:	in spelling by:	as in
[ɑ] sounded as **a** in **father**	**a** + final consonants either silent or sounded, except in **bras**	matelas, pas, hélas
	â (except in verb endings)	pâle, mâle
	a in endings **-asse, -ation,**	passe,　nation,

---

[1] Close **a** is a sound between the **a** in **pat** and the **a** in **father**.

-assion, -ason, -azon	passion, gazon
a in endings **-abre, -adre, -acle, -able** (not suffix), **-avre**	sabre, cadre, oracle, sable, havre
i in **-roi, -roî** (many exceptions)	trois, croître
y in **-roy** (many exceptions)	croyez

Exercise:

âne	cas.	gras	gaz
gâteau	passe	chasse	ration	domination
sable	gaze	cable	froideur	poids
bois	débâcle	climat	lilas	mois

CLOSE **o** [o] SOUND. It is represented:

in phonetics by:	in spelling by:	*as in*
[o] sounded as **o** in **rose**	**o** final in sound	numéro, dos
	ô	pôle, rôle
	o + s + vowel	rose, pose
	o in ending **-otion**	potion
	o sometimes in endings **-ome, -one**	arome, zone
	o in **grosse, fosse**	
	au,[1] **eau**, if not followed by **r**	caution, autant, beau

Exercise:

	franco	domino	galops	sabot
drôle	diplôme	arome	vôtre	rôder
épaule	saut	héros	lotion	notion
zone	eau	auberge	clos	bravo
émotion	aube	folio	pot	caution

OPEN **o** [ɔ] SOUND. It is represented:

in phonetics by:	in spelling by:	*as in*
[ɔ] sounded as **o** in **not**	**o** in closed syllables	porte, poste
	o in nonfinal open syllables	voler, propre
	au + r	aura, aurore
	au in **Paul**	
	u in the Latin termination **-um**	album, maximum
	oo in **alcool**	

---

[1] **Au** + sounded **l** is pronounced as an open **o** in Paul [pɔl]

Exercise:	fort	donne	sotte	auréole
pomme	colosse	aurons	colonel	minimum
rhum	lors	opium	Paul	soleil
nord	oracle	héroïque	Laure	alcoolique

CLOSE **ou** [u] SOUND.   It is represented:

in phonetics by:	in spelling by:	*as in*
[u] sounded as	ou	sou, vous, nous, roue, soucoupe
oo in soon	où	où
	oû	goût, voûte
	aoû	août

Exercise:	tout	partout	tous	bout
bouche	loup	voûte	glouglou	où
goût	nous	coucou	bourré	ou

The Neuter Vowel, Mute e.   The neuter vowel mute **e** is either completely silent or sounded [ə] or [œ].

When *silent*, it is represented:

by no phonetic symbol	in spelling by:	*as in*
	e final, with or without s	porte, portes, malade, malades
	e in verb endings -e, -es, -ent [1]	parle, parles, parlent
	e in future and conditional of verbs whose stems end in a vowel	étudierai, jouerais, crieraient
	ë in ciguë, aiguë	
	e silent in word groups, see pp. xxxvi–xxxvii	

Exercise:	pâte	rapide	plaies	remuerait
jouerez	grandes	frappent	pliera	passes
jolie	absolue	paieront	craie	aiguës

When *sounded*, the mute **e** assumes the sound [ə] as a rule.   It is only when it is particularly stressed that [ə] is pronounced [œ] instead of [ə]: Dis-le! [dilœ]   Bien sur, je partirai! [bjɛ̃syːr ʒœ partire].

---

[1] S and **nt** are silent.

Sounded mute e is represented:

in phonetics by:	in spelling by:	*as in*
[ə] sounded as e in **over** or as final a in **Anna**	e before **ri** [rj] and **li** [lj]	de rien, appeliez
	e before noun endings **-lier, -nier**	chandelier, batelíer denier
	e before an aspirate **h**	le huit, une haute
	e before **un** and **onze**, used as nouns	le un, le onze
	e in monosyllabic words	me, se, le
	on (exceptionally)	monsieur
	eu (exceptionally)	peut-être
	ai (exceptionally)	faisant
	e in prefixes **des-,** **res-** + s	dessous, dessus, ressentir, ressortir
	e in **cresson**	

Exercise:

	que	te	le	centenier
le onze mai	le huit juin	ressent	ressort	faiseur
monsieur	cresson	dessous	appeliez	batelier
de rien	denier	peut-être	ressortir	dessus

The Mixed Vowels. French has three mixed vowels, **u** [y], close **eu** [ø], and open **eu** [œ]. They have no English counterparts, except, perhaps, open **eu** in **bu(r)n**.

Mixed Vowel Sound **u** [y]. To sound this vowel correctly, put your tongue into the position of close **i** and at the same time protrude your lips as much as possible.

It is represented:

in phonetics by:	in spelling by:	*as in*
[y]. There is no English equivalent.	u	nu, rude, une
	û	flûte
	ü	Esaü
	eu and eû in past participle, past definite, and imperfect subjunctive of **avoir**	eu, eus, eûmes, eusse, eussions, eût

Exercise:	bu	lu	su	vu
dû	mû	lune	unité	eussiez
usine	eurent	eûtes	tunique	brûle
mûr	issu	fût	fussent	bûche

MIXED VOWEL SOUND **eu** OR CLOSE **eu** [ø]. To pronounce close **eu** correctly, put your tongue in the position of close **e** and, at the same time, protrude your lips to a somewhat lesser degree than for French **u** [y].

Close **eu** is represented:

in phonetics by:	in spelling by:	*as in*
[ø]. There is no English equivalent.	**eu** or **œu** final	feu, vœu
	eu or **œu** + final silent consonants	peut, veut, nœud, œufs
	eu in endings –**euse**, –**eute**, –**eutre**, and derivatives	flatteuse, émeute, neutre
	eu in a few words like **jeudi, meunier**	
	eu in prefixed **eu**- with or without **r** following	euphonique, **Eu**phrate, **Eu**rope
	eû	jeûne

Exercise:	Dieu	lieu	bleu	pieu
vœu	deux	œufs	neutre	pleutre
yeux	cieux	jeûne	émeute	meute
jeudi	eux	creux	bœufs	Eugénie

MIXED VOWEL SOUND **eu** OR OPEN **eu** [œ]. To sound open **eu** properly, put your tongue in the position of open **e** and, at the same time, protrude your lips a little less than for open **o**.

It is represented:

in phonetics by:	in spelling by:	*as in*
[œ] sounded as **u** in **bu(r)n**	**eu, œu** in closed final syllables	peur, bœuf, cœur, œuf
	eu, œu in a few nonfinal open syllables	veuvage, œuvre
	eu + **il** or **ill**	cerfeuil, veuille
	œ + **il** or **ill**	œil, œillet
	ue + **il** or **ill** preceded by **c** or **g**	écueil, cueillir orgueil

Exercise:	orgueilleux	chœur	cœur	heure
bœuf	écueil	fleuve	peuvent	sœur
feuille	veuillez	meurt	gueule	veuvage
fureur	heureux	œuvre	meurtre	œil
jeunesse	œillet	jeune	beurrer	épeuré

The Nasal Sounds. There are four nasal sounds in French: an, en [ã], in [ɛ̃], on [ɔ̃], and un [œ̃].

Two questions must be answered before the individual nasal sounds can be considered: (1) When does nasalization occur? and (2) When does nasalization not occur?

Nasalization occurs:

1. When **a, e, i, y, o, u** are followed by final **m** or **n**:

Adam	thym	nom	parfum
an	vin	non	un

2. When **a, e, i, o, u** are followed by **m** or **n** + a consonant other than **m** or **n**:

camper	importe	comte	humble
temps	infini	conte	enfant

3. In prefixes **em-, en-, rem-,** when followed by any letter of the alphabet:

enivrer	emporter	emmener	rembrunir
emménager	emprunt	ensevelir	emmancher

There is no nasalization:

1. When **a, e, i, o, u** + **m** or **n** are immediately followed by a vowel or another **m** or **n**:

âme	femme	immortel	uni
année	ennemi	solennel	pomme
bonifier	tonner	analyse	énergie

2. When **a, e, i, o, u** + **m** or **n** are parts of foreign words, especially if **m** is final:

Amsterdam	pensum	spécimen	amen
Bethléem	maximum	abdomen	album

The nasal sounds have their *near-equivalents* in English *can't, sang, song,* and *sung.* These are poor equivalents of the French nasal sounds, however, because their nasalization is incomplete—

they undergo only a beginning of the nasalization under the influence of assimilation. The French nasalization is complete.

Nasal Sound **an, en** [ɑ̃]. It is represented:

in phonetics by:	in spelling by:	*as in*
a in **can't**	**am, an** final	**A**dam, **an**, b**an**
[känt]	**am, an, em, en** + final silent consonants	ch**amps**, ch**ant**, t**emps**, d**ent**
	am, an, em, en + sounded consonant other than **m** or **n**	c**am**per, c**an**tique, **en**sem**ble**

Exercise:

plan	Adam	sang	vent
venge	semble	rend	gens	pendant
quand	attend	tante	planche	lampe
remplit	tremble	commande	s'en allant	embaumant

Nasal Sound **in** [ɛ̃]. It is represented:

in phonetics by:	in spelling by:	*as in*
[ɛ̃] sounded as **an** in **sang**	**im, in, yn** + consonant other than **m** or **n**	**im**porte, **in**time, s**yn**thèse
	in, ym final	v**in**, Rh**in**, th**ym**
	aim, ain, eim, ein final or + consonants	p**aim**polois, f**aim**, p**ain**, Rh**eims**, r**ein**
	en in endings -**ien**, -**yen**, -**éen**	ital**ien**, b**ien**, cito**yen**, europ**éen**
	en in -**ien** + consonant	v**iens**, t**ient**
	en in some foreign words	app**en**dice, ag**en**da, P**en**sylvanie
	in in -**oin** (o sounded [w])	l**oin**, c**oin**

Exercise:

impossible	Paimpol	timbre	prince
larynx	thym	fin	nymphe	ceint
saint	cinq[1]	sein	sain	lien
vaurien	tient	vient	européen	méditerranéen
soin	poing	moins	lointain	agenda

---

[1] Q is not pronounced before consonants: cinq tables [sɛ̃tɑ̃bl].

NASAL SOUND **on** [ɔ̃]. It is represented:

| in phonetics by:
[ɔ̃] sounded as
on in **song** | in spelling by:
om, on final or +
consonant
um, un in some for-
eign words | *as in*
n**om**, n**on**, c**om**te, c**on**te

l**um**bago, p**un**ch,
sec**un**do |

Exercise:	plomb	on	prompte	don
rions	tombola	dom	pompe	junte
impromptu	vont	rond	de profundis	long

NASAL SOUND **un** [œ̃]. It is represented:

| in phonetics by:
[œ̃] sounded
as **un** in **sung** | in spelling by:
um final or + consonants

un final or + consonants
(silent or sounded)
eun in a few words | *as in*
parf**um**, parf**um**s,
h**um**ble
un, br**un**, empr**un**t,
empr**un**ter
à j**eun**, M**eun**g |

Exercise:	humble	Humbert	aucun	emprunt
tribun	alun	chacun	un	opportun
à jeun	Verdun	Dunkerque	commun	bruns
parfum	défunt	lundi	importun	Meung

The Semiconsonants. There are three semiconsonants or semi-vowels in French, **i** [j], **ou** [w], and **u** [ɥ].

Semiconsonants are speech-sounds in which both the voice and the noise resulting from the stoppage of the breath are about equal in strength.

SEMICONSONANT **i** [j] SOUND. It is represented:

| in phonetics by:
[j] sounded as
y in **yes** | in spelling by:
i, y, or **ï** when initial
i in consonant + **i** +
vowel
ï, y intervocalic
ill intervocalic
ill when final in sound
but not in spelling
il final in sound and
spelling | *as in*
ionique, **y**eux, **ï**ambe
b**i**en, l**i**en, s**i**en

pa**ï**en, pa**y**er, so**y**ez
bâ**ill**er, ta**ill**er
trava**ill**e, ta**ill**e

ba**il**, éve**il** |

Note. **Ii, yi,** and **ill** are sounded [ij] in **priions, criions, fuyions, fille, bille.**

The **illi** and **y** in words like **saillir, pays,** and derivatives, and **abbaye** are sounded [ji].

Exercise:	iota	yacht	yeux	aïeux
hier	viande	bail	brille	fiacre
balaye	paye	cercueil	moitié	sien
ïambe	païen	croyez	travail	soleil
vieil	brouillard	sciure	piège	petiot

SEMICONSONANT **ou** [w] SOUND.   Sound [w] is pronounced rather lightly and with lips more protruded than for the sounding of English **w.**   It is represented:

in phonetics by:	in spelling by:	*as in*
[w] sounded as **w** in **we**	**ou** + vowel (stressed)	**ou**i, Lou**i**s
	o in **oi, oî, oin**	tr**o**is, b**o**îte, s**o**ie, s**o**in
	o in **oê, oe, oy**	p**o**êle, m**o**elle, ab**o**yer, m**o**yen
	u in **-gua, -qua** of some foreign words	ling**u**al, aq**u**atique, q**u**adrupède

Exercise:	ouï	oui	ouest	voile
bois	coin	foyer	soir	loyaux
couard	ouate	voici	moelle	poêle
couenne	ouaille	lingual	enfoui	quoi

SEMICONSONANT **u** [ɥ] SOUND.   To pronounce this sound correctly, have your tongue and lips take the position required for the pronunciation of mixed vowel **u** [y]; then enunciate at once and with special stress the following vowel.   Semiconsonant **u** [ɥ] is represented:

in phonetics by:	in spelling by:	*as in*
[ɥ]. There is no English equivalent.	**u** + a vowel	h**u**ile, l**u**i, d**u**el, n**u**ée, s**u**ave

The spelling **uy** is represented by the phonetic notation [ɥij]: fuyons [fɥijɔ̃].

Note.   In a word formed by consonant + **r** or **l** + **ou, ou** must not be considered a semiconsonant but a simple vowel: prou-esse, [pruɛs], clou-age [klua:ʒ].

When preceded by **bl, br, cl, cr, dr, fl, fr, gl, gr, pl, pr, tr,** or **vr,** etc., belonging to the same syllable, **u** + any vowel, excepting **i,** form two distinct syllables: cru-el, cru-auté, monstru-eux; *but* fruit, truite, bruit.

As a general rule, **qu** and **gu** are pronounced [k] and [g], respectively: qui [ki], que [kə], guêpe [gɛ:p], guitare [gita:r].

Such words as **aiguiser** and its derivatives are pronounced either [egɥize] or [egize].

Exercise:	pluie	nuire	salua	autrui
nuage	tortueux	linguiste	nuée	situé
puits	suède	écuyer	suite	rituel
ensuite	ambiguité	aiguiser	huitaine	estuaire

Consonants

There are eighteen consonants in French. These may be classified either according to the *mechanism* of their formation or the *place* of articulation. The table that follows points to the former when read horizontally, to the latter when read vertically.

CONSONANT CHART [1]		GUTTURALS		DENTALS		LABIALS	
		Velar	*Pal-atal*	*Pre-palatal*	*Den-tal*	*Labio-dental*	*Bila-bial*
EXPLOSIVE	*Voiceless*	**c** [k]			**t**		**p**
	Voiced	**g** [g]			**d**		**b**
FRICATIVE	*Voiceless*		**i** [j]	**ch** [ʃ]	**s**	**f**	**ou** [w]
	Voiced			**g, j** [ʒ]	**z**	**v**	**u** [ɥ]
LIQUID	*Vibrant*	**r** [R]				**r** [r]	
						l	
	Nasal		**gn** [ɲ]			**n**	**m**

Some English consonants are rather good counterparts of the French consonants, others are not. We shall discuss the latter in greater detail.

---

[1] On this chart are also shown the semiconsonants i [j], ou [w], and u [ɥ].

The Three Voiceless Explosives c [k], t [t], and p [p].   What distinguishes them from the corresponding English consonants is a total lack of aspiration.

SOUND c [k].   It is represented:

in phonetics by:	in spelling by:	*as in*
[k] pro-	c + a, o, or u	car, cor, cure
nounced as c	cc + a, o, or u	occasion, accord
in car but	c or cc + l, r	clair, acclamer,
without any		accru
aspirate	qu, cqu + a, o, i, or e	quant, qu'on, qui,
sound		que, acquis
	ch in some foreign words	écho
	ch + r in foreign words	chrétien
	k in some foreign words	kilo
	and their derivatives	
	g in liaison	sang‿impur

Exercise: canne　　corps　　quand　　court
occuper　　éclairer　　crampe　　cholérique　　kilomètre
acquièrent　　occlusion　　qui　　qu'on　　long‿espoir

SOUND t [t].   It is represented:

in phonetics by:	in spelling by:	*as in*
[t] pro-	t	tête, bête, tire, tort, tue, tant
nounced as t	tt	jette, mettent
in time but	th	thé, synthèse
without any	d in liaison	quand‿il, grand‿age
aspirate sound		

Exercise: ton　　tel　　tout　　tu
terre　　tertre　　tumeur　　tuer　　thermomètre
thème　　battent　　bâtir　　quand‿on　　grand‿ami

SOUND p [p].   It is represented:

in phonetics by:	in spelling by:	*as in*
[p] pronounced as p	p	père, pire, port, pur, par
in put but without	pp	appartenir, appel
any aspirate sound	b before s or t	absoudre, obtenir

Exercise:	parer	parier	papier	portier
apporter	supprimer	pressentir	proposer	opposer
observer	obscur	obstacle	poire	pis

The Three Voiced Explosives g [g], d [d], and b [b] and the Two Labiodentals f [f] and v [v].   The sound of these letters corresponds closely to English, except that it is somewhat more deliberate and explosive.   The lips and teeth should be set to make the sound *before* the breath is released.

Voiceless and Voiced Fricatives ch [ʃ], ge, gi [ʒ], s [s] and z [z]. The fricatives are produced by a distinct frictional rustling of the breath passing through an oral passage greatly narrowed.

Sounds **ch [ʃ]** and **ge, gi, j [ʒ]**.   They differ from the corresponding English sounds by their total lack of a dental element.   Pronounce *chercher* [ʃɛrʃe], and *juge* [ʒyʒ].   Sound [ʃ], however, has its English equivalent in the **sh** of **shell**; [ʒ] in the **s** of **treasure** and the **z** of **azure**.

Sound [ʃ] is represented:

in phonetics by: [ʃ] sounded as **sh** in **shell**	in spelling by: **ch** **sch** in foreign words **sch** [ʃ] or [sk] in **sch**éma, **sch**ématique	*as in* **ch**er**ch**er, **ch**amps, bou**ch**e, sou**ch**e **sch**isme, **sch**iste

Sound [ʒ] is represented:

in phonetics by: [ʒ] sounded as **z** in **azure**	in spelling by: **j** before **a, e, i, o, u** **g** before **e, i, y**	*as in* **j**amais, **j**e, **j**'imagine, **j**oli, **j**uste **g**èle, **g**ilet, pa**g**e, **g**ymnase

Exercise:[1]	chambre	chère	couche	chien
chemin	chuchoter	sache	cache	chiffon
janvier	gémir	girafe	jeudi	rage
neige	chute	geindre	jumeaux	choc
jour	gypseux	joie	schismatique	chinois

---

[1] [ʃ] and [ʒ] combined.

Sounds [s] AND [z]. These sounds are enunciated much more energetically and distinctly than in English; otherwise, they have their English counterparts in the s in so and in the z in zeal.

Sound [s] is represented:

in phonetics by:	in spelling by:	*as in*
[s] sounded as s in so	s initial	série, sont, su, si
	ss intervocalic	tasse, masse, tousse
	c before e, i, y	ceci, ici, cycle
	ç before a, o, u	ça, garçon, reçu
	sc before i, y, e	scier, scythe, scène
	x in numbers	dix, six, soixante

Sound [z] is represented:

in phonetics by:	in spelling by:	*as in*
[z] sounded as z in zeal	z initial or medial	zèle, zizanie
	s intervocalic	rose, pose, ruse, rase
	s in prefixes **dés-, rés-, més-, trans-, prés-** + vowel	désunion, résister, mésaventure, transit, présumer

Exercise: [1]

sans	sourd	sur	sortie
zone	gazon	zinc	mise	transiger
fils	mars	gratis	sens	six
réservoir	présage	transalpin	bêtise	vice
hélas	sciure	déçu	soixante	vise

Liquid r, l, n, and m. French has two r's, the *uvular* [R] and the *lingual* [r], neither of which has its counterpart in English.

UVULAR R [R], also called "Parisian r" or "r grasseyé." To pronounce it correctly, press the tip of your tongue against the lower front teeth, keeping it there while you cause the uvula to vibrate against the back of your tongue.

LINGUAL R [r]. It is formed by vibrating the tip of your tongue against the upper gums. Thus, while the r is pronounced, a continuous and rapid series of stoppages and openings takes place at the point of contact of the tongue with the upper gums.

Exercise:

rare	rage	arrange	ri	rond
gros	grand	car	terre	rue	très
ouverture	frais	cirage	clair	mère	vert

---

[1] [s] and [z] combined.

Liquid **l, n,** and **m.** The French liquid l differs considerably from the English **l.** The former is sounded by touching the edges of the teeth with the tip of the tongue, the back of the tongue being relatively low; the latter, by resting the tip of the tongue against the upper gums and raising its back toward the soft palate. The sides of the tongue must be lowered for the sounding of the French liquid l to permit the breath to escape laterally.

Liquid **n** presents no difficulty and has its counterpart in the English **n** in **neat.**

Liquid bilabial **m** has its equivalent in the English **m** in **me.**

Sound gn [ɲ]. This sound has no equivalent in English. To pronounce it correctly, touch the lower teeth with the tip of your tongue and press its middle part slightly against the hard palate so as to close completely the oral passage. Then, lowering the uvula toward the back of your tongue, let the air column escape through the nose. It is a serious mistake to pronounce *signifie* [sinifi]; it must be sounded [siɲifi].

Exercise:	digne	gagne	montagne	craigne
règne	peignent	joigne	cygne	compagnon
campagne	ceignez	signe	signaler	geigne

Note on the letter *h.* This letter has two forms in French, mute and aspirate. In ordinary speech neither form is given any sound, and in phonetics **h** is ignored. It is important to note, however, that there is no elision of the mute **e** before an aspirate **h** and that an aspirate **h** prevents liaison with the word preceding it (see section 2b under Liaison or Linking). By consulting his dictionary the student will be able to determine which **h's** are aspirate.

> Ils m'ont humilié. (mute h with liaison)
> [il mɔ̃tymilje]

> Ils m'ont haï. (aspirate h, no liaison)
> [il mɔ̃ ai]

CONNECTED SPEECH

When a series of words is grouped into a phrase or sentence and pronounced in connected speech, there is at times such a difference in sound that beginners are unable to understand what they hear. The reason for this difference lies in the fact that the sounds no longer have to do with the single word but with the phonetic word or the word group. The single word has lost its individuality and is stressed only when it carries the accent of the stress group to which it belongs.

Three main factors bring about this sound transformation: (1) the mute **e** in the stress group, (2) linking or liaison, and (3) the intonation of the breath group.

We can dwell only briefly on these three points.

Mute **e** *in Stress Groups* [1]

Mute **e** is silent:

1. When it is final in word-groups.

> C'est lui qui parle.   Il a regardé les livres.

2. When mute **e** is between two consonants in a single word or word-group.

> Voici la fenêtre.   Il le sait.

3. When mute **e** occupies either the position **consonant + mute e + bl** (or **br, cl, cr, dr, fl, fr, gl, gr, pl, pr, ps, sk, sm, sn, sp, sph, st, tr, ts,** and **vr**) or the position **br,** etc., **+ mute e + consonant.** In the *first* case, the inseparable consonant combination, here **dr,** belongs to the same syllable—e.g., le-dra-peau; in the *second*, to the last syllable of a word while the third consonant is the initial consonant of the next word—e.g., **cadre neuf.**

> Il prit le drapeau.   Voici un cadre neuf.
> [il pri ldra‿po]   [vwasi œ̃ caːdrnœf]
> C'est le tracas . . .   Il a ma table jaune.
> [sɛ ltraka . . .]   [il a ma tablʒoːn]

Mute **e** is pronounced:

1. Between two consonants: (a) at the beginning of a word group—e.g., Le bonheur parfait n'est pas d'ici-bas; (b) in a stressed syllable—e.g., Mes‿amis, debout! (c) in words like **ceci, celui, peser, mener, pelouse,** etc.—e.g., Savez-vous peser ceci?

2. In certain cases in monosyllabic words: (a) If there are two mute **e**'s, the one in the initial syllable of the stress group is sounded—e.g., Ne le fais pas. Je le veux; (b) within the stress group,

---

[1] Refer to *mute* **e**, pp. xxiv–xxv.

either one may be pronounced—e.g., Il ne se lave pas. Il ne se lave pas; (c) in combinations **ce ne, ce me, ce te, je ne, que de, que me,** etc., **de se, de te,** etc., **ce, je, que, de** alone are sounded —e.g., Que de choses! Ce ne peut être possible. Je ne veux pas. Et les deux hommes de se parler; (d) with more than two mono-syllabic words ending in mute **e,** sound the first and the third mute **e**—e.g., Je me le demande. Il me le remettra.

Liaison or Linking

By the word "liaison" is meant the carrying over of the last consonant of a word to a following word beginning with a vowel or mute **h.** The consonant carried over is pronounced with the word that follows: Ils‿ont des‿amis. Leurs‿amis avaient‿un‿ oiseau.

The aim of liaison is exclusively euphonic. It adds ease, flexi-bility, and suppleness to the spoken language.[1]

NOTE. In liaison **d** takes the sound of [t], **f,** of [v], **g,** of [k], **s** and **x,** of [z]. **N, p, r, t,** and **z** retain their normal value.

You should find the following general rules helpful.

1. Words that belong together by position, function, and meaning should be linked. Hence, whenever possible, there should always be a liaison between an article or adjective followed by a noun, an adverb followed by a participle or adjective, a preposi-tion and its object, a subject and its verb, a pronoun followed by a verb, component parts of a compound word, and various elements in idiomatic expressions.

Les‿oiseaux sont là-bas.	Ils‿ont‿un beau jardin.
Madame, vous‿êtes très‿aimable.	Il nous‿a parlé de vous.
Est‿il bien vrai qu'on‿arrivera tard?	Vous‿a-t-il dit qu'il partait?
Il parle sans‿accent.	J'ai un pied‿à terre ici.
Nous‿avons‿un pot-au-feu.	de moins‿en moins
de temps‿en temps	tôt‿ou tard
de plus‿en plus	Oh, les jolis‿oiseaux!
quand‿il parle [2]	dix‿amis [3]

[1] Nasalization sometimes disappears with linking: qu'on arrivera [kɔna-rivɔra].

[2] [kãtil parl]

[3] [dizami]

2.   Words whose linking might cause ambiguity, disagreeable sounds, or awkward associations should not be linked. Hence do not link:

(a) The **t** in **et** and a following word:

ennemis‿et amis   pommes‿et abricots

(b) A final consonant with a word beginning with an aspirate or words like **onze, oui,** or numeral **un** used as a noun:

Les héros sont‿arrivés.   les onze soldats
les oui et les non   les huit

(c) Words ending in a silent consonant which is not the sign of the plural:

Charles est‿arrivé.   Voici un objet admirable.

3.   The last word of a stress-group should not be linked with the first word of another stress-group:

Il est mort / à 3 heures /   Son esprit est‿étroit / et borné.
    aujourd'hui.

4.   The **s** of the plural in compound words should not be linked with the following component part:

des‿arcs-en-ciel   des vers-à-soie
des salles à manger   des machines à coudre

5.   A silent final consonant after **r** should not be linked with the next word, except **r** + **s** of the plural:

mort ou vif   de part en part
fort embarrassé   fort aimable

but: Les morts‿et les vivants.

6.   **M** or **n** which forms part of a nasal vowel should not be linked with the word that follows:

un parfum indéfini   un pronom important
un brun indescriptible   un commun intérêt

Careless liaisons often lead to puns and jokes.

Quel est le premier‿homme   Quel est le premier rhum
    du monde?   du monde?

[kɛl ɛl prəmje rɔm dy mɔ̃ːd]

Intonation

Intonation as practiced by natives can only be learned from natives. Though phonograph records may be an excellent aid, they cannot replace fully the intonation of the Frenchman.

What is meant by intonation? Intonation in its larger sense is a rise or fall in pitch. This rise or fall is not caused so much by the pitch generally inherent in vowel or consonant sounds as it is by the emotional condition of the speaker and the nature of his thoughts and sentiments.

Thoughts or sentiments, when expressed in a phrase or sentence, are presented as statements, questions, or exclamative wishes. Each of these types of human expression has an intonation of its own, varied in pitch and modulation.

1.   *In declarative sentences* there are a rise and a fall, the former ending in the highest note of the sentence, the latter in the lowest. Both the rising and the falling parts may contain several word groups which are formed into a breath-group.

La table carrée / qui est à Pierre / est peinte en rouge \.

2.   *In interrogative sentences* the rising part generally falls on the last syllable of the interrogation. When, however, there are two parallel interrogative phrases, the first takes the rising pitch; the second, the falling pitch.

Pourquoi faire cela /?   Il l'a donc fait /?
Mon ami est-il arrivé /?   Faites-vous de l'escrime / ou de
                                  la boxe \?

3.   *In exclamatory phrases or sentences* which originate from emotional disturbances, the intonation is often sudden, abrupt, intensely emotional, elliptical, and inverted in grammatical form.

(a) The stress of the intonation falls on the first syllable when it begins with a consonant:

Quelle idée!   Canaille que tu es!

When the first syllable begins with a vowel, the intonation is shifted to the next syllable whose vowel receives the full intensity of the rising inflection.

Imbécile, que venez-vous faire ici?   Abruti que vous êtes!

(b) When interjections such as **oh, ah, que, combien, comme, quel,** etc., begin an exclamatory phrase, they generally receive the emphatic stress together with the first consonant or consonant group of the next syllable.

Comme je le regrette!   Quelle perfidie!

(c) Quite often, however, the stress is shifted from the first word to the *important* word which the speaker wishes to set into relief.

Que de services rendus!   becomes   Que de services rendus!

Quel outrage !   becomes   Quel outrage!

At times, whole phrases or sentences bear the stress of a high or low pitch.

Vous voilà donc contente!   Allons donc, pas de blague.

TERMS RELATING TO
GRAMMAR

active—actif [aktif] m.

acute accent—accent aigu [aksɑ̃tegy] m.

adjective—adjectif [adʒɛktif] m.

adverb—adverbe [advɛrb] m.

alphabet—alphabet [alfabɛ] m.

apostrophe—apostrophe [apɔstrɔf] f.

article—article [artikl] m.

aspirate—aspiré [aspire], adj.

auxiliary—auxiliaire [ɔksiljɛːr], adj.

capital letter—majuscule [maʒyskyl] f.

cedilla—cédille [sediːj] f.

clause—membre de phrase [mɑ̃ːbrdəfraːz] m.

colon—deux points [døpwɛ̃] m.

comma—virgule [virgyl] f.

comparative—comparatif [kɔ̃paratif] m.

conditional—conditionnel[kɔ̃disjɔnɛl]m.

conjugation—conjugaison [kɔ̃ʒygɛzɔ̃] f.

conjunction—conjonction [kɔ̃ʒɔ̃ksjɔ̃] f.

consonant—consonne [kɔ̃sɔn] f.

dash—tiret [tirɛ] m.

declarative—explicatif [ɛksplikatif], adj.

to define—définir [definiːr]

demonstrative—démonstratif [demɔ̃stratif], adj.

diaeresis—tréma [tremɑ] m.

diphthong—diphtongue [diftɔ̃ːg] f.

disjunctive—disjonctif [dizʒɔ̃ktif], adj.

elision—élision [elizjɔ̃] f.

exclamation point—point d'exclamation [pwɛ̃dɛksklamasjɔ̃] m.

exercise—devoir [dəvwaːr] m.

expletive—explétif [ɛkspletif] m.

feminine—féminin [feminɛ̃] m.

future—futur [fytyːr] m.

future anterior—futur antérieur [fytyːrɑ̃terjœːr] m.

gender—genre [ʒɑ̃ːr] m.

grammar—grammaire [gramɛːr] f.

grave accent—accent grave [aksɑ̃graːv] m.

hyphen—trait d'union [trɛdynjɔ̃] m.

idiom—idiome [idjoːm] m.

imperative—impératif [ɛ̃peratif] m.

imperfect—imparfait [ɛ̃parfɛ] m.

indicative—indicatif [ɛ̃dikatif] m.

infinitive—infinitif [ɛ̃finitif] m.

interjection—interjection [ɛ̃tɛrʒɛksjɔ̃] f.

interrogative—interrogatif [ɛ̃tɛrɔgatif], adj.

intransitive—intransitif [ɛ̃trɑ̃zitif], adj.

irregular verb—verbe irrégulier [vɛrbiregylje] m.

italics—italique [italik] m.

masculine—masculin [maskylɛ̃] m.

to modify—modifier [mɔdifje]

mood—mode [mɔd] m.

mute letter—muette [mɥɛt] f.

nasal—nasale [nazal] f.

negative—négatif [negatif], adj.

neuter—neutre [nøːtr] m.

noun—nom [nɔ̃] m.

number—nombre [nɔ̃ːbr] m.

object—objet [ɔbʒɛ] m.

paragraph—paragraphe [paragraf] m.

parenthesis—parenthèse [parɑ̃tɛːz] f.

partitive—partitif [partitif], adj.

parts of speech—parties du discours [partidydiskuːr] f.

passive—passif [pasif] m.

past anterior—passé antérieur [paseɑ̃terjœːr] m.

past definite—passé défini [pasedefini]m.

past historic—passé historique [paseistɔrik] m.

past indefinite—passé indéfini [paseɛ̃defini] m.

past participle—participe passé [partisippase] m.

present participle—participe présent [partisipprezɑ̃] m.

perfect—parfait [parfɛ] m.

xli

period—point [pwɛ̃] m.

person—personne [pɛrsɔn] f. (première personne, deuxième personne, etc.)

personal—personnel [pɛrsɔnɛl], adj.

phonetics—phonétique [fɔnetik] f.

phrase—locution [lɔkysjɔ̃] f.

pluperfect—plus-que-parfait [plyskə-parfɛ] m.

plural—pluriel [plyrjɛl] m.

possessive—possessif [pɔsɛsif] m.

predicate—attribut [atriby] m.

preposition—préposition [prepozisjɔ̃] f.

present—présent [prezɑ̃] m.

principal clause—proposition principale [prɔpozisjɔ̃prɛ̃sipal] f.

principal parts (of a verb)—temps primitifs [tɑ̃primitif] m. pl.

pronoun—pronom [prɔnɔ̃] m.

to pronounce—prononcer [prɔnɔ̃se]

punctuation—ponctuation [pɔ̃ktɥasjɔ̃] f.

question mark—point d'interrogation [pwɛ̃dɛ̃terɔgasjɔ̃] m.

quotation marks—guillemets [gijmɛ] m.

reflexive—réfléchi [refleʃi], adj.

relative—relatif [rəlatif], adj.

semicolon—point et virgule [pwɛ̃tevirgyl] m.

sentence—phrase [frɑːz] f.

singular—singulier [sɛ̃gylje], adj.

slang—argot [argo] m.

small letter—minuscule [minyskyl] f.

to spell—épeler [eple]

subjunctive—subjonctif [sybʒɔ̃ktif] m.

subordinate clause—proposition subordonnée [prɔpozisjɔ̃sybɔrdɔne] f.

superlative—superlatif [syperlatif] m.

symbol—symbole [sɛ̃bɔl] m.

tense—temps [tɑ̃] m.

transitive—transitif [trɑ̃zitif], adj.

to translate—traduire [tradɥiːr]

verb—verbe [vɛrb] m.

vocabulary—vocabulaire[vɔkabylɛːr]m.

voice—voix [vwa] f.

vowel—voyelle [vwajɛl] f.

I. THE DEFINITE ARTICLE

There are only two genders in French, the masculine and the feminine; there are only two numbers in French, the singular and the plural.

There are three kinds of articles in French, the definite, the indefinite, and the partitive.

THE DEFINITE ARTICLE.—The definite article is **le** and **la** for the masculine and the feminine singular, respectively; **les** for both genders in the plural.

le livre, *the book*   les livres, *the books*
la porte, *the door*   les portes, *the doors*

Before masculine and feminine nouns in the singular, when they begin with a vowel or a mute *h*, **l'** is used instead of **le** or **la**.

l'ami m., *the friend*   l'honneur m., *the honor*
l'encre f., *the ink*   l'heure f., *the hour*

The definite articles **le** and **les** combine with **de** or **à** in the following way:

de + le = du, *of the, from the*
de + les = des, *of the, from the*
à + le = au, *to the, at the*
à + les = aux, *to the, at the*

Voici le livre du maître.   Here is the teacher's book.
Voilà les livres des élèves.   There are the pupils' books.
Il va au jardin.   He goes to the garden.
Il parle aux amis de Marie.   He speaks to Mary's friends.
Nous sommes au théâtre.   We are at the theater.

The use of the definite article in French differs from that in English. Thus the definite article is used in French, though not in English, in the following cases:

1. With nouns taken in a general sense:

J'aime les fleurs.	I like flowers.
Il admire les héros.	He admires heroes.

2. With abstract nouns:

La pauvreté n'est pas un vice.	Poverty is no vice.
L'amitié est un don de Dieu.	Friendship is a gift of God.

3. With names of seasons and days of the week:

Le printemps est agréable.	Spring is agreeable.
Le lundi je travaille.	I work (on) Mondays.

4. With names of continents, countries, provinces, and mountains:

L'Europe est en guerre.	Europe is at war.
La France est désolée.	France is desolate.
La Normandie est dévastée.	Normandy is devastated.
Le Mont Blanc est en France.	Mount Blanc is in France.

Note.—Chains of mountains take the article in French and English: **Les Alpes,** *The Alps*.

5. With names of sciences and languages:

La chimie est une science.	Chemistry is a science.
Il écrit bien le français.*	He writes French well.

6. With names of weight and measure:

Elle paie vingt francs la livre.	She pays twenty francs a pound.
C'est trois francs le mètre.	It costs three francs a meter.

7. With names of metals, substances, and colors:

Le fer est utile.	Iron is useful.
L'or est précieux.	Gold is precious.
Le marbre est dur.	Marble is hard.
Voici un jaune qui tire sur le vert.	Here is a yellow which verges on green.

* The definite article is omitted with *parler* unless *parler* is modified by an adverb: *il parle français;* but, *il parle bien le français*. This rule is not enforced strictly.

8. With titles preceding proper nouns, provided these titles are not used in a direct address:

Le comte de Kerville est ici.	Count de Kerville is here.
But:	
Bonjour, comte de Kerville.	Good morning, Count de Kerville.

9. With parts of body or clothing:

Il a les mains dans les poches.	He has his hands in his pockets.

In practically all other cases, the definite article is used alike in both languages.

II. VERB REVIEW

1. AUXILIARY VERBS: avoir, *to have;* être, *to be*

INDICATIVE

Present

Affirmative		*Negative*	
I have . . .	*I am . . .*	*I have not . . .*	*I am not . . .*
j'ai	je suis	je n'ai pas	je ne suis pas
tu as	tu es	tu n'as pas	tu n'es pas
il a	il est	il n'a pas	il n'est pas
elle a	elle est	elle n'a pas	elle n'est pas
nous avons	nous sommes	nous n'avons pas	nous ne sommes pas
vous avez	vous êtes	vous n'avez pas	vous n'êtes pas
ils ont	ils sont	ils n'ont pas	ils ne sont pas
elles ont	elles sont	elles n'ont pas	elles ne sont pas

Imperfect		*Past Definite*	
I had . . .	*I was . . .*	*I had . . .*	*I was . . .*
j'avais	j'étais	j'eus	je fus
tu avais	tu étais	tu eus	tu fus
il avait	il était	il eut	il fut
elle avait	elle était	elle eut	elle fut
nous avions	nous étions	nous eûmes	nous fûmes
vous aviez	vous étiez	vous eûtes	vous fûtes
ils avaient	ils étaient	ils eurent	ils furent
elles avaient	elles étaient	elles eurent	elles furent

2. PRESENT AND PAST PARTICIPLES

avoir	ayant, *having*	eu, *had*
être	étant, *being*	été, *been*
porter	portant, *carrying*	porté, *carried*
finir	finissant, *finishing*	fini, *finished*
vendre	vendant, *selling*	vendu, *sold*

III. VOCABULARY*

1.   FRENCH-ENGLISH:

l'acier *m.*, steel
aimer, to like
ainsi, thus
l'Allemagne *f.*, Germany
*aller, to go
l'Anglais *m.*, Englishman
l'anglais *m.*, English (language) .
l'Angleterre *f.*, England
l'année *f.*, year
arroser, to water
aussi, also
l'automne *m.*, fall
la bataille, battle
bien, well
bon, -ne, good
le caillou, pebble
la cendre, ash, ashes
le chapeau, hat
clair, -e, clear
conserver, to keep
contre, against
couler, to flow

le cours, course
coûter, to cost
la dame, lady
les délices *f.pl.*, delight(s)
*devenir, to become
*dire (*p.p.* dit), to say
l'eau *f.*, water
également, equally
en (*pron.*), of it, of them,
from it, from them
l'essence *f.*, gasoline
les États-Unis *m.pl.*, The United
States
l'été *m.*, summer
l'étendue *f.*, stretch
*être, to be
étudier, to study
*faire (*p.p.* fait), to do, make;
— les délices de, to be the
delight(s) of
fangeux, -se, muddy, miry
le fer, iron

* All Vocabularies refer directly to the Exercises. They are intended to simplify the student's work by making unnecessary the thumbing of the General Vocabulary, which often amounts to a considerable loss of time. Cognates which are easily recognizable are omitted. Also omitted are all verb forms other than the infinitive of regular verbs, and the present and past participles of irregular verbs. Possessive, demonstrative, interrogative, numeral, relative, and indefinite pronouns and adjectives do not appear in these Vocabularies. An asterisk before a verb indicates that it is irregular. See list of irregular verbs, pp. 218-225.

le français, French (language)
garder, to keep
la guerre, war
l'hiver *m.*, winter
infect, -e, foul
la livre, pound
mal, badly
le marais, marshland
mauvais, -e, bad
même, same
mériter de, to deserve well of
l'or *m.*, gold
oser, to dare
*plaire, to please

poli, -e, polite
la prairie, meadow
le printemps, spring (season)
quand, when
le ruisseau, brook
le sable, sand
la saison, season
le sel, salt
*sortir de, to spring from
le sou, sou
le sucre, sugar
*suivre, to follow
la tête, head
voici, here is, here are

2. ENGLISH-FRENCH:

all: at —, du tout
before (+ inf.), avant de
bird, l'oiseau *m.*
book, le livre
Brazil, le Brésil
brother, le frère
California, la Californie
child, l'enfant *m.* and *f.*
to complain, *se plaindre
to constitute (= make), *faire
courage, le courage
to desire, désirer
to eat, manger
everybody, tout le monde
evil, le mal
extreme, extrême
face, la figure, le visage, la face
fear, la peur
to find, trouver
friend, l'ami *m.*
general, le général
gratitude, la gratitude

hand, la main
happiness, le bonheur
heart, le cœur
here, ici
horse, le cheval
ignorance, l'ignorance *f.*
isn't it? n'est-ce pas?
knife, le couteau
late: to be —, *être en retard
laziness, la paresse
to lose, perdre
memory, la mémoire
merit, le mérite
Mexico, le Mexique
mother, la mère
must, (on) doit
not, non, ne . . . pas
often, souvent
patience, la patience
platinum, le platine
presumption, la présomption
to protect, protéger
to sell, vendre

sick, **malade**
sister, **la sœur**
society, **la société**
source, **la source**
success, **le succès**

ungrateful, **ingrat, -e**
useful, **utile**
valor, **la valeur**
virtue, **la vertu**
to wash, **laver**

IV. IDIOMATIC EXPRESSIONS

avoir faim, to be hungry
avoir soif, to be thirsty
avoir peur, to be afraid
avoir sommeil, to be sleepy
avoir honte de, to be ashamed of
avoir soin de, to take care of
avoir tort, to be wrong
avoir raison, to be right
avoir lieu, to take place
avoir envie de, to have a mind to

avoir besoin de, to be in need of, need
avoir sujet de, to have cause for
avoir coutume de, to be in the habit of
avoir bonne mine, to look well
avoir mauvaise mine, to look ill, bad
courir (le) risque de, to run the risk of

V. EXERCISES

1. *Fill in the dashes with the proper form of the definite article:*

1 Deux ruisseaux sortent de ——— même source; ils sont également clairs et limpides. 2. ——— premier coule sur ——— sable et ——— cailloux; il conserve sa pureté sur toute ——— étendue de son cours; il fait ——— délices et ——— ornement ——— prairies qu'il arrose. 3. ——— second traverse ——— marais fangeux, et ses eaux deviennent si infectes que personne n'ose en approcher. 4. Ainsi nous devenons bons ou mauvais suivant ——— société que nous fréquentons.

2. *Translate into idiomatic French:*

1. Children are ungrateful.
2. He likes horses.
3. My cousin sells knives.
4. Patience is a virtue.
5. Everybody desires happiness.
6. Books are friends.
7. Society is sick.
8. Laziness is a source of evil.

3. *Fill in the dashes with the proper form of the definite article whenever the latter is required:*

1. L'année a quatre saisons, ——— printemps, ——— été, ——— automne et ——— hiver. 2. C'est ——— été que je préfère. 3. Et vous, préférez-vous ——— printemps? 4. Je n'aime pas ——— mathématiques; mais ——— histoire me plaît. 5. Il étudie ——— français, il connaît ——— anglais, mais il parle mal ——— italien. 6. ——— sucre coûte six sous ——— livre; ——— sel coûte dix sous ——— livre. 7. Il n'est pas poli de garder ——— chapeau sur ——— tête quand on parle ——— dames. 8. Voici ——— or que vous désirez. 9. ——— acier, ——— fer, ——— coton, ——— essence, et ——— nickel sont indispensables en temps de guerre. 10. ——— Angleterre se défend vigoureusement contre ——— Allemagne. 11. ——— États-Unis admirent ——— courage ——— Anglais. 12. ——— France va renaître de ses cendres. 13. ——— général Albert s'est distingué dans la bataille de X., aussi ——— président B. lui a dit : ——— général Albert, vous avez bien mérité de ——— France.

4. *Translate carefully:*

1. Gratitude is the memory of the heart. 2. Platinum is found in Mexico, Brazil, and California. 3. Valor and not success constitutes (makes) merit. 4. Useful birds must be protected. 5. Presumption is the daughter of ignorance. 6. General Lewis is here. 7. Let's wash (lavons-nous) our hands and faces (singular) before eating. 8. Extreme fear is often the mother of courage.

5. *Translate into idiomatic French:*

1. He is hungry.
2. We are hungry and thirsty.
3. He runs the risk of losing.
4. He is in the habit of being late.
5. My brother looks well.
6. Sister Helen looks bad.
7. Are you not ashamed at all?
8. He is sleepy, isn't he?
9. You have cause for complaining.
10. He has a mind to talk.

I. THE INDEFINITE AND PARTITIVE ARTICLES

THE INDEFINITE ARTICLE.—In French, the indefinite article is **un,** *a, an,* for the masculine and **une,** *a, an,* for the feminine singular. **Des,** *some, any,* is used in the plural.

un livre, *a book*	des livres, (*some*) *books*
une table, *a table*	des tables, (*any*) *tables*

The indefinite article is omitted in French, although retained in English, in the following cases:

1. Before an unmodified predicate noun expressing profession, nationality, religion, etc.

Il est peintre.	He is a painter.
Il est américain.	He is an American.
Elle est luthérienne.	She is a Lutheran.

The indefinite article, however, is retained when the predicate noun is modified by an adjective or adjectival phrase, or is preceded by **ce** (instead of *il, elle, ils, elles*) + **être** in any form.

C'est un bon roman.	This is a good novel.
C'est un roman qui plaît.	This is an agreeable novel.
Ce sera un agent. . . .	It's probably a policeman. . . .

2. After the exclamative adjective **quel** *m.,* **quelle** *f., what a.*

Quel beau jour!	What a beautiful day!
Quelle belle peinture!	What a beautiful painting!

3. Before an appositive noun.

L'Avare, comédie de Molière, est célèbre.	The Miser, a comedy by Molière, is famous.

8

When an appositive phrase contrasts, distinguishes, or compares, the use of the definite article is required.

L'Avare, peut-être la meilleure comédie de Molière, fut joué en 1669.	The Miser, perhaps the best comedy by Molière, was played in 1669.

THE PARTITIVE ARTICLE.—The partitive sense is rendered in English by *some* or *any*, expressed or understood. In French, the partitive sense is rendered by **du** (= de + le), **de la, de l', des** (= de + les).

J'ai du pain.	I have some bread.
Il a de la viande.	He has meat.
Vous avez de l'encre.	You have some ink.
Nous avons des pommes.	We have apples.
Ont-ils des livres?	Do they have books?

In four cases, however, the partitive sense is expressed by **de** alone. They are

1. When the noun, expressed or understood, is preceded by an adjective.

Avez-vous de jolis tableaux?	Have you nice pictures?

Note.—**Du** and **de la** are often used in familiar speech even though the noun is preceded by an adjective: du bon pain, *good bread;* de la bonne viande, *good meat.* Petits pois, *peas;* petits pains, *rolls;* jeunes filles, *girls;* jeunes gens, *young men* as single nouns require **des**.

2. When the verb is negative.

Je n'ai pas de pain.	I have no (not any) bread.
Il n'a pas d'encre.	He has no ink.
Ils n'ont pas de pommes.	They haven't any apples.

3. When the noun is preceded by an adverb of quantity* or a noun of quantity or measure like panier (m.), *basket;* poignée (f.), *handful*; mètre (m.), *metre*; etc.

Il a beaucoup d'argent.	He has much money.
Voici un plat de viande.	Here is a dish of meat.

---

* Such as assez, *enough;* autant, *as much* or *as many;* beaucoup, *much* or *many;* tant, *so much* or *so many;* trop, *too much* or *too many;* etc.

4. When a noun is particularized by another noun.

C'est une école de filles. This is a girls' school.
Voilà une salle d'étude. There is a study hall.

II. VERB REVIEW

1. FUTURE OF *avoir* AND *être*

INDICATIVE

Future

I shall have . . .	I shall be . . .
j'aurai	je serai
tu auras	tu seras
il aura	il sera
nous aurons	nous serons
vous aurez	vous serez
ils auront	ils seront

2. REGULAR CONJUGATIONS: porter, *to carry;* finir, *to finish;* vendre, *to sell*

INDICATIVE

Present

I carry . . .	I finish . . .	I sell . . .
je porte	je finis	je vends
tu portes	tu finis	tu vends
il porte	il finit	il vend
nous portons	nous finissons	nous vendons
vous portez	vous finissez	vous vendez
ils portent	ils finissent	ils vendent

Imperfect

I carried . . .	I finished . . .	I sold . . .
je portais	je finissais	je vendais
tu portais	tu finissais	tu vendais
il portait	il finissait	il vendait
nous portions	nous finissions	nous vendions
vous portiez	vous finissiez	vous vendiez
ils portaient	ils finissaient	ils vendaient

Note.—The present and the imperfect may be translated either by the simple, the progressive, or the emphatic form of the English verb: je porte, *I carry, I am carrying, I do carry;* nous portions, *we carried, we were carrying, we did carry.*

Past Definite

I carried ...	*I finished* ...	*I sold* ...
je portai	je finis	je vendis
tu portas	tu finis	tu vendis
il porta	il finit	il vendit
nous portâmes	nous finîmes	nous vendîmes
vous portâtes	vous finîtes	vous vendîtes
ils portèrent	ils finirent	ils vendirent

Future

I shall carry ...	*I shall finish* ...	*I shall sell* ...
je porterai	je finirai	je vendrai*
tu porteras	tu finiras	tu vendras
il portera	il finira	il vendra
nous porterons	nous finirons	nous vendrons
vous porterez	vous finirez	vous vendrez
ils porteront	ils finiront	ils vendront

Note.—The following verbs have irregular future stems:

INFINITIVE	*Future Stem*	INFINITIVE	*Future Stem*
acquérir, *to acquire*	acquerr-	mourir, *to die*	mourr-
aller, *to go*	ir-	pouvoir, *to be able*	pourr-
avoir, *to have*	aur-	recevoir, *to receive*	recevr-
courir, *to run*	courr-	savoir, *to know*	saur-
cueillir, *to gather*	cueiller-	tenir, *to hold*	tiendr-
devoir, *to owe*	devr-	valoir, *to be worth*	vaudr-
envoyer, *to send*	enverr-	venir, *to come*	viendr-
être, *to be*	ser-	voir, *to see*	verr-
faire, *to do*	fer-	vouloir, *to want*	voudr-
falloir, *to be necessary*	faudr-		

III. VOCABULARY

1. FRENCH-ENGLISH:

acheter, to buy
l'an *m.*, year
assez (de), enough
l'audace *f.*, audacity
autant (de), as much as, as many as
le bas, stocking
cesse: sans —, ceaselessly

le chant, song
le crayon, pencil
le déjeuner, lunch
la douceur, sweetness, gentleness
doute: sans —, without doubt
doux, douce, sweet

---

* In the third conjugation, the final -*e* of the infinitive (vendr[e]) is dropped before the future and conditional endings are added.

la douzaine, dozen
l'écolier *m.*, student
encore, still, yet
l'encre *f.*, ink
envahir, to invade
la faute, mistake
fille: la jeune fille, girl
le flatteur, flatterer
le fromage, cheese
le garçon, boy
la ligne, line
la maison, house
le matin, morning
le mensonge, lie
mesure: n'est pas —, is no
measure
*mourir, to die
l'œuf *m.*, egg
ou, or
le panier, basket
*parcourir, to go (run) through
paresseux, -se, lazy

le petit pain, roll
le petit pois, pea
la poire, pear
remplir, to fill
le rossignol, nightingale
la rue, street
*savoir, to know
*servir, to serve
seul, -e, alone
seulement, only
le soir, evening
le soldat, soldier
le tableau, painting; — de maître, master's painting
le tissu, tissue
travailler, to work
trop (de), too much, too
many
*venir, to come
la viande, meat
le vin, wine
*vouloir, to want, wish

2. ENGLISH-FRENCH:

American, l'Américain
at, à
to bring, apporter
to build, bâtir
but, mais
Catholic, catholique
city, la ville
clothes, les habits *m.pl.*
to come, *venir
dog, le chien
dozen, la douzaine
end, la fin, le bout
enough, assez (de)
envy, l'envie *f.*
faithful, fidèle
famous, fameux, -se

George, Georges
gift, le don, le présent
to go by, porter
to help, aider
hill, la colline
house, la maison
interesting, intéressant, -e
large, grand, -e; largest, le
plus grand
long, longtemps
minute, la minute
money, l'argent *m.*
most, très
name, le nom
object, l'objet *m.*
parents, les parents *m.pl.*

peach, **la pêche**
people, **le monde**
plate, **l'assiette** *f.*
poor, **pauvre**
to possess, **posséder**
professor, **le professeur**
Protestant, **le protestant**
school, **l'école** *f.*

song, **le chant**
Spaniard, **l'Espagnol** *m.*
Swiss, **le Suisse**
too many, **trop (de)**
tragedy, **la tragédie**
very, **très**
to warm up, **réchauffer**
why, **pourquoi**

IV. IDIOMATIC EXPRESSIONS

bien entendu, of course
avoir mal à la tête, to have a headache
venir de (+ *inf.*), to have just
tenir à, to be anxious to
tout à l'heure, in a little while
s'agir de, to be a question of

tout de suite, at once, right away
tout à fait, altogether
il y a, ago
au moins, at least
du moins, at least
c'est une question de, it is a question of

V. EXERCISES

1. *Fill in the dashes with the correct form of the indefinite article:*

1. ——— écolier laborieux est toujours récompensé ——— jour ou l'autre. 2. ——— jeune fille qui ne veut pas travailler est paresseuse. 3. ——— action seule ne forme pas ——— habitude. 4. Le langage d' ——— flatteur est ——— tissu de mensonges. 5. La rose est ——— fleur qui s'épanouit ——— matin et meurt quand vient le soir.

2. *Translate:*

1. They are building a school on a hill. 2. At the end of a minute a friend came to help him. 3. He goes by a famous name. 4. Here is a faithful dog. 5. Is he not a professor? 6. What beautiful gifts! 7. Juan is a Spaniard, but Lewis is an American. 8. Le Cid, a tragedy by Corneille, has long been an object of envy. 9. New York, the largest city in (of) the United States, is most interesting. 10. Is she a Catholic or a Protestant?

3. *Fill in the dashes with the proper form of the partitive article:*

1. Avez-vous acheté ———— encre ou ———— crayons? 2. ———— soldats ont envahi ces maisons, ———— autres parcourent les rues. 3. Il y a ———— eau, ———— vin, ———— fromage et ———— viande sur la table. 4. ———— doux chants remplissent cette forêt et ces belles plaines. 5. Ce sont sans doute ———— rossignols qui chantent. 6. Il n'y a pas ———— professeurs dans cette salle de classe, mais seulement ———— élèves. 7. J'aime les petits pois, aussi maman a acheté ———— petits pois. 8. Il n'a pas ———— patience, mais il a ———— audace. 9. On trouve en Amérique ———— admirables courages parmi les pionniers. 10. On m'a servi ———— petits pains pour déjeuner. 11. ———— autres l'ont faite; ———— autres la feront encore. 12. Marie n'a pas ———— souliers; elle n'a que* ———— bas.

4. *Translate carefully:*

1. No friends at all. 2. 'Yes, I have friends, very good friends, but they are not here. 3. George doesn't possess any houses. 4. No money, no Swiss. 5. There are too many people here. 6. He brought me a dozen peaches. 7. Why haven't you enough clothes? 8. Do you come from a poor family? 9. This plate of soup warms me up.

5. *Fill in all dashes:*

1. Beaucoup ———— personnes ne savent pas se limiter; elles parlent sans cesse. 2. Trop ———— argent et pas assez n'est pas mesure. 3. Ce sont ———— tableaux ———— maître. 4. Il y a autant ———— fautes que ———— lignes. 5. C'est assez ———— fleurs et ———— douceurs. 6. Il n'a pas besoin de protecteur; c'est un garçon ———— vingt ans.

6. *Translate:*

1. Of course, the Americans have just arrived. 2. She has a headache. 3. We are anxious to see our parents at once. 4. They are altogether satisfied. 5. Is it a question of life or death? 6. At least bring some clothes to help the poor. 7. I saw the dog three days ago.

---

* **Ne . . . que,** *only,* has a restrictive sense.

I. THE NOUN—GENDER—NUMBER

There are two kinds of nouns, proper and common. Proper nouns are names of particular people and places: Jeanne, Daudet, Paris. Common nouns include all other names. They may be concrete: crayon, *pencil;* porte, *door;* they may be general: acier, *steel;* eau, *water;* they may be collective: armée, *army;* flotte, *fleet;* or they may be abstract: pauvreté, *poverty;* bonté, *kindness.*

GENDER OF NOUNS.—A noun is either masculine or feminine in French.

As a general rule, the following classes of nouns are masculine:

1. All nouns representing males: homme, *man;* père, *father;* roi, *king.*

2. Names of days of the week, seasons, months, cardinal points, metals, colors, trees: lundi, *Monday;* printemps, *spring;* janvier, *January;* nord, *north;* fer, *iron;* rouge, *red;* pommier, *apple tree.*

3. Names of cities (unless preceded by *la*), countries not ending in mute *e:* Le Havre, Paris, Portugal.

4. Names of professions ending in *-r:* boucher, *butcher;* charpentier, *carpenter.*

5. Most nouns ending in *-ment, -eau* (except eau, *water;* peau, *skin*), *-isme, -age* (except image, *picture;* cage, *cage;* page, *page;* rage, *rage;* plage, *beach;* etc.), *-acle* (except débâcle, *defeat, rout*): enseignement, *teaching;* château, *castle;* naturalisme, *naturalism;* sauvage, *savage;* spectacle, *spectacle.*

6. Adjectives, verbs, prepositions, and adverbs used as nouns: le beau, *the beautiful;* le manger, *food;* le pour et le contre, *pro and con;* le mieux, *the best.*

The following classes of nouns are feminine:

1. All nouns representing females: sœur, *sister;* chienne, *bitch.*

2. Names of fruits (except abricot, *apricot;* raisin, *grape;* citron, *lemon;* ananas, *pineapple;* coing, *quince;* etc.): pomme, *apple;* poire, *pear;* prune, *plum.*

3. Names of countries ending in mute *e* (except Mexique, *Mexico*): France, *France;* Suisse, *Switzerland.*

4. Names of sciences and arts: chimie, *chemistry;* peinture, *painting.*

5. Names expressing dimension or capacity: hauteur, *height;* brassée, *armful.*

6. Most nouns ending in -*ssion*, -*tion*, -*aison*, -*ance*, -*ence*, -*té*, -*tude*, -*ale*, and -*ole:* passion, *passion;* notion, *notion;* terminaison, *ending;* confiance, *confidence;* patience, *patience;* bonté, *kindness;* cathédrale, *cathedral;* parole, *word.*

A few masculine nouns are also applied to women. They usually are preceded by the word "femme": une femme professeur.

docteur (also doctoresse), *doctor*	philosophe, *philosopher*
écrivain, *writer*	poète (also poétesse), *poet*
médecin, *physician*	professeur, *professor*
orateur, *orator*	sculpteur, *sculptor*
peintre, *painter*	soldat, *soldier*
	témoin, *witness*

Some masculine nouns form their feminine after the fashion of adjectives.

le berger, *shepherd*	la bergère, *shepherdess*
le danseur, *dancer*	la danseuse, *dancer*
le veuf, *widower*	la veuve, *widow*

Cf. Feminine of adjectives, pp. 25-26.

Others have the same form in both genders:

Masculine	Feminine
un enfant, *child*	une enfant
le camarade, *comrade*	la camarade
un esclave, *slave*	une esclave
le compatriote, *compatriot*	la compatriote
un artiste, *artist*	une artiste

Note.—Many nouns in -*iste* are both masculine and feminine. Still others, unchanged in form, assume a new meaning when used in the feminine. The more usual ones are:

le crêpe, *crape*	la crêpe, *pancake*
le critique, *critic*	la critique, *criticism*
l'enseigne, *ensign*	l'enseigne, *sign*

le garde, *keeper* — la garde, *guard*
le guide, *guide* — la guide, *rein*
le livre, *book* — la livre, *pound*
le manche, *handle* — la manche, *sleeve*
le mémoire, *memoir* — la mémoire, *memory*
le mode, *manner, mood* — la mode, *style, fashion*
le moule, *mould* — la moule, *mussel*
le mousse, *cabin-boy* — la mousse, *moss*
l'office, *office, duty* — l'office, *pantry*
le page, *page-boy* — la page, *page*
le paillasse, *clown* — la paillasse, *straw mattress*
le pendule, *pendulum* — la pendule, *timepiece*
le poêle, *stove* — la poêle, *frying pan*
le poste, *post, station* — la poste, *post office*
le somme, *nap* — la somme, *sum*
le souris, *smile* (poetic) — la souris, *mouse*
le tour, *trick* — la tour, *tower*
le vapeur, *steamer* — la vapeur, *steam*
le vase, *vase* — la vase, *mud*
le voile, *veil* — la voile, *sail*
etc. — etc.

There are some nouns the feminine form of which differs completely from that of the masculine:

l'homme, *man* — la femme, *woman*
le frère, *brother* — la sœur, *sister*
le père, *father* — la mère, *mother*
le compagnon, *companion* — la compagne, *female companion*
le héros, *hero* — l'héroïne, *heroine*
le dieu, *god* — la déesse, *goddess*
le duc, *duke* — la duchesse, *duchess*
l'ambassadeur, *ambassador* — l'ambassadrice, *ambassadress*
le gendre, *son-in-law* — la bru, *daughter-in-law*
le parrain, *godfather* — la marraîne, *godmother*
le compère, *comrade* — la commère, *gossip*
le roi, *king* — la reine, *queen*
l'empereur, *emperor* — l'impératrice, *empress*
le baron, *baron* — la baronne, *baroness*
le tigre, *tiger* — la tigresse, *tigress*
le lion, *lion* — la lionne, *lioness*

Number of Nouns.—A noun is either in the singular or the plural.

As a general rule, the plural of a noun is formed by adding an *s* to the singular of the noun.

| le livre | les livres | l'ami | les amis |
| la porte | les portes | l'heure | les heures |

If the noun is ending in -*s*, -*x*, -*z*, its plural and singular forms are identical.

le bras, *arm*	les bras
le nez, *nose*	les nez
la voix, *voice*	les voix

The following groups of nouns have an irregular plural:

1. Nouns ending in -*au*, -*eau*, -*eu*, *œu* in the singular add *x* to form their plural.

le tuyau, *pipe*	les tuyaux	le noyau, *stone*	les noyaux
le château, *castle*	les châteaux	(of fruit)	
le cheveu, *hair*	les cheveux	le bateau, *boat*	les bateaux
le vœu, *vow*	les vœux	le feu, *fire*	les feux

2. Nouns ending in -*al* in the singular change -*al* to -*aux*.

| le cheval, *horse* | les chevaux |
| le journal, *newspaper* | les journaux |

3. Some nouns in -*ail* change -*ail* to -*aux:*

| le travail, *work* | les travaux |
| le vitrail, *stained glass window* | les vitraux |

4. Seven masculine nouns in -*ou* in the singular take an *x* in the plural:

bijou, *jewel*	caillou, *pebble*	chou, *cabbage*
genou, *knee*	hibou, *owl*	joujou, *toy*
pou, *louse*		

5. Aïeul, ciel, and œil have a double plural, one regular, the other irregular. Notice the change of meaning.

un aïeul des aïeuls, *grandfathers*   aïeux, *ancestors*
le ciel   les ciels, *skies* (in painting); in   cieux, *skies, heavens*
    ciels de lit, *bed-testers*

un œil   des œils in œils-de-bœuf,   yeux, *eyes*
   small oval or *round windows*, etc.

The formation of the plural of *compound nouns* depends a great deal upon the nature of the noun.

1.   A compound noun made up of two nouns in apposition requires both nouns in the plural.

> le chou-fleur, *cauliflower*   les choux-fleurs
> le chef-lieu, *chief town*   les chefs-lieux

2.   A compound noun made up of a noun and an adjective requires both parts in the plural.

> le coffre-fort, *safe*   les coffres-forts
> la basse-cour, *poultry-yard*   les basses-cours

3.   A compound noun made up of two nouns, one completing the other with or without a preposition, has only the first noun in the plural.

> un arc-en-ciel, *rainbow*   des arcs-en-ciel
> un chef-d'oeuvre, *masterpiece*   des chefs-d'oeuvre
> un timbre-poste, *stamp*   des timbres-poste (de la poste)

4.   Other parts of speech (such as prepositions, verbs, and adverbs) do not take the sign of the plural when the compound noun of which they are a part is in the plural.

> l'avant-bras, *forearm*   les avant-bras
> un en-tête, *heading* (of letter)   des en-têtes
> un passe-partout, *master key*   des passe-partout

II.   VERB REVIEW

1.   COMPOUND TENSES

To form compound tenses in French, combine the simple tenses of **avoir** or **être** with the past participle of the verb to be conjugated in compound tenses.

INDICATIVE

Perfect	*Pluperfect*
j'ai eu, *I have had* . . .	j'avais eu, *I had had* . . .
j'ai été, *I have been* . . .	j'avais été, *I had been* . . .

j'ai porté, *I have carried* . . .

j'ai fini, *I have finished* . . .

j'ai vendu, *I have sold* . . .

je suis allé(e), *I have gone* . . .

j'avais porté, *I had carried* . . .

j'avais fini, *I had finished* . . .

j'avais vendu, *I had sold* . . .

j'étais allé(e), *I had gone* . . .

Past Anterior

j'eus eu, *I had had* . . .

j'eus été, *I had been* . . .

j'eus porté, *I had carried* . . .

j'eus fini, *I had finished* . . .

j'eus vendu, *I had sold* . . .

je fus allé(e), *I had gone* . . .

Future Anterior

j'aurai eu, *I shall have had* . . .

j'aurai été, *I shall have been* . . .

j'aurai porté, *I shall have carried* . . .

j'aurai fini, *I shall have finished* . . .

j'aurai vendu, *I shall have sold* . . .

je serai allé(e), *I shall have gone* . . .

2. CONDITIONAL MOOD

The conditional mood has two tenses, the present and the perfect. The present conditional is formed by adding to the infinitive—after dropping the *e* mute of verbs in the third conjugation—the endings of the imperfect indicative, *-ais, -ais, -ait, -ions, -iez,* and *-aient*. It has the same irregular stems as the future, p. 11. The perfect conditional is formed by the conditional present of the auxiliary + the past participle.

Present

I should have . . .	*I should be* . . .	*I should carry* . . .
j'aurais	je serais	je porterais
tu aurais	tu serais	tu porterais
il aurait	il serait	il porterait
nous aurions	nous serions	nous porterions
vous auriez	vous seriez	vous porteriez
ils auraient	ils seraient	ils porteraient

I should finish . . .	*I should sell* . . .
je finirais	je vendrais
tu finirais	tu vendrais
il finirait	il vendrait
nous finirions	nous vendrions
vous finiriez	vous vendriez
ils finiraient	ils vendraient

Perfect

I should have had . . .	*I should have been . . .*
j'aurais eu . . .	j'aurais été . . .
nous aurions eu . . .	nous aurions été . . .
I should have carried . . .	*I should have finished . . .*
j'aurais porté . . .	j'aurais fini . . .
nous aurions porté . . .	nous aurions fini . . .
I should have sold . . .	*I should have gone . . .*
j'aurais vendu . . .	je serais allé(e) . . .
nous aurions vendu . . .	nous serions allé(e)s . . .

III. VOCABULARY

1. FRENCH-ENGLISH:

l'argent *m.*, money
la bague, ring
le bœuf, beef
le boucher, butcher
le boulanger, baker
le champ, field
le chanteur, singer
le chat, cat
le chien, dog
le chrétien, Christian
le citoyen, citizen
*conduire, to conduct, lead
coucher, to put to bed
coûter, to cost
*couvrir (*p.p.* couvert), to cover
la croix, cross
le cuisinier, cook
déchirer, to tear
donner, to give
l'espion *m.*, spy
l'étranger *m.*, stranger, foreigner
le fermier, farmer

le feu, fire
le fils, son
le lionceau, lion's cub
marcher, to walk
le marteau, hammer
le nez, nose
le Normand, Norman
le nuage, cloud
l'oiseau *m.*, bird
l'ouvrier *m.*, worker
par, by
le parleur, speaker, talker
le patron, boss
la peau, skin
petit, -e, small
la pierre, stone
le sceau, seal
tourner, to turn
le travail, work
usage : faire — de, to use
le veston, jacket
le villageois, villager
la voix, voice
le voleur, thief

2. ENGLISH-FRENCH:

about, **vers**

afternoon, **l'après-midi** *m.*
and *f.*

to believe, *****croire**

ever, **jamais**

to leave, *****partir**

to look, **regarder**

to meet, **rencontrer**

never, **ne . . . jamais**

o'clock, **l'heure** *f.*

people, **les gens** *m.pl.*

to see, *****voir**

to stay, **rester**

story, **l'histoire** *f.*

truth, **la vérité**

uncle, **l'oncle** *m.*

what, **ce que, ce qu'**

yesterday, **hier**

IV. IDIOMATIC EXPRESSIONS

à côté de, beside, next to

du côté de, in the direction of

à peine, hardly

en effet, indeed, in fact

c'est-à-dire, that is to say

quant à, as for

en somme, in short

envoyer chercher, to send for

qu'avez-vous? what is the matter with you?

il y a, there is, there are

V. EXERCISES

1. *Put the following nouns into the feminine:*

*****le cuisinier	l'ami	le chrétien
le chien	l'ouvrier	l'étranger
le flatteur	le danseur	le voleur
le chat	le parent	le villageois
le Français	le cousin	le chanteur
le fermier	l'espion	le citoyen
le boucher	le boulanger	le patron

2. *Translate carefully:*

1. Le garde de cette maison a un fils qui est de la garde républicaine. 2. Le bœuf coûte quarante sous la livre. 3.

---

* The meaning of these words is given in the General Vocabulary.

Ce poêle n'est plus à la mode. 4. Ce mousse aime à s'étendre sur la mousse. 5. Le page tourne les pages du livre de la reine. 6. Le paillasse est couché sur sa paillasse. 7. Le guide conduit son cheval par la guide. 8. Louis a déchiré la manche du veston et Jean a cassé le manche du marteau. 9. Sans le pendule on ne peut faire marcher la pendule. 10. Je vous donne cette somme d'argent avant d'aller faire un somme.

3. *Translate:*

1. My brother, the duke, met his sister, the baroness. 2. The heroine is the daughter-in-law of Albert's godmother. 3. We have seen the empress with the duchess of K. and the ambassadress of R. 4. Rome had her gods and goddesses. 5. The companion of the king's son-in-law is my father's friend.

4. *Put the following nouns into the plural:*

*l'ami	l'arsenal	le feu
la voile	le bas	l'eau
le parrain	la noix	le ciel
l'amiral	la source	le sceau
le travail	la peau	l'aïeul
le rival	le mal	le vitrail
le nez	la croix	l'œil

5. *Put the following sentences into the plural:*

1. La bague est un bijou. 2. Le lionceau est le petit du lion. 3. Le Normand aime le travail des champs. 4. Le hibou est un oiseau. 5. Le caillou est une petite pierre. 6. Le ciel de ce tableau est couvert de nuages. 7. Que le ciel est beau! 8. En France on fait encore usage du ciel de lit. 9. Nous avons un œil-de-bœuf dans la porte de notre porche. 10. Le pou est un insecte désagréable.

6. *Translate into idiomatic French:*

1. He is walking beside his uncle. 2. Do you ever look in

---

the direction of the river? 3. He had hardly seen him when he left. 4. I spoke to him this afternoon—that's to say about four o'clock. 5. As for me, I have never seen him. 6. In short, that's what he said yesterday. 7. In fact, he has sent for him. 8. What is the matter with them? 9. There are many people who do not believe him. 10. There isn't much truth in his story.

I. THE QUALIFYING ADJECTIVE—FORMATION OF THE FEMININE AND THE PLURAL—POSITION—COMPARISON—COMPARATIVE SENTENCE

An adjective is a word that qualifies a noun to describe, limit, or distinguish it from others of the same class.

There are various kinds of adjectives: qualifying, possessive, demonstrative, interrogative, numeral, and indefinite.

THE QUALIFYING ADJECTIVE.—A qualifying adjective may either serve as a qualifier of a noun or as a predicate. In both cases it must agree in gender and number with the noun which it qualifies or of which it is a predicate. Hence this question, how are the feminine and the plural of adjectives formed?

FORMATION OF THE FEMININE.—As a general rule, the feminine of adjectives is formed by adding an *e* to the masculine form of the adjective unless the adjective in the masculine already ends in *e*, in which case the masculine and feminine forms are alike.

grand, *tall*	grande	poli, *polite*	polie
fort, *strong*	forte	absolu, *absolute*	absolue
malade, *sick*	malade	faible, *weak*	faible

but:

| aigu, *acute* | aiguë |

There are, however, *exceptions* to this general rule. Thus,

1. Adjectives ending in -*el*, -*eil*, -*en*, -*on*, -*et*, and -*s* double their consonant and add *e*.

cruel, *cruel*	cruelle	solennel, *solemn*	solennelle
pareil, *similar*	pareille	vermeil, *rosy*	vermeille
ancien, *ancient*	ancienne	païen *pagan*	païenne
bon, *good*	bonne	net, *neat*	nette
gros, *stout, big*	grosse	bas, *low*	basse

Contrary to the above mentioned rule,

frais, *fresh*	fraîche	tiers, *third*	tierce
complet, *complete*	complète	concret, *concrete*	concrète
replet, *replete*	replète	inquiet, *uneasy*	inquiète
discret, *discrete*	discrète	secret, *secret*	secrète

2. Adjectives ending in *-f*, *-g*, *-x*, and *-c* change *-f* to *-ve*, *-g* to *-gue*, *-x* to *-se*, and *-c* to *-che* or *-que*.

vif, *vivid*	vive	actif, *active*	active
long, *long*	longue	oblong, *oblong*	oblongue
heureux, *happy*	heureuse	peureux, *timorous*	peureuse
blanc, *white*	blanche	public, *public*	publique

but :

doux, *sweet*	douce	roux, *red*	rousse
grec, *Greek*	grecque		

3. Adjectives ending in *-er* change *-er* to *-ère*. Adjectives ending in *-eur,* if derived from verbs, change *-eur* to *-euse;* otherwise they add an *e* in the feminine. Some are quite irregular.

cher, *dear*	chère	danseur, *dancing*	danseuse
léger, *light*	légère	flatteur, *flattering*	flatteuse

but :

meilleur, *better*	meilleure	protecteur, *protecting*	protectrice
acteur, *acting*	actrice	moteur, *motive*	motrice

4. The following adjectives with double masculine form their feminine from the second masculine (which is used only before nouns in the singular beginning with a vowel or a mute *h*), by doubling the last consonant and adding *-e*.

Masculine	*Masculine*	*Feminine*
beau, *beautiful*	bel	belle
nouveau, *new*	nouvel	nouvelle
vieux, *old*	vieil	vieille
fou, *crazy*	fol	folle
mou. *soft*	mol	molle

Formation of the Plural.—Generally, the plural of masculine and feminine adjectives is formed by the addition of an *s*.

petit, *small*	petits	petite	petites
bon, *good*	bons	bonne	bonnes

Some adjectives, however, form their plural irregularly.

1. Masculine adjectives ending in -*s* or -*x* remain unchanged:

gros, *stout*	gros	frais, *fresh*	frais
dangereux, *dangerous*	dangereux	honteux, *ashamed*	honteux

2. Masculine adjectives ending in -*eau* and -*eu* take an *x* in the plural.

beau, *beautiful*	beaux	hébreu, *Hebrew*	hébreux
nouveau, *new*	nouveaux		

Note.—Bleu, *blue*, takes an *s* in the plural.

3. Masculine adjectives ending in -*al* change -*al* to -*aux*.

légal, *legal*	légaux	loyal, *loyal*	loyaux
égal, *equal*	égaux	royal, *royal*	royaux

Note.—Fatal, *fatal;* glacial, *icy;* natal, *native;* etc., take an *s* in the plural masculine.

Position of Adjectives.—As a general rule, adjectives are placed after the noun which they qualify, in French.

une histoire amusante	*an amusing story*
une invention américaine	*an American invention*

There are, however, some *exceptions*.

1. The following small adjectives are, as a rule, placed before the nouns which they qualify or modify:

autre, *other*	gros, *stout*	petit, *small*
beau, *beautiful*	jeune, *young*	plusieurs, *several*
bon, *good*	joli, *pretty*	tel, *such a*
chaque, *each*	long, *long*	vieux, *old*
court, *short*	mauvais, *bad*	vilain, *ugly*, etc.

Note.—When two small adjectives are connected by **et**, both adjectives are placed after the noun which they qualify: un homme jeune et beau, *a handsome young man.*

When an adjective is modified by an adverb, it follows the noun: un château plutôt petit, *a rather small castle.*

When one of the above mentioned adjectives is used together with an adjective that follows the noun, it keeps its position before the noun: un gros livre jaune, *a big yellow book.*

2. A few adjectives take up a different meaning when placed before or after the noun which they qualify.

un brave homme	*worthy*	un homme brave	*brave*
un cher ami	*dear*	une robe chère	*expensive*
le dernier roi	*last*	le mois dernier	*past, last*
un grand homme	*famous*	un homme grand	*tall*
un pauvre garçon	*pitiable*	un garçon pauvre	*penniless*
la propre chambre	*own*	une chambre propre	*clean*
la bonne femme	*simple*	la femme bonne	*good*

COMPARATIVE AND SUPERLATIVE.—To form the comparative of a qualifying adjective, whether masculine or feminine, singular or plural, prefix **plus** or **moins** to the adjective in the positive.

petit	plus petit	*smaller*
polie	plus polie	*more polite*
générales	moins générales	*less general*
beaux	moins beaux	*less beautiful*

To form the superlative of a qualifying adjective in the positive, prefix **le plus, la plus, les plus** or **le moins, la moins, les moins** to the adjective.

lent	le plus lent	*slowest*
gaie	la plus gaie	*gayest*
forts	les plus forts	*strongest*
belles	les plus belles	*most beautiful*
utile	le moins utile	*the least useful*
vieille	la moins vieille	*the least old*
grands	les moins grands	*the least tall*
seules	les moins seules	*the least lonely*

A few adjectives, however, form their comparatives and superlatives irregularly.

bon, *good*	meilleur, -e, *better*	le meilleur, *the best*
mauvais, *bad*	pire, *worse*	le pire, *the worst*

	plus mauvais, -e, *worse*	le plus mauvais, *the worst*
petit, *small*	moindre (in importance, quantity), *smaller*	le moindre, *the least*
	plus petit, -e, (in size), *smaller*	le plus petit, *the smallest*

THE COMPARATIVE IN A SENTENCE.—A comparison in a sentence may be one of superiority, inferiority, or equality.

1. To form a comparison of *superiority* put **plus** before the adjective and **que** after it.

Louis est plus grand que sa sœur.	Louis is taller than his sister.
Ce livre est plus intéressant que le mien.	This book is more interesting than mine.

2. To form a comparison of *inferiority* place **moins** before the adjective and **que** after it, or use the negative form of the verb + **si** before the adjective.

Elle est moins intelligente que son frère.	She is less intelligent than her brother.
Elle n'est pas si (aussi) intelligente que son frère.	She is not so intelligent as her brother.

Note.—This second manner of expressing a comparison of inequality is just a negatived comparison of equality. Instead of **aussi** a simple **si** may also be used with the verb in the negative.

3. To form a comparative of *equality* place **aussi** before the adjective and **que** after it.

Son jardin est aussi beau que le mien.	His (or her) garden is as beautiful as mine.

Note.—In the sentence J'ai plus de trente livres, *I have more than thirty books*, **plus de** . . . is an adverbial expression, not a comparative phrase.

II. VERB REVIEW

1. THE PRINCIPAL PARTS

All regular and most irregular verbs have five forms, called principal parts, from which are drawn all derived tenses.

PRINCIPAL PARTS:	*Infinitive*	*Pres. Part.*	*Past Part.*	*Present*	*Past Def.*	
	porter	portant	porté	porte	portas	2nd
	finir	finissant	fini	finis	finis	pers.
	vendr(e)	vendant	vendu	vends	vendis	sing.

DERIVED TENSES:					
1. *Future*	porterai				
	finirai				
	vendrai				
2. *Conditional*	porterais				
	finirais				
	vendrais				
3. *Imperfect*		portais			
		finissais			
		vendais			

4. *All Compound Tenses*

1° Past Indefinite	ai	porté
		fini
		vendu
2° Pluperfect	avais	porté
		fini
		vendu
3° Past Anterior	eus	porté
		fini
		vendu
4° Future Anterior	aurai	porté
		fini
		vendu
5° Conditional Perfect	aurais	porté
		fini
		vendu
6° Perfect Subjunctive	aie	porté
		fini
		vendu
7° Pluperfect Subjunctive	eusse	porté
		fini
		vendu

5. *Imperative*		*Present*
	2nd person singular	porte
		finis
		vends
	1st person plural	portons
		finissons
		vendons
	2nd person plural	portez
		finissez
		vendez

6. *Present Subjunctive* (*from 3d pers. plur of Present*)	porte
	finisse
	vende

7. *Imperfect Subjunctive*	*Past Def.*
	portasse
	finisse
	vendisse

2. IRREGULAR VERBS

Present		*Principal Parts*
aller, *to go*		aller, allant, allé, vais, allai
vais	allons	
vas	allez	
và	vont	
devoir, *to owe*		devoir, devant, dû, dois, dus
dois	devons	
dois	devez	
doit	doivent	
faire, *to do, make*		faire, faisant, fait, fais, fis
fais	faisons	
fais	faites	
fait	font	

III. VOCABULARY

1. FRENCH-ENGLISH:

accourir, to come hastening
l'âne *m.*, donkey
***apercevoir,** to perceive, see
apporter, to bring
attraper, to catch
autour de, around
l'aventurier *m.*, adventurer
le capitaine, captain
charmant, -e, charming
doucement, cautiously
***s'ébattre,** to gambol, play
l'enfant *m.* and *f.*, child
enfin, finally
épuisé, -e, exhausted
extrêmement, extremely
fatigué, -e, tired
fier, -ère, proud
fois: à la fois, both
le frelon, hornet
la gaîté, gaiety
le gamin, urchin
grand, -e, famous

la guêpe, wasp
habiter, to dwell
jeter: — les hauts cris, to give vent to one's indignation
marcher, to walk
le médecin, physician
le milieu, middle
où, where
perdre, to lose
piquer, to sting
le plaisir, pleasure
plein, -e, full
plusieurs, several
reposer, to rest
le rosier, rose-tree
saisir, to seize
séduisant, -e, tempting
la semaine, week
***se souvenir de,** to remember
souvent, often
subitement, suddenly

sur, on, upon
le tour, round
tranquille, quiet
trouver, to find
se trouver, to be (location)

*venu, -e (inf. *venir) come
vermeil, -le, bright red
vers, toward
*voir, to see
voltiger, to fly about

2. ENGLISH-FRENCH:

to believe, *croire
to convince, *convaincre
country, le pays
day, le jour
dry, sec, sèche
each, chaque
England, l'Angleterre *f.*
family, la famille
generous, généreux, -se

to go away, *s'en aller, *partir
handsome, beau, bel, belle
man, l'homme *m.*
mountain, la montagne
to play, jouer
to print, imprimer
rich, riche
student, l'étudiant *m.*
tobacco, le tabac
uncle, l'oncle *m.*

IV. IDIOMATIC EXPRESSIONS

à peu près, almost, nearly
c'est entendu, agreed, very well
tiens! well!
à toute heure, at any time
tout à l'heure, in a little while
allons! come!
avoir l'air de, to appear, look like
au contraire, on the contrary
être en train de (+ inf.), to be busy
voyons! surely!
il a beau parler, it is useless for him to talk, he talks in vain

V. EXERCISES

(a) FORMATION OF THE FEMININE AND THE PLURAL OF ADJECTIVES:

1. *Put the adjective into agreement with the noun which it modifies:*

*pauvre fille	mère indulgent	générosité royal
mer profond	patronne aimable	vie pénible

* The meaning of these words is given in the General Vocabulary.

joli maison	question obscur	volonté absolu
femme fort	nuit étoilé	dame obligeant
chambre aéré	demeure sain	tête obstiné

2. *Form sentences with the above* (1.) *phrases, using the qualifying adjectives as predicate adjectives* (*Example: la fille est pauvre*).

3. *Fill in each dash with the correct form of the adjective in the preceding phrase:*

*un jour solennel	une fête————
un ami discret	une femme————
un teint vermeil	une lèvre————
un visage frais	une rose————
un regard inquiet	une attitude————
un ancien camarade	une histoire————
un temple païen	une nation————
un tiers témoin	une————personne

4. *Put both the noun and the adjective into the feminine:*

*un père heureux
un roi hautain
un acteur vif
un oncle flatteur
un neveu léger
un parrain doux
un dieu fier
un frère cadet
un prince dépensier
un marquis vieillot
un serviteur gentil
un garçon roux
un chat faux

5. *Put the following selection into the feminine, using as characters "une jeune fille" and "une guêpe":*

Un jour, un joli petit gamin, vif et plein de gaîté, s'ébattait dans un parc. Tout à coup il aperçoit un frelon. Il veut attraper l'insecte. Mais le frelon voltige autour du charmant enfant, fait mille et mille tours et vient enfin, fatigué

---

* The meaning of these words is given in the General Vocabulary.

et épuisé, se reposer sur une rose vermeille. Marchant doucement vers le rosier où se trouvait son ennemi, notre petit aventurier saisit subitement et à la fois, la rose et le frelon. Mais, celui-ci le pique et l'imprudent de jeter les hauts cris. Son père accourt. Après avoir consolé son fils, il lui dit: "Mon fils, souviens-toi qu'au milieu des plaisirs les plus séduisants on trouve souvent du poison."

(b) POSITION OF QUALIFYING ADJECTIVE:

1. *Prefix the following nouns with the proper form of the adjectives in parentheses:*

* (beau) un oiseau	(vieux) les amis	(fou) un ami
les officiers	un couteau	les affaires
la voile	une porte	une ambition
le vase	les tables	un projet
un amant	l'ouvrier	les dépenses

2. *Have all adjectives agree with the nouns that follow*
(Model: fertile, un champ fertile, des vallées fertiles, etc.):

*fertile	champ, vallées, jardins, contrée
aigu	cri, sons, douleur, souffrances
frais	peinture, œufs, vent, boissons
blanc	murs, page, drap, cravates
doux	airs, main, paroles, regard
grec	ville, héros, temples, armées

3. *Translate:*

*a cruel tyrant	a narrow path	a gay fellow
last year	a round balloon	a stout soldier
a rosy peach	a black dress	a celebrated man
an expensive book	a pretty object	a nasty person

4. *Explain the position of the adjectives in the following sentences:*

1. Plusieurs médecins sont venus voir le petit garçon. 2. Le grand capitaine s'est distingué dans des batailles furieuses. 3. Une victoire glorieuse a récompensé ses longs efforts. 4. Le pauvre garçon a perdu son bon père la semaine

* The meaning of these words is given in the General Vocabulary.

dernière. 5. Quel homme brave et quel pauvre homme!
6. Il a maintenant sa propre chambre, qui n'est pas toujours
une chambre propre. 7. Voici une tête extrêmement jolie.
8. Il habite une belle maison blanche.

5. *Translate:*

1. The beautiful days are gone. 2. Here is some good dry
tobacco. 3. His last book was printed last year. 4. He
is a tall and handsome man. 5. Each student comes from
a good family.

(c) Comparative, Superlative, and Comparative Sentence:
1. *Give the comparative and the superlative of superiority and in-*
feriority of the following adjectives:

méchant	lents	vifs
bonne	mauvaise	franc
polie	fière	froide
folles	basses	douces
frais	gentil	net

2. *Translate carefully:*

1. He is not so polite as his sister. 2. Alice is more
generous than her comrades. 3. The mountains of my
country are higher than these mountains. 4. Is England
as rich as the United States? 5. They have more money
than you, but less intelligence. 6. My friend is charming,
is he not? 7. You are very rich, but you are not so rich as
my uncle.

3. *Point out all comparisons of superiority, inferiority, and*
equality; then translate:

1. La guerre apporte des maux plus terribles que vous ne
pensez. 2. Le verre est moins transparent que le cristal.
3. Un océan est plus étendu qu'une mer. 4. Est-ce que
les légumes sont aussi nourrissants que la viande? 5. La
lune n'est pas si brillante que le soleil. 6. L'âne est de son
naturel aussi humble, aussi patient, aussi tranquille que le
cheval est fier, ardent, impétueux.

4. *Translate into idiomatic French:*

1. Well, you look like a sick man. 2. Of course, I'll see you in a little while. 3. Come, don't do that! 4. Are you playing? No, on the contrary; I'm busy working. 5. This spectacle took place at five o'clock or nearly at five. 6. Surely, you don't believe it! 7. It was useless for him to speak; he convinced no one.

LESSON V

I. THE POSSESSIVE, DEMONSTRATIVE, AND INTERROGATIVE ADJECTIVES

THE POSSESSIVE ADJECTIVE.—The possessive adjectives add an idea of possession to the nouns which they modify.

Possessive adjectives vary according to the gender, number, and person of the nouns which they limit.

SINGULAR			PLURAL	
Masculine	*Feminine*		*Masculine and Feminine*	
mon	ma	*my*	mes	*my*
ton	ta	*thy, your*	tes	*your*
son	sa	*his, her, its*	ses	*his, her, its*
notre		*our*	nos	*our*
votre		*your*	vos	*your*
leur		*their*	leurs	*their*

In French, possessive adjectives agree in gender, number, and person with the nouns which they limit.

Jeanne parle avec son père.	Jean speaks with her father.
Je parle avec ma mère.	I speak with my mother.
Émile parle avec sa sœur.	Emile speaks with his sister.
Ce sont vos livres.	These are your books.

Notice that in French the possessive adjectives agree in gender and number, not with the *possessor* but with the *possessed object*.

Mon, ton, son must be used before any feminine noun in the singular that begins with a vowel or mute *h*. This is also the case with feminine adjectives in the singular beginning with a vowel or mute *h*, when they precede the nouns which they modify.

mon amie (*f.*)	mon aimable amie
ton histoire (*f.*)	ton autre histoire
son origine (*f.*)	son humble origine

37

Note.—Possessive adjectives are replaced by the definite article —with or without a reference pronoun—when they prefix a noun denoting parts of one's own body or clothes: il a les mains dans les poches, *he has his hands in his pockets;* il se fait couper les cheveux, *he has his hair cut.*

DEMONSTRATIVE ADJECTIVES.—A demonstrative adjective points out objects definitely.

Demonstrative adjectives vary according to the gender and number of the objects they point out.

SINGULAR			PLURAL	
Masculine	*Feminine*		*Masculine and Feminine*	
ce	cette	*this, that*	ces	*these, those*
cet		*this, that*		

Cet is used when masculine nouns in the singular begin with a vowel or an *h* mute: cet ami, *this friend;* cet homme, *this man.*

For the sake of precision and to distinguish a nearby object from a more remote one, **-ci** or **-là** is added to the noun prefixed with a demonstrative adjective.

ce jardin-ci,	*this garden*	cette maison-ci,	*this house*
ce jardin-là,	*that garden*	cette maison-là,	*that house*
ces lits-ci,	*these beds*	ces femmes-ci,	*these women*
ces lits-là,	*those beds*	ces femmes-là,	*those women*

Demonstrative adjectives must be repeated before each noun which they modify: ce jardin et cette maison; ces jardins et ces maisons.

INTERROGATIVE ADJECTIVES.—An interrogative adjective combines with a noun and aids in forming a question.

There is only one interrogative adjective in French, **quel?** *what?* which assumes various forms according to the gender and number of the nouns which it modifies.

SINGULAR		PLURAL	
Masculine	*Feminine*	*Masculine*	*Feminine*
quel	quelle	quels	quelles

quel jour? *what day?*	quels jours? *what days?*
quelle dame? *what lady?*	quelles dames? *what ladies?*

Quel, quelle, quels, and **quelles,** are also used as predicate adjectives before **être.** They then assume the meanings of *who, which,* or *what.*

Quel est ce peintre?	Who is this painter?
Quelle est votre plume?	Which is your pen?
Quelles sont les rivières de la France?	What are the rivers of France?

Note. — Besides being an interrogative adjective, **quel** may function as an exclamative adjective: quel beau jour! *what a beautiful day!* quelles belles robes! *what beautiful dresses!* Notice the absence of the indefinite article in the singular.

II. VERB REVIEW

1. INTERROGATIVE FORM OF VERBS

Est-ce que is commonly used for the first person singular when verbs are conjugated interrogatively: est-ce que j'ai? *have I?* est-ce que je suis? *am I?* est-ce que je porte? *do I carry?* est-ce que je finis? *do I finish?* est-ce que je vends? *do I sell?* One may use **est-ce que** throughout the various tenses.   Ai-je? suis-je? dis-je? sais-je? fais-je? vais-je? etc., may also be used instead of est-ce que j'ai? etc.[1]

To conjugate a verb interrogatively in simple tenses, put the subject pronoun after the verb and connect it with the verb by a hyphen.

Present	*Imperfect*	*Past Definite*
Do I scold? . . .	*Did I finish? . . .*	*Did I sell? . . .*
est-ce que je gronde?	est-ce que je finissais?	est-ce que je vendis?
grondes-tu?	finissais-tu?	vendis-tu?
gronde-t-il?	finissait-il?	vendit-il?
grondons-nous?	finissions-nous?	vendîmes-nous?
grondez-vous?	finissiez-vous?	vendîtes-vous?
grondent-ils?	finissaient-ils?	vendirent-ils?

---

[1] Verbs in -er may have their interrogative form in the 1*st* person singular of the present indicative in **-é-je:** parlé-je? *do I speak?*

When the last letter of the verb ending is a vowel, a euphonic **t** is used between that vowel and the third person pronoun in the singular.

a-t-il?	porte-t-il?	porta-t-il?
a-t-elle?	porte-t-elle?	porta-t-elle?

To conjugate a verb interrogatively in compound tenses, put the subject pronoun after the auxiliary and connect it with that auxiliary by means of a hyphen.

a-t-il eu?	avait-il porté?	auriez-vous vendu?
ont-ils été?	avions-nous fini?	seront-ils partis?

2. Irregular Verbs[1]

Present   *Principal Parts*

pouvoir, *to be able*   pouvoir, pouvant, pu, puis *or* peux, pus

puis or peux	pouvons
peux	pouvez
peut	peuvent

vouloir, *to want*   vouloir, voulant, voulu, veux, voulus

veux	voulons
veux	voulez
veut	veulent

dire, *to say, tell*   dire, disant, dit, dis, dis

dis	disons
dis	dites
dit	disent

III.   VOCABULARY

1. French-English:

amener, to bring along	**brumeux, -se,** foggy
apporter, to bring	**cela,** that
l'aquilon *m.*, north wind	**ce que,** that which, what
l'arbre *m.*, tree	**chacun, -e,** each, every
l'argent *m.*, money	**la charrue,** plough
le blé, wheat	**le chien,** dog
la bonté, kindness	**la colline,** hill

[1] Compounded irregular verbs are conjugated like the simple irregular verbs. *Redire* is conjugated like *dire.* There are very few exceptions.

devant, before
l'élève *m.* and *f.*, pupil
entendre, to hear
l'heure *f.*, hour, o'clock, time
incertain, -e, uncertain
le jeu, game
jouer, to play
le jouet, toy
joyeux, -se, joyful
là-bas, yonder
le lit, bed
lointain, -e, distant
le mât, mast
même, same
la mer, sea
nouveau, nouvel, nouvelle, new
l'oiseau *m.*, bird
par delà, beyond
parler, to speak

*partir, to leave, go away
le pays, country
le paysage, landscape
le pré, meadow
la propriété, estate, property
la proue, prow
raconter, to tell
recommencer, to begin again
regarder, to look at
remplir, to fill
*rire, to laugh
le sillon, furrow
la sœur, sister
*sortir, to go out
la tempête, tempest
la terre, earth
toujours, always
tracer, to trace
voyager, to travel

2. ENGLISH-FRENCH:

again, de nouveau
always, toujours
breakfast, le petit déjeuner
chair, la chaise
to change, changer
cigar, le cigare
constantly, constamment
father, le père
field, le champ
hat, le chapeau
headache, le mal de tête; to
have a —, avoir mal à la
tête
to help, aider
to listen to, écouter
mouth, la bouche

new, nouveau, nouvel, nouvelle
only, ne . . . que
painting, la peinture
picture, le tableau, la photographie
to plough, labourer
red, rouge
short, court
summer, l'été *m.*
today, aujourd'hui
tomorrow, demain; — morn-
ing, demain matin
where, où
work, le travail
to work, travailler

IV. IDIOMATIC EXPRESSIONS

vouloir bien, to be willing, like to
faire beau, mauvais, to be fine weather, bad weather
faire le malade, to pretend to be sick
faire semblant de travailler, to pretend to work
faire mine de ne pas comprendre, to pretend not to understand
vouloir dire, to mean
se mettre à, to begin, set about

V. EXERCISES

1. *Complete the sentences by translating all words in parentheses; then render the sentences into English:*

   1. (My) sœur est malade. 2. (Her) amie est arrivée. 3. Louise regarde (her) livres. 4. Ils ont amené (their) chien. 5. Où se trouve (your) nouvelle propriété? 6. (Our) amies sont parties. 7. Apportez-moi (her) encre. 8. Paul parle avec (his) mère. 9. Émilie est sortie avec (her) père. 10. Lui a-t-il raconté (his) histoire?

2. *Translate:*

   1. Where are your hats? 2. My hat is on the chair. 3. I saw her father yesterday; he had just finished his work. 4. He has always a (le) cigar in his mouth. 5. Have you seen their new pictures? 6. My story is very short. 7. Your eyes are red.* 8. She again has her headache.

3. *Point out all the demonstrative adjectives of the following selection:*

   > Vois, ce spectacle est beau!   Ce paysage immense,
   > Qui toujours devant nous finit et recommence;
   > Ces blés, ces eaux, ces prés charmants aux yeux;
   > Ce chaume où l'on entend rire un groupe joyeux;
   > Cet oiseau qui voyage et cet oiseau qui joue;
   > Ici cette charrue et là-bas cette proue,
   > Traçant en même temps chacune leur sillon;

---

* (= you have the eyes red.)

Ces arbres et ces mâts, jouets de l'aquilon;
Et là-bas, par delà les collines lointaines,
Ces horizons remplis de formes incertaines,
Tout ce que nous voyons, brumeux ou transparent . . .
————regarde, c'est la terre.
Victor Hugo.

4. *Fill in the dashes with the proper form of the demonstrative adjective:*

*————noble ouvrage   ————prétendues promesses
————ancien ami   ————intéressant voyage
————sons pénétrants   ————pays immense
————homme malheureux   ————formes trompeuses
————énorme pierre   ————animal malfaisant

> ————ombres errantes
> ————regards méchants
> ————colline lointaine
> ————bel oiseau
> ————officier français

5. *Form twelve sentences with the words below according to this model:*

spectacle   beau   Ce spectacle-ci est beau; ce spectacle-là n'est pas beau. *Translate each sentence:*

*paysage	immense	charrues	lourdes
blés	jaunes	sillon	long
eau	limpide	mâts	hauts
prés	verts	arbres	grands
chaume	vieux	horizon	bleu
groupes	joyeux	temps	brumeux

6. *Translate:*

1. Quelle heure est-il? 2. Savez-vous quelle est la principale industrie du pays? 3. Quels sont ces hommes? 4. Quel livre est-ce? 5. Quelle bonté, cher ami! 6. Avec quel argent avez-vous acheté cela? 7. Dites-moi quelles sont les frontières de la France. 8. Quelle mer n'a pas de tempêtes? 9. Quels sont vos jeux préférés? 10.

* The meaning of these words is given in the General Vocabulary.

Sur quel lit vous étendez-vous? **11.** Quels sont les élèves qui sont absents?

7. *Translate into idiomatic French:*

1. Has Paul just finished his breakfast? 2. He told John that they were willing to help you. 3. Isn't the weather changing constantly this summer? Yesterday, the weather was bad; today it is fine; tomorrow it will be bad again. 4. He only pretended to be listening (two ways). 5. What does this mean? It means that they do not want to work. 6. Did they begin to plough the fields? 7. Has she seen the keeper? No, she will see the keeper and speak to him tomorrow morning.

I. NUMERAL AND INDEFINITE ADJECTIVES

NUMERAL ADJECTIVES.—A numeral adjective denotes some exact number. Numeral adjectives are of two kinds, cardinal and ordinal.

CARDINAL numbers indicate *how many* or *how much*. They are

1	un, -e	40	quarante
2	deux	41	quarante et un
3	trois	42	quarante-deux
4	quatre	50	cinquante
5	cinq	51	cinquante et un
6	six	52	cinquante-deux
7	sept	60	soixante
8	huit	61	soixante et un
9	neuf	62	soixante-deux
10	dix	70	soixante-dix
11	onze	71	soixante et onze
12	douze	72	soixante-douze
13	treize	80	quatre-vingts
14	quatorze	81	quatre-vingt-un
15	quinze	82	quatre-vingt-deux
16	seize	90	quatre-vingt-dix
17	dix-sept	91	quatre-vingt-onze
18	dix-huit	92	quatre-vingt-douze
19	dix-neuf	100	cent
20	vingt	1,000	mille
21	vingt et un	10,000	dix mille
22	vingt-deux	100,000	cent mille
30	trente	1,000,000	un million
31	trente et un	10,000,000	dix millions
32	trente-deux	100,000,000	cent millions
		1,000,000,000	un billion, un milliard

Cardinal numbers are invariable with the exception of **un, vingt,** and **cent.**

Un takes the gender of the noun which it limits: un livre, *one book;* une livre, *one pound;* vingt et une pommes, *twenty-one apples.*

Vingt and **cent** generally take the *s* of the plural only when another number which multiplies them precedes and no other number follows: quatre-vingts, but quatre-vingt-deux; deux cents, but deux cent deux.[1]

When substituting for ordinal numbers, **vingt** and **cent** never take the *s* of the plural: l'an deux cent (= l'an deux centième); page quatre-vingt (= page quatre-vingtième).

Mille is invariable. When used to designate a date of the Christian era, **mille** or **mil** may be used: l'an mil (mille) neuf cent cinquante (1950). But **mille** must be used in the expression l'an mille, *the year one thousand.*

ORDINAL numbers indicate *which one* of a number.

They are formed by adding **-ième** to the last consonant of the corresponding cardinal number: sept, septième; quatre, quatrième. Exceptions are **un, cinq,** and **neuf,** which are changed into premier, cinquième, and neuvième, respectively.

Unième, however, is used instead of **premier** in compound ordinal numbers: vingt et unième, quatre-vingt-unième.

Un millier, *a thousand;* un million, *a million;* un billion or un milliard, *a billion* are numeral nouns and are masculine. They are always followed by **de** before a noun: deux millions de soldats, *two million soldiers;* des milliers d'habitants, *thousands of inhabitants.*

Deuxième, not **second,** is usually used in a series of more than two: j'ai vu le deuxième et le troisième accident. **Deuxième,** not **second,** is used in compound ordinal numbers: vingt-deuxième, *twenty-second.*

Cardinal, not ordinal, numbers are used in dates or titles with the exception of premier, *first:* le deux mai, *May 2nd;* Henri II (deux); but le premier mai, *May 1st;* Henri I (premier).

By adding **-aine** to the last consonant of certain cardinal numbers, nouns are formed which convey the idea of *about* + number: une huitaine, *about eight;* une vingtaine, *about twenty.* Douzaine (*f.*), *dozen,* is used as a definite measure.

---

[1] *Quatre-vingts-deux* and *deux cents deux* are also tolerated. The dropping of the hyphen or hyphens is permissible.

INDEFINITE ADJECTIVES.—The indefinite adjective modifies in a vague and general way the noun with which it is associated.

Some indefinite adjectives are used as adjectives only, others as adjectives and pronouns. (For indefinite pronouns only, see p. 81.)

Adjectives only:		*Both adjectives and pronouns:*	
chaque	*each, every*	aucun, -e	*no, no one*
divers, -e	*various*	autre	*other*
même	*same*	certain, -e	*certain*
quelconque	*any, any whatever*	maint, -e	*many a*
		nul, -le	*no, no one*
quelque	*some*	plusieurs	*several*
quelques	*a few*	tel, -le	*such a*
		tout, -e	*whole, all*
		tous, toutes *m., f., pl.*	*all*

Note.—**Quelque** is of more limited force than **des**, *some, any:* donnez-moi quelques livres, *give me a few books;* donnez-moi des livres, *give me some books*.

Nul and **aucun,** adjectives or pronouns, require **ne** before their verb: nul homme ne le croit, *no man believes it;* but not when they stand alone: As-tu reçu une lettre? — Aucune. *Did you receive a letter? — None.*

II. VERB REVIEW

1. NEGATIVE-INTERROGATIVE FORM OF VERBS

When verbs are conjugated in their negative-interrogative form, in simple tenses, **ne** precedes the interrogative form of the verb and **pas** follows it.

n'ai-je pas?   ne suis-je pas?   ne portes-tu pas?
n'avons-nous pas?   ne sommes-nous pas?   ne portons-nous pas?

When **est-ce que** (**est-ce qu'**) is used to formulate a question, **ne** (**n'**) comes directly before the verb form, and **pas** after.

est-ce que je ne suis pas?   est-ce que je ne porte pas?
est-ce que nous n'avons pas?   est-ce que vous ne vendez pas?

In compound tenses, **ne** (**n'**) precedes the auxiliary and **pas** comes immediately after the interrogative form of the verb.

n'avez-vous pas porté?   n'auront-ils pas fini?
n'auraient-ils pas vendu?   ne sera-t-il pas parti?

Of course, if there are direct or indirect object pronouns preceding the interrogative form of the verb, **ne** (**n'**) must be placed immediately before them.

ne l'avez-vous pas apporté?   ne leur parlez-vous pas?
ne le lui dites-vous pas?   n'y seront-ils pas allés?

2. IMPERSONAL VERBS

Impersonal verbs are verbs that are conjugated in the third person singular only. **Il** is their subject. They are either regular or irregular and are used in all verb tenses.

Il pleuvra demain.   It will rain tomorrow.
Il est deux heures.   It is two o'clock.

Usually, impersonal verbs denote natural phenomena and time, or they impart a special impersonal sense to certain verbs.

il pleut, *it is raining.*   il est trois heures, *it is three o'clock.*
il neige, *it is snowing.*   il est midi, *it is noon.*
il gèle, *it is freezing.*   il est minuit, *it is midnight.*
il grêle, *it is hailing.*   il est tard, *it is late.*
il vente, *it is windy.*   il est tôt, *it is early.*
il tonne, *it is thundering.*   il est deux heures moins dix, *it*
il dégèle, *it is thawing.*   *is ten minutes to two.*
il bruine, *it is drizzling.*

il y a, *there is, there are*
il est, *there is, there are*
il faut, *it is necessary*
il importe, *it matters*
il arrive (que), *it happens*

3. IRREGULAR VERBS

Present

connaître, *to be acquainted with, know*

connais	connaissons
connais	connaissez
connaît	connaissent

Principal Parts

connaître, connaissant, connu, connais, connus

savoir, *to know*   savoir, sachant, su, sais, sus

sais	savons
sais	savez
sait	savent

mettre, *to put*   mettre, mettant, mis, mets, mis

mets	mettons
mets	mettez
met	mettent

III. VOCABULARY

1. FRENCH-ENGLISH:

avril *m.*, April
juin *m.*, June
*lire, to read

mort, -e (*p.p.* of *mourir), dead
le roi, king
la vie, life

2. ENGLISH-FRENCH:

alms, l'aumône *f.*
anything better, ne . . . rien de mieux
to ask for, demander
at once, tout de suite
battlefield, le champ de bataille
better, mieux
bookshelf, le rayon
custom, la coutume
to do, *faire
done, fait, -e (*p.p.* of *faire)
each, chaque (*adj.*)
else: anything —, n'importe quoi, autre chose
equal, égal, -e
to fall, tomber
glove, le gant
lost, perdu, -e
man, l'homme *m.*

minute, la minute
modesty, la modestie
to mourn, pleurer
must, doit (*pres. 3rd pers. sing.* of *devoir)
now, maintenant
real, réel, -le, vrai, -e
really, réellement
to require, demander
sleep, le sommeil
something, quelque chose;
—else, quelque chose d'autre
street, la rue
surely, sûrement
through, par
town: in —, en ville
twice, deux fois
to understand, *comprendre
well, bien

IV. IDIOMATIC EXPRESSIONS

peu importe, little matters, it matters little
se passer de, to do without
s'attendre à, to expect
à quoi bon? what's the use?
en vouloir à, to have a grudge against, be offended at
manquer de, to come near, almost
faire de son mieux, to do one's best
l'échapper belle, to have a narrow escape
à la belle étoile, in the open
à l'aventure, at random, aimlessly

V. EXERCISES

1. *Write out in full the following numbers:*

17	21	72	67	100
80	433	562	7,291	183
5,103	287	7,008	1,117	6,777
77,839	9,729	473,000	3,000,649	984,921

2. *Write out in full all numbers, cardinal and ordinal:*

1. Lisez la page 300. 2. Il faut étudier la vie de Louis VII. 3. Elle est morte le 2 juin 1937. 4. Ce n'est pas de Charles Ier, mais de Louis II qu'il parlera. 5. Votre leçon est à la page 80. 6. Louis XI était un grand roi. 7. Nous partirons le 16 avril 1950. 8. Le 10 ou le 12 avril, peu importe.

3. *Translate:*

1. Each country has its customs. 2. Modesty is a virtue which we require in others. 3. The same man did it twice. 4. Many a mother mourns a son lost on the battlefield. 5. Any alms at all. 6. Charles has some real friends. 7. All men are equal before God. 8. Ask for something else.

4. *Translate carefully:*

1. It's surely going to rain tomorrow. 2. This doesn't concern us at all, does it? 3. Why don't you put these

books on the bookshelves?—You know which books I mean,
don't you? 4. When you are better acquainted with Louis,
you will understand his work. 5. It is five minutes to
seven now; at midnight your work must be done.

5. *Translate idiomatically:*

1. It's raining now.—It matters little; aren't you coming
with me? 2. Do you ever do without your gloves? · 3. Is
he not going to come?—No!—Then what's the use to wait?
4. Will he not be offended at John, if John doesn't come?
5. Is he really going to sleep in the open? 6. Didn't you
expect to see your sister in town? 7. They are acquainted
with his work, aren't they? 8. He almost fell twice while
walking aimlessly through the streets. 9. We know very
well that we had a narrow escape. 10. Start studying
your lessons at once.

I. THE PERSONAL PRONOUNS AND THEIR POSITION

There are several kinds of pronouns, the personal, possessive, demonstrative, relative, interrogative, and indefinite pronouns.

A pronoun, being used instead of a noun, must assume the gender, number, and person of its antecedent.

PERSONAL PRONOUNS.—Personal pronouns are either conjunctive or disjunctive. Conjunctive pronouns are such personal pronouns as are connected with the verb in the capacity of a subject, or a direct or indirect object; disjunctive are such personal pronouns as have no direct connection with the verb.

Je le vois.	I see him.
Il lui parle.	He talks to him.
Il vient avec moi.	He comes with me.

I. CONJUNCTIVE PRONOUNS.—The conjunctive pronouns have various forms according to their functions in the sentence.

Subject		Direct Object		Indirect Object	
je	*I*	me	*me*	me	*to me*
tu	*you*	te	*you*	te	*to you*
il	*he*	le	*him, it*	lui	*to him, to it*
elle	*she*	la	*her, it*	lui	*to her, to it*
nous	*we*	nous	*us*	nous	*to us*
vous	*you*	vous	*you*	vous	*to you*
ils	*they*	les	*them*	leur	*to them*
elles	*they*	les	*them*	leur	*to them*
				y	*to* or *at it*
				en	*of it* or *them, from it* or *them*

The reflexive pronoun **se** is used for both the singular and the plural, the masculine and the feminine. It may act as direct or indirect object.

Se, reflexive pronoun, has the following meanings:

Singular	*Plural*
himself, to himself	themselves, to themselves
herself, to herself	each other, to each other
itself, to itself	one another, to one another

Y and **en.**—**Y** is both a pronoun and an adverb. As a pronoun, **y** stands for a noun governed by any preposition except **de.** Its meaning varies according to the context. Thus,

1. When **y** stands for the name of a place previously mentioned, it is translated by *there*, which is sometimes understood in English.

Vous voyez cette maison?—	Do you see that house?—
J'y demeure.	I live there (in it).
Paul est-il à la cuisine?—	Is Paul in the kitchen?—
Oui, il y est.	Yes, he is (there).

Note.—**Y** standing for a place already mentioned must always be expressed in French.

2. When **y** refers to things or ideas and follows verbs which require **à** (such as obéir à, *to obey;* renoncer à, *to renounce;* répondre à, *to answer*, etc.), it is best rendered by *it, them*, which are often understood in English.

Obéissez à la loi.—	Obey the law.—
J'y obéis.	I do obey (it).
Répond-il jamais au téléphone?—	Does he ever answer the tele-
Non, il n'y répond jamais.	phone?—No, he never does.

En is both a preposition and a pronoun. As a pronoun, its meaning varies according to its context. Thus,

1. When **en** stands for a noun governed by the preposition **de,** it is usually rendered by *of it, of them, from it, from them*, often understood in English. This is particularly the case when the noun for which **en** stands is followed by a word expressing quantity or number.

A-t-il des livres?—	Has he books?—
Oui, il en a deux.	Yes, he has two (of them).
Ont-ils des pommes?—	Have they apples?—
Oui, ils en ont beaucoup.	Yes, they have many (of them).

2. When **en** replaces a noun used in the partitive sense, it takes the meaning of *some* or *any*, expressed or understood in English.

Avez-vous de la viande?—	Have you some meat?—
Oui, j'en ai.	Yes, I have (some).
Ont-ils des livres?—	Have they some books?—
Non, ils n'en ont pas.	No, they haven't (any).

POSITION OF CONJUNCTIVE PRONOUNS.—The position of conjunctive pronouns in the sentence may be twofold, that in relation to the verb, or the one in relation to the various conjunctive pronouns used as direct or indirect objects.

1. IN RELATION TO THE VERB, all conjunctive pronouns are placed immediately before the verb in its simple as well as compound tenses.

Je le vois.	I see him.
Il nous voit.	He sees us.
Nous les voyons.	We see them.

Je l'ai vu.	I have seen him.
Il nous a vus.	He has seen us.
Nous les avons vus.	We have seen them.

In the *affirmative imperative*, however, the conjunctive pronouns follow the verb and are usually connected with it by a hyphen:

Donnez-le.	Give it.
Regardons-les.	Let's look at them.
Prenez-la.	Take it.

Donne-lui une plume.	Give him a pen.
Parlez-leur.	Speak to them.
Rendez-les.	Give them back.

Note.—In affirmative imperatives, the tonic or stressed pronouns **moi** and **toi** are used instead of **me** and **te**; but, when **moi** and

toi are followed either by **y** or **en**, the *-oi* is elided: donnez-moi, *give me;* donnez-m'en, *give me some.*

2. IN RELATION TO OTHER CONJUNCTIVE PRONOUNS, conjunctive pronouns take up the following order or relative position:

First come:	me, te, nous, vous, se,
then	le, la, les,
then	lui, leur,
then	y,
finally	en.

Il me le donne.	He gives it to me.
Je te la donne.	I give it to you.
Ils nous les donnent.	They give them to us.
Elle s'y dévoue.	She devotes herself to it.
Nous le lui donnons.	We give it to him.
Ils les leur donnent.	They give them to them.
Il lui en donne.	He gives him some.
Il leur en donne.	He gives them some.

In *affirmative imperatives,* the direct object pronoun always precedes the indirect.

Rendez-le-moi.	Give it back to me.
Prenez-la-lui.	Take it away from her.
Rapportons-le-leur.	Let's bring it back to them.
Prête-les-nous.	Lend them to us.

II. DISJUNCTIVE PRONOUNS.—The French disjunctive pronouns are

Subject		Object	
moi	*I*	moi	*me*
toi	*you*	toi	*you*
lui	*he*	lui	*him*
elle	*she*	elle	*her*
nous	*we*	nous	*us*
vous	*you*	vous	*you*
eux	*they m.*	eux	*them m.*
elles	*they f.*	elles	*them f.*

By adding **-même,** *self,* or **-mêmes,** *selves,* to the above mentioned disjunctive pronouns we form the intensive disjunctive pronouns: lui-même, *himself;* vous-mêmes, *yourselves;* etc.

The disjunctive pronouns are used:

1. Alone, as subject or object, the verb being understood:

Qui parle?—Moi.	Who is speaking?—I.
Qui cherchent-ils?—Lui.	Whom are they seeking?—Him.

2. With prepositions:

Avec qui voyagez-vous?— Avec elle.	With whom are you traveling?— With her.
Vous travaillez contre nous.	You are working against us.

3. After **ce + être** in its various tenses:

C'est lui qui l'a fait.	It is he who did it.
Ce sera lui qu'on accusera.	It will be he whom they will accuse.
Ce sont eux qui arrivent.	It is they who are coming.

4. For emphasis:

Moi, je travaille; lui joue.	*I* am working; *he* is playing.
Mon livre à moi est sur la table.	*My* book is on the table.

5. In compound subjects and objects:

Mon frère et moi nous partons.	My brother and I are leaving.
Je les vois, lui et elle.	I see them, him and her.

6. When the subject pronoun is separated from its verb by an adjective or an adverb:

Il est coupable.	He is guilty.
Lui seul est coupable.	He alone is guilty.
Je le sais.	I know it.
Moi aussi je le sais.	I also know it.

7. When the direct object is **me, te, se, nous, vous,** the indirect object of the sentence takes **à +** a disjunctive pronoun.

Il nous a présentés à eux.	He introduced us to them.
Elle se présente à nous.	She introduces herself to us.
But: Tu te dévoues pour elle.	You sacrifice yourself for her.

II. VERB REVIEW

1. ORTHOGRAPHIC PECULIARITIES (Also see p. 65.)

There are four verb groups that have some orthographic peculiarities which must be mentioned.   They are

1. VERBS ENDING IN THEIR INFINITIVE IN -CER AND -GER.— These verbs retain throughout their conjugation the *c* and *-ge* sounds of the infinitive.   This is obtained by putting a cedilla (˛) under the *c* (ç) and by adding an *e* after the *g* (*ge*) whenever an *a* or *o* follows *c* or *g* respectively.

commencer	commençais,	commençons,	commençant
manger	mangeais,	mangeons,	mangeant

2. VERBS WITH INFINITIVES ENDING IN -YER.—Verbs ending in *-yer* in their infinitive do not retain the *y* throughout their conjugation.   *Y* is changed to *i* whenever it is directly followed by a mute *e*.   This happens in part in the five following tenses: the present and future indicative, the imperative, the present subjunctive, and the conditional present.

nettoyer, *to clean*

Pres.	*Fut.*	*Imper.*	*Pres. Subj.*	*Condit. Pres.*
nettoie	nettoierai	nettoie	nettoie	nettoierais
nettoies	nettoieras,		nettoies	nettoierais,
nettoie	etc.		nettoie	etc.
nettoient			nettoient	

Verbs ending in *-ayer* may either keep the *y* unchanged or change it to *i*: je paye or je paie; je payerai or je paierai, etc.

2. PRONOMINAL FORM OF VERBS

Pronominal verbs are conjugated in the same way as the verbs in the active voice.   But, in addition, they are accompanied both by a subject and an object pronoun.

il se lave,	*he washes himself*	nous nous lavons, *we wash ourselves*
elle se lave,	*she washes herself*	vous vous lavez, *you wash yourselves*
tu te laves,	*you wash yourself*	(See pp. 216–218.)

In compound tenses, the pronominal verbs are conjugated with **être,** *to be,* instead of **avoir,** *to have.*

je me suis lave,   *I washed myself*
nous nous sommes lavés, *we washed ourselves*

The past participle of pronominal verbs in compound tenses must agree in gender and number with the direct object in front of the verb.

elle s'est lavée,	*she washed herself*
nous nous sommes salués,	*we greeted each other*
elles se sont regardées,	*they looked at each other*

But there is no agreement when **se** is an indirect object:

elles se sont écrit	*they wrote to each other* or *one another.*
elles se șont dit à elles-mêmes,	*they said to themselves*

Note.—**Se** with reciprocal verbs is rendered in English by *each other* or *one another*, as required. Examples: Louis et Marie se sont parlé, *Louis and Mary spoke to each other*. Les trois garçons se sont salués, *the three boys greeted one another*.

3. IRREGULAR VERBS

Present   *Principal Parts*
prendre, *to take*   prendre, prenant, pris, prends, pris

prends	prenons
prends	prenez
prend	prennent

partir, *to leave**   partir, partant, parti, pars, partis

pars	partons
pars	partez
part	partent

venir, *to come**   venir, venant, venu, viens, vins

viens	venons
viens	venez
vient	viennent

III. VOCABULARY

1. FRENCH-ENGLISH:

causer, to cause
***se connaître à,** to be a good judge of
le coucou, cuckoo

***déplaire,** displease
donc, then
écouter, to listen to
l'enfant *m.* and *f.,* child

---

* Conjugated with **être** in compound tenses.

l'ennemi *m.*, enemy
l'ennui *m.*, worry
la fleur, flower
le frère, brother
goûter, to enjoy
ne . . . guère, hardly
ne . . . jamais, never
se moquer de, to make fun of
s'en moquer, not to care
pardonner, to pardon

pauvre, poor
pour, as to
pratiquer, to practice
*redire : trouver à — (in *inf.*
only), to criticize
*revenir, to come back
le superflu, superfluity
la vertu, virtue
la voix, voice

2. ENGLISH-FRENCH:

affair, l'affaire *f.*
aid, l'aide *f.*
to blame, blâmer
to borrow, emprunter à
to buy, acheter
cards: to play —, jouer aux cartes
to complain, *se plaindre
to converse about, *s'entretenir de
to end in, finir par (+ *inf.*)
to fight, *se battre
finally, finalement
to be glad to, se réjouir de
to help, aider

to help oneself, *se servir de
to introduce, présenter à
to knock at, frapper à
to lend, prêter
to be mistaken, se tromper
only, ne . . . que, seulement
to sit, *s'asseoir
to stay, rester (Conjugate with être.)
to telephone, téléphoner
to think of, penser à, penser de (opinion)
together, ensemble
to use, employer
to wish, *vouloir, désirer
without, sans

IV. IDIOMATIC EXPRESSIONS

y perdre son latin, not to be able to make head or tail of it
assister à, to attend
prendre un parti, to make up one's mind
de parti pris, deliberately
rebrousser chemin, to turn back
je n'y puis rien, I can't help it
pas que je sache, not that I know of
faire la connaissance de, to become acquainted with

il a fait leur connaissance, he got acquainted with them
faire partie de, to belong to
il se fait tard, it's getting late

V. EXERCISES

1. *Replace the words in italics by the proper personal pronouns:*

   1. *La vie* est belle, il faut aimer *la vie.* 2. Il cherche *les fleurs*, mais il ne peut trouver *les fleurs.* 3. Il faut pratiquer *la vertu* si l'on veut goûter *la vertu.* 4. Il faut savoir pardonner *à ses ennemis.* 5. Il ne parle jamais au *frère de Louise.* 6. Nous ne donnons pas toujours *notre superflu aux pauvres.* 7. Ne regardez pas ainsi *votre frère.*

2. *Translate:*

   1. Here he is. 2. Do you see him? 3. No, I do not see him. 4. Did he not lend it to them? 5. There are some here. 6. Didn't you borrow some from him? 7. Sit down! 8. Speak to me! 9. Tell me about it. 10. Don't you wish some? 11. Think of it! 12. Are you going to give us some there? 13. Did you use some? 14. Does he play cards? 15. Yes, he plays. 16. My friend is here; I am very happy (of it). 17. Here is a beautiful page; read it to them. 18. Do you want some? 19. Please, help yourselves.

3. *Choose the proper personal pronoun in parentheses; then translate:*

   1. Qui (y, en) parle? 2. Ne faites pas cela; je m' (y, en) oppose. 3. Il a un piano, mais il n' (y, en) joue guère. 4. La leçon est bonne, profitez- (y, en). 5. Louis est parti pour la France; moi j' (y, en) reviens. 6. N' (y, en) pensez donc pas. 7. Jouez-vous aux dominos?—Non, je n' (y, en) joue pas. 8. Qu' (y, en) pensez-vous? 9. A l'écouter, on (y, en) perd son latin. 10. Je m' (y, en) moque. 11. Il aime la France; il (y, en) va tous les ans.

4. *Translate:*

   1. Who is speaking?—I. 2. My brother and I bought it. 3. He also helped us. 4. Did you see them, and did you

speak to them? 5. It is they who are knocking at the door.
6. Without her, you can't go. 7. They alone stayed
home. 8. Why fight against them? 9. His brother and
I went to school together. 10. It is I who phoned. 11.
I am also going there. 12. I am coming from there.

5. *Replace the dashes by the proper personal pronouns:*

 Qu'est-ce donc qui déplaît dans le chant des coucous?
   Pour ———, ——— ——— trouve assez doux.
 ——— ne sais pas ce qu'on peut ——— trouver à redire.
   Mon enfant, ——— vais ——— ——— dire:
 Dans la voix du coucou, ce qui cause l'ennui,
   C'est qu' ——— parle toujours de ———.
         (L. Ratisbonne).

6. *Translate:*

1. Why doesn't he introduce him to them? 2. Will he
never think of himself? 3. Come to me, if you ever are
in need of aid. 4. They think only of themselves. 5.
Charles will introduce us to them.

7. *Translate into idiomatic French:*

1. She is always complaining; I can't make head or tail of
it. 2. They will come and attend the ceremony. 3.
They conversed a long time about this affair, then finally
came to a decision. 4. If you turn back, John will be glad
to see you. 5. It's getting dark. 6. Why wouldn't you
want to belong to our club? 7. Has he become acquainted
with them?—No, not that I know. 8. They blame me
for being late; I can't help it. 9. Was he mistaken, or did
he do this deliberately. 10. It is getting late, but I am
not late.

I. POSSESSIVE AND DEMONSTRATIVE PRONOUNS

POSSESSIVE PRONOUNS.—A possessive pronoun stands in place of a noun modified by an adjective denoting possession.

The possessive pronouns derive their gender and number from the nouns which they replace; their person is determined by the person of the possessor.

SINGULAR			PLURAL	
Masculine	*Feminine*		*Masculine*	*Feminine*
le mien	la mienne	*mine*	les miens	les miennes
le tien	la tienne	*yours*	les tiens	les tiennes
le sien	la sienne	*his, hers, its*	les siens	les siennes
le nôtre	la nôtre	*ours*	les nôtres	les nôtres
le vôtre	la vôtre	*yours*	les vôtres	les vôtres
le leur	la leur	*theirs*	les leurs	les leurs

All possessive pronouns must agree in gender, person, and number with their antecedents.

> mon chapeau, *my hat* = le mien, *mine*
> sa table, *his* or *her table* = la sienne, *his, hers*
> nos crayons, *our pencils* = les nôtres, *ours*
> vos plumes, *your pens* = les vôtres, *yours*

To express emphatically the idea of ownership, the possessive pronoun is used instead of à + the disjunctive pronoun.

> A qui est ce livre?—Il est à moi.—Non, c'est le sien.

> Whose book is this?—It belongs to me.—No, it's his.

62

DEMONSTRATIVE PRONOUNS.—There are two kinds of demonstrative pronouns, the variable and the invariable.

VARIABLE DEMONSTRATIVES				INVARIABLE DEMONSTRATIVES	
SINGULAR		PLURAL			
Masculine	*Feminine*	*Masculine*	*Feminine*	ceci	*this*
celui	celle	ceux	celles	cela (ça)	*that*
the one	*the one*	*the ones*	*the ones*	ce	*he, she, it,*
		these	*these*		*this, that,*
		those	*those*		*these, those*

The above forms of the *variable* demonstrative pronoun never stand alone. They require for their complete sense a modifier such as

1. A relative clause:

celui qui est ici	the one who is here
celle que vous voyez	the one whom (which) you see
ceux dont vous parlez	the ones (those) of whom you speak
celles que vous préférez	those whom you prefer

2. A prepositional phrase:

celui de mon oncle	that of my uncle
celles à Marguerite (colloquial)	the ones of Marguerite
ceux de ma sœur	those of my sister
celle du médecin	that of the physician

3. **-ci or -là.** To distinguish more clearly *this* from *that*, and *these* from *those*, -ci, *here*, and -là, *there*, are added to the variable demonstrative pronouns:

Je n'aime pas celui-ci.	I don't like this one.
Il aime celui-là.	He likes that one.
Voyez-vous celle-là?	Do you see that one?
Je préfère ceux-ci à celles-là.	I prefer these to those.

The two invariable demonstrative pronouns **ceci,** *this,* and **cela,** *that,* are used as subjects or as direct and prepositional objects.

Ceci se fait en un instant.	This is done in a minute.
Cela est plus difficile.	That is more difficult.
Pourquoi a-t-il fait cela?	Why did he do that?
Pour ceci vous serez récompensé.	You will be rewarded for this.

NOTE.—The English phrases *this is, that is* are rendered by **voici** and **voilà** in French, when they are followed by a noun or a possessive pronoun: voici votre crayon, *this is your pencil;* voilà le mien, *that is mine.*

The *invariable* demonstrative pronoun **ce,** meaning *he, she, it, this, that, these, those,* is used as subject of the verb **être,** *to be:*

1. When **être** is immediately followed by a proper noun or a common noun modified by a limiting adjective.

Qui est-ce?—C'est Louis.	Who is it?—It's Louis.
C'est Paul qu'on cherche.	It's Paul they're looking for.
Qui vient nous voir?—Ce sont nos amis, ceux de Lauzon.	Who is coming to see us? Our friends, the ones from Lauzon.

2. When **être** is followed by an adjective.

| C'est évident. | That's evident. |
| C'est difficile à comprendre. | This is difficult to understand. |

EXCEPTIONS.—If **être,** however, is followed by an adjective referring to a noun previously mentioned, **il, elle, ils, elles** must be used instead of **ce,** according to the gender and number of that noun.

| Voici une table; elle est belle. | Here is a table; it is beautiful. |
| Voyez-vous cette maison; elle est bien bâtie. | Do you see this house; it is well built. |

Or, if **être** is followed by an adjective + an infinitive with an object, the impersonal **il** is used instead of **ce,** and **de** instead of **à.**

| Il est intéressant de le lire. | It is interesting to read it. |

Finally, if the adjective is expanded by a **que** clause, the impersonal construction **il est** must replace **c'est.**

| Il est clair que j'ai tort. | It's clear, I am wrong. |

3. When **être** is followed by a pronoun, an adverb, or an infinitive.

Est-ce elle?—Non, ce sont eux.	Is it she?—No, it is they.
C'est bien, n'est-ce pas?	That's good, isn't it?
C'est bien mal à vous.	This is very bad of you.
Voir c'est croire.	To see is to believe.

Note.—**Est-ce** is always used instead of **sont-ce** in questions: est-ce eux qui viennent? *Is it they who are coming?*

II. VERB REVIEW

1. ORTHOGRAPHIC PECULIARITIES (continued)

3. VERBS WITH STEM VOWELS MUTE e OR é.—In verbs with stem vowel mute *e,* the *e* becomes *è* whenever it is followed in the next syllable by a mute *e.*

mener; *to lead*

Pres.	Fut.	Imper.	Pres. Subj.	Pres. Cond.
mène	mènerai	mène	mène	mènerais
mènes	mèneras, etc.		mènes	mènerais, etc.
mène			mène	
mènent			mènent	

In verbs with stem vowel *é, é* is changed to *è* whenever *é* is followed in the next syllable by an *e* mute.   In the future and conditional present there is no change.

céder, *to yield*

Pres.	Imper.	Pres. Subj.
cède	cède	cède
cèdes		cèdes
cède		cède
cèdent		cèdent

préférer, *to prefer*

préfère	préfère	préfère
préfères		préfères
préfère		préfère
préfèrent		préfèrent

4. VERBS ENDING IN -ELER, -ETER.—The mute *e* in *-eler* and *-eter* is changed to the open *e* sound whenever the mute *e* is followed by another mute *e* in the next syllable. This is done by doubling the *l* or *t*.

appeler, *to call*

Pres.	*Fut.*	*Imper.*	*Pres. Subj.*	*Pres. Cond.*
appelle	appellerai	appelle	appelle	appellerais
appelles	appelleras, etc.		appelles	appellerais, etc.
appelle			appelle	
appellent			appellent	

jeter, *to throw*

Pres.	*Fut.*	*Imper.*	*Pres. Subj.*	*Pres. Cond.*
jette	jetterai	jette	jette	jetterais
jettes	jetteras, etc.		jettes	jetterais, etc.
jette			jette	
jettent			jettent	

2. IMPERATIVE MOOD

The imperative, which has the function of expressing orders or requests, is ordinarily composed of three forms derived from the present indicative. These three forms are taken from the second person singular and the first and second persons plural. In the second person singular of verbs belonging to the first conjugation, the *s* of the ending is dropped, unless followed by **y** or **en**.

porter	porte, *carry*	portons, *let's carry*	portez, *carry*
finir	finis, *finish*	finissons, *let's finish*	finissez, *finish*
vendre	vends, *sell*	vendons, *let's sell*	vendez, *sell*

A few imperatives are irregular. They are

avoir	aie	ayons	ayez
être	sois	soyons	soyez
aller	va	allons	allez
savoir	sache	sachons	sachez
vouloir*			veuillez

Note.—**Vas** is used instead of **va** before **y**: vas-y, *go there, go on.*

---

* The imperative of **vouloir** is more particularly used in the second person plural; then it assumes the meaning of *please*.

3. IRREGULAR VERBS

Present		*Principal Parts*
voir, *to see*		voir, voyant, vu, vois, vis
vois	voyons	
vois	voyez	
voit	voient	
rire, *to laugh*		rire, riant, ri, ris, ris
ris	rions	
ris	riez	
rit	rient	
suivre, *to follow*		suivre, suivant, suivi, suis, suivis
suis	suivons	
suis	suivez	
suit	suivent	

III. VOCABULARY

1. FRENCH-ENGLISH:

blesser, to wound
le bonheur, happiness
le chagrin, pain
le cœur, heart
constamment, constantly
coupable, guilty
***croire,** to believe
dicter, to dictate
l'été *m.,* summer
le fardeau, burden
l'hiver *m.,* winter

insupportable, unbearable
meilleur, -e, better
le mortel, mortal
la nuit, night
le pauvre, poor
***peindre,** to paint
***permettre** (*p.p.* **permis**), to permit
la propriété, property
renoncer à, to renounce
le soir, evening

2. ENGLISH-FRENCH:

after, **après**
attractive, **attrayant, -e**
departure, **le départ**
to dream, **rêver**
easy, **facile**
Englishman, **l'Anglais** *m.*
gentleman, **un homme comme il faut**
important, **important, -e**
interesting, **intéressant, -e**
just as, **tout comme**

often, **souvent**
parents, **les parents** *m.pl.*
physician, **le médecin**
rapidly, **rapidement**
say: that is to say, **c'est-à-dire**
so, **si, tellement**
to steal, **voler**
theater, **le théâtre**
time: in time, **à temps**

IV. IDIOMATIC EXPRESSIONS

être de retour, to be back
finir par (+ *inf.*), to end up by, finally
penser, to think
penser de, to think of (opinion)
penser à, to think about, of; to direct one's thought to
obéir à, to obey
entendre dire, to hear (it) said
en plein air, outdoors, in the open
donner sur, to face, look out upon
à partir de, beginning from, from . . . on

V. EXERCISES

1. *Translate all words in parentheses; then read the whole sentence:*

1. Les pauvres ont (their) chagrins, le riche a (his), tous les mortels ont (theirs). 2. Respecte (his) propriété, si tu veux qu'il respecte (yours). 3. Nous avons (our) fardeaux, vous avez (yours). 4. Il faut écouter l'opinion des autres, mais ne pas renoncer pour cela à (yours), si vous croyez (yours) meilleure que (theirs). 5. La vanité des autres nous est insupportable parce qu'elle blesse (ours). 6. Le bonheur de ceux qu'on aime est aussi (ours).

2. *Translate:*

1. Here is mine and there is yours. 2. I see your house and hers. 3. Not your book, but theirs has been stolen. 4. Why speak about mine and thine? 5. Ours have arrived.

3. *Fill in the dashes with the proper demonstrative pronouns:*

1. Il n'y a d'avarice permise que ———— du temps. *2.* Les nuits d'été sont moins longues que ———— d'hiver. 3. ———— qui parlent constamment ne sont pas ———— qu'on admire. 4. Corneille et Racine sont deux grands poètes dramatiques: ———— peint les hommes tels qu'ils sont, ———— tels qu'ils devraient être. 5. Ce jeune homme est ———— qui est coupable.

4. *Translate all pronouns in parentheses; then translate the entire sentence into English:*

1. (He who) fait toujours (what = that which) il veut, fait rarement (what) il doit.   2.   Parler sans penser à (what) on dit est folie.   3.   Les meilleurs discours sont (those which) le cœur a dictés.

5. *Translate:*

1. Do this rapidly.   2. Why didn't he say this to me?
3. That's very interesting.   4. All this is yours.   5. That is to say that he will not be here in time.   6. It will be just as you like it.   7. It's our friends.   8. It is they.   9. Is it they?   10. This is done in a minute.   11. Will you do this?   12. The ones of whom you were in need are absent.   13. It is important; in fact, it is so important that you should study it.   14. It's very easy to do it.   15. Here is a book; it's most attractive.   16. Who is this gentleman?   17. He is an Englishman.   18. He is a physician.

6. *Translate into idiomatic French:*

1. Be back in time to take your sister to the theater.   2. From now on, I shall lead an outdoor life.   3. They finally obeyed their parents.   4. What are you thinking of?—I'm not thinking, I'm dreaming.   5. Please tell me what you are thinking of my adventure?   6. I have just heard it said that you will not yield in this affair.   7. I shall often think of you after your departure.   8. Why do you laugh so often?   Only fools laugh so often.

I. THE RELATIVE PRONOUN

A relative pronoun is one that relates to, and connects its clause with, a noun or a pronoun before it. The word to which it relates is called an ANTECEDENT.

Relative pronouns vary in their form according to the nature of their antecedents and their own function in the sentence.

There are two kinds of relative pronouns, the simple and the compound.

SIMPLE RELATIVE PRONOUNS.—The simple relative pronouns are invariable.   They are

qui	*who, which, that* (subject)
que	*whom, which, that* (object)
de qui, dont	*whose, of whom, of which*
quoi	*what, which* (object of a preposition)
où	*in which, to which* (*where*), etc.

THE RELATIVE PRONOUN DONT.—**Dont** is the equivalent of **de qui, de quoi, duquel, de la quelle, desquels,** and **desquelles.** It is generally used for both persons and things.

l'homme dont je parle	the man of whom I am speaking
le chien dont je parle	the dog of which I am speaking
la maison dont je parle	the house of which I am speaking
les livres dont je parle	the books of which I am speaking

Whenever a relative clause headed by **dont** has **être** as a verb, its subject must be prefixed by the article and placed immediately before the verb.

l'homme dont le fils est ici	the man whose son is here
la maison dont la porte est ouverte	the house the door of which is open

But, when a relative clause headed by **dont** is governed by a transitive verb, its object must follow the verb.

l'homme dont j'ai vu le fils	the man whose son I have seen
la maison dont j'ai vu la porte ouverte	the house the door of which I saw open

Dont cannot be used to render *whose* preceded by a preposition. The compound relative pronoun **lequel,** etc., must replace it.

l'homme contre le fils duquel . . .	the man against whose son . . .

THE RELATIVE PRONOUN OÙ.—**Où** often replaces **à, dans, sur, vers,** etc., $+$ a relative pronoun in expressions of time and place.

la maison où (dans laquelle) je demeure	the house where (in which) I live
la montagne où (sur laquelle) il vit	the mountain on which he is living
le moment où (auquel) il se montra	the moment when he appeared
le siècle où (dans lequel) nous vivons	the century in which we live

COMPOUND RELATIVE PRONOUNS.—The compound relative pronouns are made up of the definite article, combined or not with **de** or **à,** and the forms of **quel.** They must agree in gender and number with their antecedent.

SINGULAR			PLURAL	
Masculine	*Feminine*		*Masculine*	*Feminine*
lequel	laquelle	*which*	lesquels	lesquelles
duquel	de laquelle	*of which*	desquels	desquelles
auquel	à laquelle	*to which*	auxquels	auxquelles

The above compound relative pronouns have also the meaning of *who, whom, of whom, whose, to whom,* and *that.*

Relative pronouns are never omitted in French.

The compound relative pronouns are ordinarily used for things; for persons, mostly to avoid ambiguity.

le chien auquel il donne du pain	the dog to which he gives bread
la chatte à laquelle il parle	the she-cat to which he is speaking
Le fils de Marie Leffier, lequel était malade, est ici.	Mary Leffier's son, who was sick, is here.

Note.—Compound relative pronouns must always be used after parmi, *among;* entre, *between;* sans, *without.* They also should be used instead of **dont** whenever the relative pronouns refer to a noun already preceded by a preposition: les garçons à l'éducation desquels vous vous consacrez, *the boys to whose education you devote yourself.*

The compound relative pronouns **ce qui, ce que,** *what* (*that which*); **ce dont,** *of* or *about what,* are used for things. **Ce** and **qui, que** or **dont** belong to different clauses: **ce** belongs to the main clause while **qui, que,** and **dont** are found in the subordinate clause.

Voici ce qui est arrivé.	Here is what happened.
Il sait ce que vous faites.	He knows what you are doing.
Je sais ce dont il a besoin.	I know what he is in need of.

II. VERB REVIEW

1. Idiomatic Uses of aller, *to go;* pouvoir, *to be able;* and savoir, *to know.*

    1.   The verb ALLER conveys various meanings:

      (a) **Aller** is used to denote an immediate future.

| Je vais revenir dans une heure. | I shall come back in an hour. |
| Nous allons partir à l'instant. | We shall leave in an instant. |

      (b) It is used in expressions of health.

Comment allez-vous, mon ami?	How are you, my friend?
Est-ce que votre père va bien?	Is your father well?
Il va de plus en plus mal.	He is getting worse and worse.

Note.—**Etre bien** is not the equivalent of **aller bien.** It means *to be comfortable, well off,* or *to look well.*

      (c) It denotes fitness and assumes the meaning of *to fit, be becoming.*

Comme cette robe lui va bien!	How becoming her dress is!
Vraiment, ce chapeau vous va à merveille.	To tell the truth, this hat fits you marvelously.

(d) Finally, **aller,** in its natural sense, denotes locomotion.

Je vais à New York.	I am going to New York.
Allez-vous à cheval demain?	Are you going on horseback tomorrow?

2. The verb POUVOIR may be used to

(a) Express a respectful wish or permission.

Puis-je vous voir maintenant?	May I see you now?
Mon père, pouvons-nous sortir ce soir?	Father, may we go out this evening?

(b) Convey the idea of physical ability.

Il s'est cassé le bras, mais il peut nager quand même.	He broke his arm, but he is able to swim anyhow.
Il n'est pas malade, il peut travailler.	He is not sick, he is able to work.

(c) Suggest possibility.

Il peut se faire qu'il soit parti.	He may have left.
Il pourrait arriver qu'elle ne vienne pas aujourd'hui.	It might happen that she won't come today.

3. The verb SAVOIR has the following meanings:

(a) It denotes possession of knowledge.

Je sais ce qu'ils font.	I know what they are doing.
Il sait que Paris est la capitale de la France.	He knows that Paris is the capital of France.

(b) Followed by an infinitive, **savoir** means *to know how to*.

Savez-vous nager?	Do you know how to swim?
J'ai su faire cela autrefois.	I knew how to do this formerly.

(c) **Savoir** sometimes replaces **pouvoir** in polite refusal.

Mon ami, je ne saurais vous le
dire.

My friend, I can't tell you.

3. Irregular Verbs

Present		*Principal Parts*
croire, *to believe*		croire, croyant, cru, crois, crus
crois	croyons	
crois	croyez	
croit	croient	
courir, *to run*		courir, courant, couru, cours, courus
cours	courons	
cours	courez	
court	courent	
vivre, *to live*		vivre, vivant, vécu, vis, vécus
vis	vivons	
vis	vivez	
vit	vivent	

III. VOCABULARY

1. French-English:

ancien, -ne, old
autrui, others, other people
l'avenir *m.*, future
bâtir, to build
le bureau, office, writing-desk
le chemin, path, road
*combattre, to fight
comme, as, like
*connaître, to be acquainted
with, to know
*découvrir, to discover
*se défaire de, to get rid of
le défaut, defect, fault
désolé, -e, desolate
*entretenir, to speak
la femme, woman, wife
fort (*adv.*), very
ici-bas, in this world

l'idole *f.*, idol
s'intéresser à, to be interested in
lot: le gros —, first prize
lutter, to wrestle
le médecin, the physician
mention: *faire — de, to
mention
mûr, -e, ripe
nuisible, harmful
*prendre: — garde à, to pay
attention to
ramasser, to gather, pick up
le rocher, rock
le sang, blood
sembler, to seem
surpris, -e (*p.p.* of *surprendre), surprised

2. ENGLISH-FRENCH:

to abandon, **abandonner**
  anything: — better, **rien de**
    mieux, de meilleur
to belong to, ***être à**
  bountiful, **plein (-e) de bonté**
  bridge, **le pont**
to buy, **acheter**
  called: to be —, **s'appeler**
  car, **l'automobile** *m.* or *f.*
  cat, **le chat**, *f.*, **la chatte**
to choose, **choisir**
to climb, **gravir**
to commit, ***commettre**
  common, **commun, -e**
  confidence: to have —, **avoir**
    confiance
  country: in the —, **à la**
    campagne
  crime, **le crime**
to cross, **traverser**
to drink, ***boire**
to drive, ***conduire**
  green, **vert, -e**
to head for, **se diriger vers**
  kindness, **la bonté**

to live, **demeurer**
  miserable, **misérable**
  moment, **le moment**
  mountain, **la montagne**
  next, **prochain, -e**
  officer, **l'officier** *m.*
  old: to be 800 years —,
    *avoir huit cents ans
  palace, **le palais**
to pardon, **pardonner**
  picture, **l'image** *f.*
to practice, **pratiquer**
  sale: for —, **à vendre**
  shutter, **le volet**
  soldier, **le soldat**
to stay, **rester**
  steep, **à pic, raide**
  suit, **l'habit** *m.*
  surprised, **surpris, -e**
  toward, **vers**
  tower, **la tour**
to trust, **avoir confiance en**
  uniform, **l'uniforme** *m.*
  wherever, **partout où**
  window, **la fenêtre**

IV. IDIOMATIC EXPRESSIONS

à toute vitesse, at full speed
être bien aise (de), to be glad (to)
tous les deux, tous deux, both
se moquer de, to make fun of
sauter aux yeux, to be obvious, evident; **cela saute —,** it is
  obvious —
pleuvoir à verse, to be pouring
il y a une semaine, a week ago
d'aujourd'hui en huit, a week from today

quel jour du mois est-ce? ⎫
le combien sommes-nous ⎬ what day of the month is it?
quelle date sommes-nous? ⎭
c'est aujourd'hui le 27 septembre, today is the 27th of September

V. EXERCISES

1. *Translate all relative pronouns in parentheses while reading the sentences:*

1. Suis les exemples (which) tes parents te donnent. 2. Cueillez les fruits (which) sont mûrs. 3. Voici les livres (which) vous devez étudier. 4. Voilà (of what) je voulais vous entretenir. 5. La pauvre femme, (whom) vous venez de voir et (who) a perdu un fils à la guerre, est désolée. 6. L'avenir est une chose (of which) on ne pense pas assez. 7. Ce sont là des choses (to which) vous ne prenez pas garde. 8. Le rocher sur (which) cette maison est bâtie est solide. 9. Ce chemin sur (which) vous courez si gaîment c'est la vie. 10. La vanité est une idole (to which) nous offrons tous des sacrifices. 11. Que de parasites ici-bas contre (which) nous avons à lutter tous les jours! 12. Voilà un document (in which) vous vous intéresserez. 13. Les livres (of which) vous avez fait mention sont en effet fort intéressants. 14. La fille de M. Lemoine, (who) m'a reçu hier si aimablement, a gagné le gros lot. 15. Avez-vous connu le fils de Madame X . . . (who) part demain pour Paris?

2. *Translate:*

1. The cat with which you are playing is pretty. 2. The mountain upon which you are going to climb is steep. 3. The boys among whom they are going to stay are Americans. 4. God, in whom you trust, is bountiful. 5. The soldiers in whom they had confidence abandoned them. 6. The two men between whom you are to choose are here. 7. Kindness, without which life is miserable, must be practiced by all.

3. *Fill in the dashes with the proper translation of* what:

1. Je sais ———— ———— vous pensez. 2. Pourquoi ne

ramassez-vous pas ———— ———— est sur la table? 3. Il
ne parle jamais de ———— ———— il fait. 4. N'êtes-vous
pas surpris de ———— ———— il dit? 5. ———— ———— vous
trouverez sur ce bureau est à vous. 6. Il combat toujours
contre ———— ———— il considère comme injuste. 7. Qui
connaît ———— ———— il joue? 8. Il a besoin de ————
———— vous lui refusez.

4. *Fill in the dashes with the best fitting relative pronoun:*

1. Il y a des dangers ———— on n'ose parler. 2. La
famille ———— vient mon ami est très ancienne. 3. Le
médecin ———— vous parlez a découvert la circulation du
sang. 4. Napoléon ———— les armées semblaient in-
vincibles a fini sa vie à Sainte-Hélène. 5. Il y a des
défauts ———— on doit se défaire parce qu'ils sont nuisibles
à autrui.

5. *Translate:*

1. He is coming from the house the windows of which have
green shutters. 2. The man whose son is with us is a
general. 3. The palace the doors of which are open is for
sale. 4. The officers whose green uniforms I admired
yesterday are crossing the bridge. 5. The book on the
pages of which I saw pictures seems interesting. 6. The
castle from whose tower I can see the Seine (River) is eight
hundred years old. 7. The town for which you are heading is called Périgueux. 8. At the moment he appeared,
I was surprised to see him. 9. The house in which I am
living is my uncle's. 10. I shall find you wherever you go.

6. *Translate into idiomatic French:*

1. When he is in the country, he likes to drive at full speed.
2. We are very glad to know that our common friend is
here. 3. We both are going to be sick if we drink this.
4. It is evident that he couldn't commit this crime. 5.
Do you know what day of the month it is? 6. Tomorrow
it will be August the seventh and I shall know how to drive a
car. 7. She wouldn't pardon him for making (to have made)

fun of her. 8. He left here a week ago; may I leave next week? 9. It is obvious that we are all well. 10. Did you ever see such a downpour? 11. This suit is very becoming to you; you couldn't buy anything better. 12. He isn't sick, is he?—No, he couldn't be in better health.

I. INTERROGATIVE AND INDEFINITE PRONOUNS

INTERROGATIVE PRONOUNS.—Interrogative pronouns are used to ask questions about the subject, the predicate, or the object of the verb.

There are two kinds of interrogative pronouns, the simple and the compound. The simple interrogative pronouns are:

For Persons			*For Things*	
qui?	*who?*	*whom?*	qu'est-ce qui?	*what?*
de qui?	*whose?*	*of whom?*	de quoi?	*of what?*
à qui?	*to whom?*		à quoi?	*to what?*

The simple interrogative pronoun has an emphatic form, which is often used in daily discourse.

For Persons		*For Things*	
qui est-ce qui?	*who?*	qu'est-ce qui?	*what?*
de qui est-ce que?	*whose?*	de quoi est-ce que?	*of what?*
	of whom		
à qui est-ce que?	*to whom?*	à quoi est-ce que?	*to what?*
qui est-ce que?	*whom?*	qu'est-ce que?	*what?*

Note.—**De qui?** may also denote origin and authorship, while **à qui?** often refers to ownership. De qui est cette pièce?—Elle est de Racine. *Who is the author of this play?—Racine.* À qui est ce livre?—À moi. *Whose book is this?—Mine.*

The compound interrogative pronouns are identical in form with the compound relative pronouns. They are:

	SINGULAR	
Masculine	*Feminine*	
lequel?	laquelle?	*which one?*
duquel?	de laquelle?	*of which one?*
auquel?	à laquelle?	*to which one?*

	PLURAL	
Masculine	*Feminine*	
lesquels?	lesquelles?	*which ones?*
desquels?	desquelles?	*of which ones?*
auxquels?	auxquelles?	*to which ones?*

Note.—**Qu'est-ce que** and **qu'est-ce que c'est que** call for definitions: Qu'est-ce que le Louvre? *What is the Louvre?* Qu'est-ce que c'est que le Louvre?

WORD ORDER IN INTERROGATIVE SENTENCES.—The word order in interrogative sentences varies according to the nature of the question.

1. When the subject of the interrogative sentence is a noun, that noun is placed before the verb and is repeated after the verb under the form of a subject pronoun, agreeing in gender, number, and person with its antecedent.

| Paul est-il ici? | Is Paul here? |
| La table est-elle belle? | Is the table beautiful? |

Est-ce que, prefixed to the declarative form of a sentence, is commonly used to introduce interrogative sentences.

| Est-ce que Paul est ici? | Is Paul here? |
| Est-ce que la table est belle? | Is the table beautiful? |

2. In interrogative sentences which begin with **où, comment, combien, quand,** etc., the noun or pronoun subject goes after the verb when no noun objects are mentioned.

Où sont les enfants?	Where are the children?
Où sont-ils?	Where are they?
Quand viendra-t-il?	When will he come?

If the interrogative sentence contains also a noun object, the noun subject goes before the verb and the noun object after.

| Quand les enfants préparent-ils leurs devoirs? | When do the children prepare their lessons? |

INDEFINITE PRONOUNS.—Indefinite pronouns designate persons and things indefinitely. They have no common characteristics other than their indefiniteness.

Indefinite pronouns are either purely pronominal or adjectival pronouns.

The purely pronominal ones are:

> autre chose (*m.*), *something else*
> autrui, *others, other people*
> chacun, -e, *each (one), everyone*
> on, *one, people, we, you, they*
> personne, *someone*
> rien, *something*
> quelqu'un, -e, *someone, somebody*
> quelques-uns, *some, some people*
> quelques-unes (*f.*), *some, some people*
> quiconque, *whoever, whosoever*
> qui que, *whoever*
> l'un, -e, *one*
> les uns, *some*
> les unes (*f.*), *some*
> l'autre, *another*
> les autres, *others*
> grand' chose, *much*
> quelque chose, *something*

1. **Autrui** is not ordinarily used without a preposition. As antecedent, it is referred to by **il** not by **on,** in the dependent clause.

| Je ne convoite pas le bien d'autrui. | I do not covet other people's property. |
| Faisons pour autrui ce que nous voudrions qu'il fît pour nous. | Let's do unto others as we would be done by. |

2. **On** (for the sake of euphony, **l'on** after **si, ou, où,** and **que**)

is generally masculine; occasionally it represents the feminine.   It is followed by the verb in the singular.

On est toujours content quand on a ce qu'on aime.	One is always happy when one has what he likes.
Mademoiselle, est-on contente aujourd'hui?	Miss, are you happy to-day?
Partout on devrait tous être égaux devant la loi.	Everywhere we should all be equal before the law.

3.   **Personne,** *someone, somebody*.   When **personne** assumes the meaning of *nobody, not anybody*, it has its verb preceded by **ne (n').** It is never followed by **pas.**   With **personne,** the verb is always in the singular.   When used without a verb, **personne** (*nobody*) stands alone.

Je doute que personne le sache.	I doubt that someone (any-one) knows it.
Personne n'est ici.	Nobody is here.
Qui est ici?—Personne.	Who is here?—Nobody.

4.   **Rien,** *something, nothing*.   When used with the verb in the negative, it has the meaning of *nothing*.   Used alone it retains the same sense.   Preceded by a verb in the affirmative it assumes the sense of *something*.

Ici rien n'est considéré important.	Here nothing is considered important.
Que faites-vous?—Rien.	What are you doing?—Nothing.
Il n'est pas homme à donner rien pour rien.	He is not the man to give something for nothing.

5.   **Quiconque,** *whoever*, is an indefinite relative pronoun.   Although generally used in the masculine, it is sometimes feminine.

Quiconque dit cela ment.	Whoever says this is lying.
Elle est dévouée à quiconque est généreuse parmi ses amies.	She is devoted to whom-ever is generous among her lady friends.

The indefinite adjectival pronouns are:

aucun, -e	*nobody, no one, none*
autre	*other*
même	*same*
nul, -le	*nobody, no one*
pas un, -e	*not one*
plusieurs	*several*
tel, -le	*such a*
tout, -e	*all, whole, everything, every*
un	*one*

1. **Aucun, nul,** and **pas un** take **ne** before their verb.

Aucun d'eux n'est arrivé.	None of them arrived.
Nul ne l'a vu.	Nobody saw him.
Pas un n'est mort.	Not one died.

2. **Même,** *same*, as a pronoun, is preceded by the definite article.

C'est le même que vous connaissez.	It's the same one you know.

Note.—**Même,** *even*, is an adverb; it is placed in front of the word which it modifies: Même lui ne peut le faire. *Not even he can do it.*

3. **Tout, toute, tous, toutes,** *whole, all, everything.* In **tous,** pronoun, the *s* is always sounded.

Tout est fini.	All (everything) is ended.
Tous sont arrivés.	All have come.
Toutes sont parties.	All left.
Toute femme le sait.	Every woman knows it.
Toute la maison brûle.	The whole house is burning.

II. VERB REVIEW

1. IDIOMATIC USES OF devoir, *to owe,* and connaître, *to be acquainted with.*

1. DEVOIR assumes various meanings, the most usual ones of which are

(a) *To owe.*

Vous me devez de l'argent.	You owe me some money.
Il nous doit au moins de la reconnaissance.	He owes us at least some gratitude.

(b) *To have to, must.*

Vous devez faire cela maintenant.	You must do that now.
Vous devrez obéir à la loi.	You will have to obey the law.

(c) *Ought to, should.*

Il devrait venir à l'heure.	He ought to (should) come on time.
Nous devrions nous parler plus souvent.	We should speak to each other oftener.

(d) *Ought to have, should have.*

J'aurais dû vous avertir.	I should have warned you.
On aurait dû vous punir.	They ought to have punished you.

(e) *Was to* (= was supposed to).

Il devait venir.	He was to come.
Nous devions lui parler.	We were to speak to him.

(f) *Had to.*

Nous avons dû y aller à pied.	We had to go there on foot.
Je sais que vous avez dû travailler hier soir.	I know that you had to work last night.

(g) *Must,* implying supposition.

Il n'a pas mangé depuis trois jours; il doit avoir faim.	He hasn't eaten for three days; he must be hungry.

2. CONNAÎTRE must not be mistaken for **savoir** although both verbs are translated by *to know*.

(a) **Connaître** means *to know*, but in the sense of *to be acquainted, familiar with* by means of the five senses.

Connaissez-vous ce morceau de musique?	Are you familiar (by hearing) with this piece of music?
Nous connaissons très bien ce monsieur.	We are very well acquainted (by sight) with this gentleman.
Il connaît ces vins.	He knows (by taste) these wines.

(b) **Connaître** in expressions like se connaitre en, s'y connaître is rendered by *to be a good judge of.*

Il se connaît fort bien en architecture.	He is a very good judge of architecture.
On m'a dit qu'il se connaissait en peinture.—Oui, il s'y connaissait bien.	I was told that he was a good judge of painting.—Yes, he was a good judge of it.

2. IRREGULAR VERBS

Present	*Principal Parts*
falloir, *to be necessary, must*	falloir, (none), fallu, il faut, fallut
il faut	

boire, *to drink*		boire, buvant, bu, bois, bus
bois	buvons	
bois	buvez	
boit	boivent	

battre, *to beat*		battre, battant, battu, bats, battis
bats	battons	
bats	battez	
bat	battent	

III. VOCABULARY

1. FRENCH-ENGLISH:

*s'en aller, to go away, leave
  s'amuser, to have a good time
  approfondir, to go deeply into
  appuyer, to support
  avec, with
  l'avis *m.*, opinion
  beaucoup, much, many
  la chaleur, heat
  content, happy, contented
  discuter, to discuss
  disputer, to discuss, argue
  s'éclairer, to enlighten oneself
  l'habitude *f.*, habit

  heureux, -se, happy
*s'instruire, to learn
  même: pas —, not even
  milieu: au —, in the middle
le mot, word
  l'ombre *f.*, shadow
  opiniâtrément, obstinately
  pareil, -le, like
  passer: en passant, casually
  peu de, few; en — —, in a few
  peur: de — de, for fear of; *faire —, to frighten

pour que, so that, in order that

puisse (*pres. subj. 3d pers. sing.* of *pouvoir) is able

quelque chose, something

*retenir, to retain, remember

rien, something, nothing

traiter, to treat

2. ENGLISH-FRENCH:

against, contre

to ask for, demander

box, la boîte

car, l'automobile *m.* or *f.*

council, le conseil

coward, le couard, le poltron

cowardly, en couard

desirable, désirable

dollar, le dollar

to earn one's living, gagner sa vie

European, européen, -ne

event, l'événement *m.*

expensive, cher, chère

experience, l'expérience *f.*

to fight, *se battre

fortune, la fortune

generous, généreux, -se

to happen, arriver

to hear, entendre

to hunt, chasser; to go hunting, *aller à la chasse

laborious, industrieux, -se

latest, dernier, -ère

now: by —, maintenant

to rest, se reposer

to return, rendre

someone, quelqu'un

tired, fatigué, -e

train, le train

IV. IDIOMATIC EXPRESSIONS

être à même de, to be in a position to, able to

tirer parti de, to profit by

être des nôtres, to be one of the party

tout de même, all the same

au bout de, at the end of

se faire attendre, to make people wait for oneself

entendre parler (de), to hear about

se tirer d'affaire, to get along

s'en tirer, to get along, to manage

faire grand cas de, to attach great importance to

à qui le dites-vous? Don't I know?

V. EXERCISES

1. *Fill in the dashes with the proper form of the interrogative pronoun:*

    1. ————est venu vous voir? 2. ————pensez-vous?
    3. ————fait cet élève? 4. À————parle Robert? 5.
    À————travaillez-vous? 6. À————est cette maison?
    7. ————est sur cette table? 8. ————discutez-vous?
    9. Voici un tableau;———— ————est-il? 10. A————
    était ce tableau quand tu l'as acheté?

2. *Fill in the dashes of the above exercises with the emphatic form of the interrogative pronoun.*

3. *Translate:*

    1. Who has just arrived? 2. Against whom is he fight-
    ing? 3. Of whom is he thinking? 4. What is in this
    box? 5. Of what were you speaking? 6. What is he
    doing this morning? 7. Which one of the two men is more
    industrious? 8. What is more desirable, fortune or virtue?
    9. Which one of these four ladies do you know? 10. Here
    are two houses for sale; which one is the more expensive?
    11. He asks what you were talking about yesterday. 12.
    They don't want to know what happened to him. 13.
    What is the Panthéon? 14. What is this?

4. *Point out all indefinite pronouns in the following selection; then translate:*

    Dans la conversation, on parle de tout pour que chacun ait
    quelque chose à dire; on n'approfondit pas les questions de
    peur d'ennuyer les autres; on les propose comme en passant;
    on les traite avec rapidité; chacun dit son avis et l'appuie en
    peu de mots; nul n'attaque avec chaleur celui d'autrui; nul
    ne défend opiniâtrément le sien. On dispute pour s'éclairer,
    chacun s'instruit, chacun s'amuse, tous s'en vont contents.

    (J. J. Rousseau)

5. *Translate carefully:*

    1. Did you see someone?—No, I haven't seen anybody.
    2. Respect other people's property. 3. People always
    talk more than they act. 4. They knock at the door.

5. Haven't you heard anything?—No, nothing. 6. To-day is Sunday; nobody is working on Sunday. 7. Who is here?—Nobody. 8. Something is better than nothing. 9. We should all be generous when we are rich. 10. Who-ever acts cowardly is a coward.

6. *Discuss the following sentences; then translate them:*

1. Alors, madame, est-on heureuse au milieu de ces richesses? 2. Il n'a pas l'habitude de donner rien pour rien. 3. Il est fort douteux que quelqu'un puisse le faire. 4. Honneur à quiconque donne sa vie pour sa patrie. 5. Quiconque a beaucoup vu peut avoir beaucoup retenu. 6. Chacun fut de son avis. 7. Est-il rien de pareil? 8. Une ombre, un rien lui faisait peur. 9. L'avenir n'est à personne, pas même aux rois.

7. *Translate idiomatically:*

1. Are you in a position to undertake this trip? 2. It is necessary to profit by your experience. 3. We are going hunting; are you going to be one of the party? 4. One has to work to earn a living. 5. At the end of this tiring day we should rest. 6. Do you know that Mr. Lewis always makes people wait for him? 7. Did you hear about the latest European events? People should be tired of war. 8. He doesn't attach great importance to councils and yet he gets along. 9. You owe me a hundred dollars; you ought to have returned the money by now. 10. Having no car, he had to take the train.

I. THE VERB—CONJUGATIONS—VOICES—MOODS—TENSES—VERBAL ENDINGS

The verb is a word used to express the act, being, or state of its subject.

CONJUGATIONS.—There are three conjugations in French, the infinitives ending in -*er, -ir* (pres. part. -*issant*), and -*re* respectively. The third conjugation also comprises verbs in -*ir* (pres. part. -*ant*) and others in -*oir*. Most of the French verbs are regularly conjugated; a few have irregular forms and therefore are called irregular verbs. See *Appendix,* pp. 218-225.

VOICES.—According to the relation of the subject to the action performed, a verb is either in the active, passive, or pronominal voice.

When the subject is acting, the verb is said to be in the active voice.

Il finit son travail.   He is finishing his work.

When the subject is acted upon, the verb is said to be in the passive voice.

Le travail sera terminé   The work will be finished later.
    plus tard.

When the subject is acting reflexively, or when two distinct subjects are acting reciprocatingly, the verb is said to be in the pronominal or reflexive voice.

Elle se lave.   She is washing herself.
Ils se saluent.   They are greeting each other.

MOODS.—Conjugations have moods to express the various manners in which an action or state may present itself.

Thus, the *indicative* mood expresses an affirmation, an interrogation, or a negation as a positive fact.

Il a diné.   He has dined.   Il n'a pas diné.   He hasn't dined.
A-t-il diné? Has he dined?   Il n'avait pas diné. He hadn't dined.

The *conditional* mood expresses an action or state as dependent in its fulfillment on a condition still to materialize.

Si j'avais un livre, je le lirais.   If I had a book, I should read it.

The *subjunctive* mood represents the action or state as subordinated, in the main clause, to a verb which expresses either necessity, doubt, or emotion.

Il faut qu'il parte.   He must leave.
Je doute qu'il parte.   I doubt he will leave.
Je veux que vous partiez.   I want you to leave.

The *imperative* mood expresses the action or state as an order, a request, an exhortation, a prohibition, a permission, etc.

Partez aujourd'hui.   Leave today.
Ayez la bonté de partir.   Please, leave.
Ne partez pas.   Don't leave.
Qu'il parte s'il le désire.   Let him go if he so wishes.

The *infinitive* mood expresses the meaning of the verb in a general way without any distinction of person, number, or time.

Les enfants aiment jouer.   Children like to play.

Finally, the *participial* mood denotes an action or state as continued or as complete, without regard to time.

Il va de porte en porte, chan-   He goes from door to door sing-
    tant des chansons.   ing (some) songs.
Un palais bâti de pierres,   What I want is a palace built
    voilà ce que je veux.   with stones.

TENSES.—Each mood comprises a number of tenses which varies from four to two.

Tenses are verbal forms which serve to point out distinctions of time: present, past, and future.

As the present has no continuance, no space, there is only one tense to express present time. The past and future admit of several shades of past or future time, of anteriority or posteriority, of action or being. This explains and justifies the existence of primary and secondary tenses.

PRIMARY TENSES: PRESENT	PERFECT	FUTURE

SECONDARY TENSES:

1. Simple   { (a) *Imperfect*
                { (b) *Past Definite*

2. Compound   { (a) *Pluperfect*
                   { (b) *Past Anterior*   *Future Anterior*

VERBAL ENDINGS.—The stem of the verb is that part which usually remains unchanged. The endings are the part of the verb which varies according to the mood, the tense, the number, the person, and in some cases according to the gender.

Verb endings are not sufficient in French to express persons, numbers, tenses, etc.; the personal subject pronoun or a noun subject is required.

ils marchent	they walk
vous marchez	you walk

II. VERB REVIEW

1. IDIOMATIC USES OF falloir, *to be necessary;* faire, *to make, to do.*

   1. The verb FALLOIR may denote

      (a) Necessity. It is rendered either by *to be necessary* or *must*.

Il est tard, il faut partir.	It's late; we must leave (it's necessary to leave).
Il faut savoir s'il viendra.	One must know whether he is coming.

(b) Want. The person in want is referred to by an indirect object or reference pronoun which often becomes the subject of the English sentence.

Il me faut une plume.	I need a pen.
Il leur fallut un guide.	They needed a guide.
Il me faut un jour pour faire cela.	It takes me a day to do that.

(c) Lack, in expressions like s'en falloir, *to be far from;* tant s'en faut, *far from it;* or peu s'en faut, *nearly, not far from it.*

Je ne suis pas riche; il s'en faut.	I'm not rich, far from it.
Il n'est pas intelligent, tant s'en faut.	He is not intelligent, very far from it.
Vous alliez tomber ou peu s'en fallait.	You were going to fall, or you were not far from it.

Note.—**Falloir** is found in idioms like un homme comme il faut, *a gentleman;* une dame comme il faut, *a ladylike person;* un jeune homme comme il faut, *a well-mannered youth.*

2. FAIRE is used in many senses.   It takes the meaning of

(a) *To make or to do.*

Il a fait cette assertion.	He made this statement.
Faites-le vite.	Do it rapidly.

(b) *To cause to, to have . . . + past participle.*

Vous faites bâtir une maison, n'est-ce pas?	You are having a house built, are you not?
Il fait écrire une lettre.	He has a letter written.

Note.—In its causative sense, **faire** is of common use. When the infinitive that follows **faire** and completes its sense has a direct object, the "doer" of the action is referred to as the indirect object: Je lui (doer) fais acheter une maison. *I have him buy a house.*

Faire in the causative sense assumes sometimes the reflexive form with a passive meaning: Il se fait faire un habit. *He has a suit made (for himself).*

(c) *To pretend to be.*

Il fait le malade.	He pretends to be sick.
Vous faites le réformateur.	You pretend to be a reformer.

(d) *To be*, in expressions of weather.

Comme il fait chaud aujourd'hui!	How warm it is today!
Il fait froid.	It is cold.

Note.—**Faire** enters into many idiomatic expressions such as faire un voyage, *to take a trip;* faire des emplettes, *to go shopping;* etc.

2. IRREGULAR VERBS.

Present

craindre, *to fear, be afraid of*

crains	craignons
crains	craignez
craint	craignent

croître, *to grow*

croîs	croissons
croîs	croissez
croît	croissent

plaire, *to please*

plais	plaisons
plais	plaisez
plaît	plaisent

Principal Parts

craindre, craignant, craint, crains, craignis

croître, croissant, crû, croîs, crûs

plaire, plaisant, plu, plais, plus

III. VOCABULARY

1. FRENCH-ENGLISH:

argent: *faire de l'—, to make (some) money
s'arrêter, to stop
bien: Eh bien, well
le bureau, desk, office
car, for, because
donc, therefore, then
habile, smart, skillful

se lever, to get up
lutter, to wrestle
manger, to eat
pendant, during
retard: *être en —, to be late
le revers, reverse
la vie, life

2. ENGLISH-FRENCH:

to become, *devenir
  before, **avant de** (+ *inf.*)
  body, **le corps**
to climb, **gravir**
  debt, **la dette**
  duty, **le devoir**
  genius, **le génie**
to go out, *sortir
  guide, **le guide**
  interest, **l'intérêt** *m.*
  mind, **l'esprit** *m.*
  neck, **le cou**

nothing, **ne . . . rien**
one (*pron.*), **on**
outside, **dehors**
to rain, *pleuvoir
satisfied, **satisfait, -e**
South America, **l'Amérique
  du Sud** *f.*
strong, **fort, -e**
tired, **fatigué, -e**
true, **vrai, -e**
to be well-mannered, **avoir de
  bonnes manières**

IV. IDIOMATIC EXPRESSIONS

prendre son courage à deux mains, to summon
  one's courage
s'occuper de, to look after
de bonne heure, early
bon marché, cheap
au beau milieu de, in the very middle of
et ainsi de suite, and so on
sur-le-champ, immediately
avoir une occasion de, to have an opportunity to
en faire autant, to do likewise

V. EXERCISES

1. *Translate:*

1. It is necessary to think before speaking. 2. One must eat to live and not live to eat. 3. We need a guide to climb this mountain. 4. He is no genius, far from it. 5. We are far from being satisfied with our books. 6. I shall do it if I must. 7. Make him do his duty. 8. Is it cold or warm outside? 9. Don't always pretend to be tired when you have to go out. 10. He had a new suit made. 11. I nearly broke my neck when I fell from the tree. 12. When are you going to take a trip to South America?

2. *Translate into English:*

1. Vous vous croyez donc bien habile!—Eh bien, tout le monde en peut faire autant. 2. Voici une occasion de faire un peu d'argent, si vous m'en croyez. 3. Rien n'est bon marché en temps de guerre. 4. Je me lève toujours de bonne heure, car je crains d'arriver en retard à mon bureau. 5. S'il vous plaît, occupez-vous bien de mes affaires pendant mon absence. 6. Quand on a eu des revers de fortune, il faut prendre son courage à deux mains et recommencer à lutter. 7. Il s'arrêta au milieu de son discours. 8. C'est tous les jours la même vie: on se lève, on mange, on va au travail, on parle, on lit et ainsi de suite.

3. *Translate into idiomatic French:*

1. What are you afraid of? A true soldier fears nothing. 2. Children grow in body and mind; thus they become useful to their home and country. 3. To please, one has to be well-mannered. 4. This book of yours is of great interest. In fact it grows in interest as one reads on. 5. Do not make him believe that we must fear those who are stronger than we.

I. THE PRESENT AND IMPERFECT INDICATIVE—THEIR USES

The correct use of the French tenses constitutes one of the difficulties which a student of French has to overcome if he wishes to write, speak, understand, or read with accuracy and enjoyment.

1. VERB FORMS OF THE PRESENT AND IMPERFECT INDICATIVE, p. 10

2. USE OF THE PRESENT AND IMPERFECT INDICATIVE

THE PRESENT INDICATIVE.—As in English, the present indicative is used in French

1. To denote an action in its entire carrying out.

Louis parle.	Louis is speaking (now).
Je regarde ce tableau.	I am looking at this picture (now).

2. To denote a state or action in progress without considering either its duration, or its beginning and end.

Il neige à gros flocons.	It is snowing in large flakes.
Le ciel est bleu.	The sky is blue.

3. To indicate that the state or action expressed by the verb in the present is always true, or at least usually so.

Pierre qui roule n'amasse pas mousse.	A rolling stone gathers no moss.
Deux et deux font quatre.	Two and two are four.

4. To denote a state or action as beginning in the past and still in progress. In this particular case, the perfect tense is used in English.

Nous sommes ici depuis trois mois.	
Il y a trois mois que nous sommes ici.	We have been here for three months.
Voilà trois mois que nous sommes ici.	

In addition to the above mentioned uses, the present indicative assumes sometimes the functions of other tenses. Thus,

1. It denotes an immediate past, especially with verbs like **arriver, rentrer, venir de, revenir, sortir,** etc.

Il arrive de Paris; il est encore tout essoufflé.	He has (just) arrived from Paris; he is still out of breath.
Vous l'avez manqué; monsieur vient de partir à l'instant.	You missed him; monsieur has just left this very minute.

2. It assumes the sense of an immediate future.

Entendu!—Je vous vois demain au restaurant.	Fine!—I'll see you tomorrow at the restaurant.
Dans une heure je vous présente à Georges.	In one hour I shall introduce you to George.

Note.—After **quand** and **lorsque** (*when, whenever*), the future is used when an idea of futurity is contained in the sentence: Nous partirons quand elle viendra. *We shall leave when she arrives.*

Notice the use of the present in English after *when*, even though an idea of futurity is contained in the phrase.

3. It replaces a past tense to render a narrative more vivid. The English also uses the present in animated narratives.

Le voici enfin de retour: il se précipite vers la porte de sa maison, l'ouvre, entre dans le vestibule et se trouve soudain devant sa femme et ses enfants.	Here he is, back again: he dashes toward the door of his house, opens it, enters into the vestibule, and finds himself suddenly facing his wife and his children.

THE IMPERFECT INDICATIVE.—To express the past time, French possesses, in addition to its primary tense, the past indefinite (or perfect), four secondary tenses, the imperfect, the past definite (or *passé simple*), the pluperfect, and the past anterior. Each of these tenses has, besides the general rôle of expressing the past, specific functions the knowledge of which is important to interpret accurately the written or spoken word.

What characterizes the imperfect and distinguishes it from any other past tense, such as the past definite and the past indefinite, is its function of presenting a state or an action, in the past,

1. As occurring repeatedly or habitually.

Nous fumions souvent.	We smoked frequently.
Louis et moi, nous parlions toujours de l'Amérique.	Louis and I spoke always of America.

2. As being in progress when some other action or event took place or was taking place.

J'étudiais en Turquie quand la guerre éclata.	I was studying in Turkey when the war broke out.
J'étudiais tandis que mon ami lisait.	I was studying while my friend was reading.

3. As being the object of description.

La troupe errante venait de planter ses tentes sur la rive du fleuve. Entre les roues des chariots on voyait briller le feu. La horde apprêtait son souper.	The wandering troup had just pitched its tents on the bank of the river. Between the wheels of the wagons one could see a bright fire. The horde was preparing its supper.

In addition to the above mentioned functions, the imperfect is used now and then to replace

1. A conditional past.

Si j'avais dit un mot, on vous tuait (on vous aurait tué).	If I had said a word, they would have killed you.
Si l'on ne vous avait pas arrêté, vous tombiez (vous seriez tombé).	If they hadn't stopped you, you would have fallen.

2. A present in a direct discourse, when the latter is changed into an indirect discourse.

Il nous a dit: "Je pars demain."	He said to us: "I'm leaving tomorrow."
Il nous a dit qu'il partait demain.	He said to us that he was leaving (would leave) tomorrow.

3. An apparent future or present in the past.

Il prit place dans un bateau qui partait à trois heures.	He took a seat on a boat which was going to leave at three o'clock.
Il m'a assuré qu'il revenait dans un instant.	He assured me that he would be back in a minute.

4. A past definite or indefinite.

Deux minutes après, le général se dressait avec difficulté, marchait lentement vers la porte, puis, s'arrêtant, s'écriait . . .	Two minutes after, the general stood up with difficulty, walking slowly toward the door; then, stopping, cried out . . .

II. VERB REVIEW

1. Intransitive Verbs of Motion

In French, intransitive verbs denoting change of state or condition—verbs that do not take a direct object—use **être** instead of **avoir** in their compound tenses. The most common ones are:

Infinitive	*Past Participle*
aller, *to go*	allé
arriver, *to arrive*	arrivé
descendre, *to go down*	descendu
entrer, *to enter*	entré
monter, *to go up*	monté
mourir, *to die*	mort
naître, *to be born*	né
partir, *to leave*	parti
rester, *to stay*	resté

retourner, *to return*	retourné
sortir, *to go out*	sorti
tomber, *to fall*	tombé
venir, *to come*	venu

Note.—**Descendre, entrer, monter,** and **sortir** assume the sense of *to take down, to take in, to take up,* and *to take out* when conjugated with **avoir.**

To these verbs add all their compounds like **revenir,** *to come back;* **devenir,** *to become,* etc.

Note.—In all compound tenses of intransitive verbs expressing change of state or condition, the past participles must agree in gender and number with the subject of the verb: elle est allée, *she went.*

2.　IDIOMATIC USES OF vouloir, *to want,* and plaire, *to please.*

1.　The verb VOULOIR denotes

(a)　A command.

Je veux qu'il parte tout de suite.	I want him to leave at once.
Nous le voulons absolument.	We want it absolutely.

(b)　A mere wish.

Nous voudrions bien vous parler un instant.	We should like to speak to you a moment.
Que je voudrais être en bonne santé!	How I should like to be in good health!

(c)　An invitation.

Voulez-vous dîner avec moi, mon ami.	Have dinner with me, my friend.
Veux-tu prendre un apéritif avec Louis et moi?	Won't you have an appetizer with Louis and me?

Vouloir enters into a number of idiomatic expressions. (See idiomatic expressions, p. 103.)

2. PLAIRE assumes more particularly the sense of

(a) *To please*.

On ne peut plaire à tout le monde.	One cannot please all the world and his wife.
Elle cherche à lui plaire, n'est-ce pas?	She tries to please him, doesn't she?

(b) *To like*. When **plaire** takes the sense of *to like*, it has an indirect object which in English is often subject of the sentence.

Cette région me plaît beaucoup.	I like this region very much.
Est-ce que Paris vous plaît?	Do you like Paris?

3. IRREGULAR VERBS

Present   *Principal Parts*

mourir, *to die*   mourir, mourant, mort, meurs, mourus

meurs	mourons
meurs	mourez
meurt	meurent

naître, *to be born*   naître, naissant, né, nais, naquis

nais	naissons
nais	naissez
naît	naissent

III. VOCABULARY

1. FRENCH-ENGLISH:

allumer, to light
l'approche *f*., drawing near
l'arrêt *m*., stop
le bout, end
le bruit, noise
brûler, to burn
se cabrer, to rear
chanceler, to stagger
chez, at the house of; — moi, at my home
la colère, anger
la côte, slope

coup: à —s redoublés, repeatedly
la course de taureaux, bullfight
davantage, more
depuis, since
dessécher, to dry up
la douleur, grief, suffering
éclatant, shining
s'élancer, to dash
*s'enfuir, to flee
l'épi *m*., ear (of grain)

l'étoile *f.*, star
éviter, to avoid
la fanfare, brass band
guérir, to cure
s'irriter, to get angry
journée: de la —, all day
jurer, to swear
le laboureur, farmer
larme: fondre en —s, to dissolve, burst into tears
léger: à la légère, lightly, light-heartedly
malheureux, -se, unhappy
modérer, to moderate
morne, morose
*se mourir, to be dying
nouveau: de —, anew
*paraître, to appear, seem
peur: *prendre —, to become afraid
pied: à —, on foot
*pleuvoir, to rain
*poursuivre, to pursue
se précipiter sur, to dash on
près: de —, closely

proie: en — à, a prey to
récolter, to harvest
se réfugier, to seek shelter
se rendre, to surrender
rentrer, to re-enter, return
*reprendre, to scold
respirer, to breathe
rougir, to blush
sauter, to jump
scintiller, to scintillate
semer, to sow
signe: faire —, to signal
le sommeil, sleep
la sottise, stupidity; dire une —, to say a silly thing
tôt, early
tout à coup, suddenly
troublé, -e, disquieted
veiller, to watch
vert, -e, green
vide, empty
le voile, veil
la vue, sight; à la — de, at the sight of

2. ENGLISH-FRENCH:

army, l'armée *f.*
audacity, l'audace *f.*
back: to be —, *être de retour
to bend, plier
to blind, aveugler
to break, rompre
confusion, la confusion
to co-operate, coopérer
to criticize, critiquer
to dare, *se permettre, oser
dash, l'élan *m.*
to dash, s'élancer

defense, la défense
for, pour
frontier, la frontière
home, à la maison
to invite, inviter à
to open, *ouvrir
prosperity, la prospérité
reed, le roseau
to rush toward, s'élancer
sure, sûr, -e
to totter, chanceler
weapon, l'arme *f.*
to withstand, résister

IV. IDIOMATIC EXPRESSIONS

s'en vouloir de, not to forgive oneself for
veuillez, please
vouloir du mal à, to bear ill will to
plaît-il? I beg your pardon; what did you say?
s'il vous plaît, (if you) please
comme il vous plaira, please yourself, as you like it
à Dieu ne plaise (que), God forbid (that)

V. EXERCISES

1. *Put the verbs in parentheses into the present indicative; then give the reason for the use of the present:*

*1. Nous (modérer) difficilement nos passions. 2. Il (*venir) d'arriver. 3. Il (*pleuvoir) à verse. 4. Quand le vent (*être) brûlant, il (dessécher) les plantes. 5. C'(*être) un fait, la terre (tourner) autour du soleil. 6. (Regarder) donc, il (*faire) un beau soleil. 7. Le laboureur (semer) en automne et il (récolter) en été. 8. Tout nous (prouver) que Dieu (exister). 9. Les jours (*se suivre) et ne (se ressembler) pas. 10. Ils (rougir) quand on les (*reprendre). 11. Les épis vides (lever) la tête. 12. A l'approche du printemps la campagne (*devenir) verte. 13. Par économie, il n'(allumer) qu'un seul feu dans la maison. 14. Le général (*se mourir), tout (chanceler), les soldats (*prendre) peur, (*s'enfuir), la défaite (*être) complète. 15. Il (sortir) de chez son ami il y a trois minutes. 16. Nous (rentrer) de Paris encore tout fatigués. 17. C'(*être) bien, nous nous (*voir) demain au Café des Arts. 18. Elles (travailler) depuis deux heures. 19. Nous (*partir) tôt demain matin. 20. Voilà deux ans qu'il (étudier) le français.

2. *Explain the use of the present indicative in the following selection after reading it once; then translate.*

Course de taureaux. Le signal est donné; la barrière s'ouvre, le taureau s'élance au milieu du cirque; mais au

---

* All irregular verbs are preceded by an asterisk.

bruit de mille fanfares, aux cris, à la vue des spectateurs, il s'arrête, inquiet et troublé; il semble également en proie à la surprise et à la fureur. Tout à coup il se précipite sur un cheval qui se cabre et l'évite; le cavalier le blesse et se réfugie à l'autre bout. Le taureau s'irrite, le poursuit de près, frappe à coups redoublés la terre, et se jette sur le voile éclatant que lui présente un combattant à pied. Celui-ci le blesse de nouveau. La malheureuse bête tombe enfin, épuisée d'efforts, de colère et de douleur.

(Florian)

3. *Translate carefully, using the present indicative whenever possible:*

1. I shall leave tomorrow morning. 2. We shall be back in a minute. 3. Prosperity often blinds people. 4. What audacity is his! . . . he dashes to the defense of the bridge and withstands a whole army. 5. "I bend but do not break," said the reed. 6. Turenne is falling; confusion is complete; fortune is tottering . . . 7. War is declared: all are running for weapons, and, in a generous dash, they are rushing toward the frontiers to defend their country.

4. *Put the verbs in parentheses into the imperfect indicative; then explain the use of the imperfect:*

1. J'(examiner) ce livre quand on a frappé à la porte. 2. Nous (*partir) quand Georges est arrivé. 3. Il (*vivre) seul et (refuser) de recevoir qui que ce fût: c'(*être) un misanthrope. 4. Il (neiger), (neiger) toujours et les soldats qui (avancer) lentement (*paraître) autant de spectres sur un horizon morne. 5. Jeudi, il (entrer) triomphalement dans sa capitale, deux jours après il en (*sortir) secrètement détesté de tout le monde. 6. La nuit (tomber), mais la bataille (continuer) toujours. 7. C'(*être) une soirée incomparable: d'innombrables étoiles (scintiller) au firmament et (sembler) veiller sur le sommeil des mortels qui (respirer) tranquillement parce qu'ils se (*sentir) pénétrés de la paix des nuits.

5. *Explain the usage of the imperfect in the following sentences:*

1. Si on ne vous avait pas appelé à temps, vous vous jetiez dans cet abîme. 2. Si vous aviez insisté davantage, on vous condamnait. 3. Si Louis ne vous avait pas fait signe, vous disiez une sottise. 4. Si le secours n'était pas arrivé à temps, l'armée se rendait. 5. Si vous n'aviez pas tant parlé à la légère, on vous croyait.

6. *Change the following into indirect discourse sentences* (Model sentence: Il me dit: "Ce tableau est un chef-d'oeuvre" = Il me dit que ce tableau était un chef-d'oeuvre):

1. Vous nous avez dit: "Je vais faire cela pour vous faire plaisir." 2. Il vint me dire: "L'opération de Pierre est une merveille." 3. Le medecin est venu me déclarer: "Louis est hors de danger." 4. Tout le monde nous a crié: "Les aviateurs sont ici." 5. Il nous a rassurés en disant: "L'ordre est parfait, la paix règne partout, le peuple semble content." 6. "Est-ce que les dernières nouvelles sont bonnes?" demanda-t-il.

7. *Explain the usage of the imperfect in the following sentences:*

1. En sautant dans une auto qui quittait Paris à six heures du matin, il me dit qu'il revenait avant le coucher du soleil. 2. Le garçon quitta soudain la chambre; dix minutes après il revenait pâle et sombre et se dirigeait péniblement vers le seul fauteuil, puis, fondait en larmes. 3. Il a juré qu'il ne partait pas de la journée de demain. 4. Il ne voulut rien savoir du train qui partait à sept heures; il avait décidé de prendre l'autobus qui traversait Liancourt trois heures plus tard. 5. On l'avait porté à l'hôpital; une heure après, il sortait guéri et, à la surprise de tous, descendait rapidement et sans aide la côte de N . . . et continuait sa route sans arrêt.

8. *Translate into idiomatic French:*

1. Why has he a grudge against me?—I haven't done anything to harm him. 2. God forbid that I dare criticize

him.   3.   He doesn't forgive himself for having said that.
4.   Please tell him to do that for me.   5.   He may be sure
that I bear him no ill will.   6.   They are willing to co-
operate with us.   7.   Has he invited you for dinner?—
What did you say? I didn't hear you well.   8.   You may
come with us or stay home; please yourself.   9.   Open the
door, if you please.

THE PERFECT AND PAST DEFINITE
—THEIR USE

1. Verb Forms of the Perfect and Past Definite, pp. 19-20 and 11.

2. Use of the Perfect and Past Definite

The Perfect or Past Indefinite.—The perfect, often called "conversational tense" because it is constantly used in conversation, letter-writing, informal narratives, etc., expresses an action or state in the past just as the past definite does, but it adds some specific features to its expression of a past action which distinguish it from any other tense of the past.

The action in the past expressed by the perfect is presented:

1. As now completed, but with reference to the present implied. The English present perfect is its equivalent.

J'ai acheté une automobile.	I have bought an automobile.
Nous avons atteint tous deux l'âge de vingt ans.	We have both reached the age of twenty.

2. As having taken place at some time in the past.

Je l'ai déjà rencontré, ce jeune homme-là.	I have already met that young man.
Le général s'en est aperçu, il y a quelque temps.	The general noticed it some time ago.

In addition to the above functions, the perfect sometimes takes the place of the future anterior, especially after **si**.

Si demain vous ne lui avez pas écrit, je lui écrirai.	If you haven't written him by tomorrow, I shall write to him.
J'ai fini dans cinq minutes.	I shall be through in five minutes.

Note.—In proverbs, the perfect is used now and then instead of the present: L'oisiveté n'a jamais nourri son homme. *Idleness has never fed anybody.*

THE PAST DEFINITE.—The past definite is also called "historical tense" because it is used primarily in narratives and historical literature. It is perhaps best described when called "literary tense." In fact, it is seldom used in daily conversation. Like the imperfect and the perfect it situates the action or state expressed by the verb into the past. It differs from both tenses by presenting an action or a state in the past:

1. As absolutely completed without any reference whatsoever to the present.

La porte s'ouvrit tout à coup bruyante et claire.	Suddenly the door burst wide open noisily.
Il souffleta l'insolent et ferma la porte.	Slapping the face of the insolent man, he closed the door.

2. As having taken place at a definite point of time in the past.

A minuit, le chef de la troupe sortit de sa tente. "Debout," s'écria-t-il, "il est temps de partir!" Aussitôt la bande s'épandit à grand bruit, plia les tentes et s'ébranla.	At midnight the leader of the troop came out of his tent. "Be up!" he shouted; "it is time to leave." Immediately the troop scattered around noisily, folded its tents, then got under way.

The past definite is often used to express a rapid succession of actions or events and is more particularly suited to indicate the succession of events.

On déclara la guerre. Aussitôt un souffle embrasé parcourut le pays. Tous se crurent en état de combattre, tous voulurent s'engager. On les reçut, on les enrôla, on les équipa, on les arma, ils partirent tous pour les frontières.	War was declared. At once the country was set ablaze with patriotism. All considered themselves capable of fighting: they all wanted to enlist. In fact, they were accepted, enlisted, equipped, and armed; they all marched to the frontiers.

The past definite is sometimes used to express duration or repetition of a completed action. In no way can the past definite be used when the action in the past is going on; this function is reserved to the imperfect tense.

Telle fut la tradition de l'église pendant cinq siècles.	Such was the tradition of the church for five centuries.
Louis XIV régna soixante-douze ans.	Louis XIV reigned for seventy-two years.
Louis XIV entreprit de nombreuses guerres durant sa longue vie.	Louis XIV undertook numerous wars during his long life.

II. VERB REVIEW

1 PASSIVE VOICE

The passive voice is formed with the auxiliary **être** + the past participle of any transitive verb. In the passive voice, the past participle must agree in gender and number with the subject of the verb.

The tenses of the passive voice are:

INDICATIVE

Present
I am (being) punished . . .
je suis puni(e)
tu es puni(e)
il est puni
elle est punie

nous sommes puni(e)s
vous êtes puni(e)s
ils sont punis
elles sont punies

Imperfect
I was (being) punished . . .
j'étais puni(e)
tu étais puni(e)
il était puni
elle était punie

nous étions puni(e)s
vous étiez puni(e)s
ils étaient punis
elles étaient punies

Past Definite
I was punished . . .
je fus puni(e), etc.
nous fûmes puni(e)s, etc.

Future
I shall be punished . . .
je serai puni(e), etc.
nous serons puni(e)s, etc.

Perfect
I *have been punished* . . .
j'ai été puni(e), etc.
nous avons été puni(e)s, etc.

Pluperfect
I *had been punished* . . .
j'avais été puni(e), etc.
nous avions été puni(e)s, etc.

Past Anterior
I *had been punished* . . .
j'eus été puni(e), etc.
nous eûmes été puni(e)s, etc.

CONDITIONAL

Present
I *should be punished* . . .
je serais puni(e), etc.
nous serions puni(e)s, etc.

Perfect
I *should have been punished* . . .
j'aurais été puni(e), etc.
nous aurions été puni(e)s, etc.

INFINITIVES

Present
to be punished
être puni(e)

Perfect
to have been punished
avoir été puni(e)

PARTICIPLES

Present
being punished
étant puni(e)

Past
having been punished
ayant été puni(e)

Note.—The agent of a verb in the passive voice is introduced by **par**, as a rule; but **de** is used with verbs denoting emotion and with such verbs as **accompagner, couvrir, assister,** etc.

Aux États-Unis le président est élu par le peuple.

In the United States the president is elected by the people.

Louise est aimée de tous.

Everybody likes Louise. (Louise is liked by everybody.)

2. IRREGULAR VERBS

Present
mouvoir, *to move*

meus	mouvons
meus	mouvez
meut	meuvent

Principal Parts
mouvoir, mouvant, mû, meus, mus

pleuvoir, *to rain*		pleuvoir, pleuvant, plu, il pleut,
il pleut		il plut

vêtir, *to clothe*		vêtir, vêtant, vêtu, vêts, vêtis
vêts	vêtons	
vêts	vêtez	
vêt	vêtent	

lire, *to read*		lire, lisant, lu, lis, lus
lis	lisons	
lis	lisez	
lit	lisent	

III. VOCABULARY

1. French-English:

agrandir, to enlarge
l'aide de camp *m.*, aide-de-camp
apaiser, to appease
apprêter, to get ready
apprivoisé, -e, tamed, tame
*atteindre, to reach
aussitôt, at once
aventure: à l' —, at random
le bois, woods
briller, to shine
le calme, calmness
le casque, helmet
causer, to bring about
choisir, to choose
le conquérant, conqueror
creuser, to dig, hollow out
la crinière, mane
le début, the beginning
s'ébranler, to move off
écumant, -e, foaming
embrasé, -e, blazing
s'emparer, to take hold of
empêcher, to prevent
l'enclume *f.*, anvil
endormi, -e, asleep

enflammé, -e, inflamed
l'envie *f.*, desire, intention
s'épandre, to spread, scatter
l'épée *f.*, sword
errer, to wander about
*s'éteindre, to die out
s'étendre, to spread
le fleuve, river
fois: à la —, at the same time
frémir, to tremble
le gazon, lawn
le gîte, lodging, home
le hennissement, neighing
la horde, horde
le hurlement, howling
la lance, spear
lever, to lift
la lumière, light
le maintien, upholding
le malheur, misfortune
marquer, indicate
le naseau, nostril (of an animal)
opposé, -e, opposite
l'ours *m.*, bear

pâtir, to suffer
plier, to fold
point: au — du jour, at dawn
la poitrine, chest
le politique, politician
quelquefois, sometimes
*renvoyer, to send back, dismiss
le repli, fold
résonner, to resound
la rive, bank

rouler: les yeux roulent du sang, the eyes are shot with blood
secouer, to shake
le son, sound
sonner, to sound, ring
la steppe, steppe
la Suède, Sweden
tantôt, a little while ago
la tente, tent
verser, to pour
le vieillard, old man

2. ENGLISH-FRENCH:

ally, l'allié *m.*
companion, le compagnon
danger, le danger; in —, en danger
to end in, by, finir par
to enter, entrer (dans)
to hasten, *accourir
late: too —, trop tard

night, la nuit
poor, le pauvre
to prevent, empêcher
to rage, sévir
side: to her —, auprès d'elle
study hall, la salle d'étude
supervisor, le surveillant
victory, la victoire

IV. IDIOMATIC EXPRESSIONS

contre toute attente, without any warning, contrary to all expectation
n'en plus pouvoir, to be exhausted*
cela ne me fait ni froid ni chaud, it's all the same to me.
rentrer chez soi, to go (back) home
à la belle saison, in summer, in fine weather
chanter à pleine gorge, to sing loudly
courir la prétentaine, to gad about, run around
rendre visite, to call on, pay a visit
se faire un plaisir de, to take pleasure in
faire la leçon, to teach a lesson

---

* Notice word order: *je n'en peux plus,* I am exhausted.

V. EXERCISES

1. *Explain why the perfect is used in the following sentences:*

   1. De tout temps les petits ont pâti de la sottise des grands.
   2. J'ai cru que mes présents apaiseraient son avidité. 3. Le général a choisi son aide de camp. 4. Cette jeune fille-là ne m'a pas été présentée. 5. Nous avons atteint le sommet de cette montagne plus d'une fois.

2. *Translate the following sentences into conditional sentences with the past indefinite in the "si" clause* (Model: Vous serez parti demain ou je vous renverrai = Si vous n'êtes pas parti demain, je vous renverrai):

   1. Vous aurez fait cela demain ou je le ferai moi-même.
   2. Vous m'aurez fait une visite dans dix jours ou je ne vous parlerai plus jamais. 3. La prise de la Bastille aura marqué le début de la Révolution française ou rien ne l'indiquera jamais. 4. Il aura été arrêté tantôt ou personne ne l'arrêtera jamais.

3. *Study the use of the perfect and past definite in the following selection; then translate:*

   Charles XII, roi de Suède, a porté toutes les vertus des héros à un excès où elles sont aussi dangereuses que les vices opposés. Sa fermeté, devenue opiniâtre, fit ses malheurs dans l'Ukraine, et le retint cinq ans en Turquie; sa libéralité a ruiné la Suède; son courage, poussé jusqu'à la témérité, a causé sa mort; sa justice a été quelquefois jusqu'à la cruauté, et, dans les dernières années, le maintien de son autorité approchait de la tyrannie. Ses grandes qualités ont fait le malheur de son pays. Il n'attaqua jamais personne, mais il ne fut pas aussi prudent qu'implacable dans ses vengeances. Il a été le premier qui ait eu l'ambition d'être conquérant sans avoir l'envie d'agrandir ses états. Sa passion pour la gloire, pour la guerre et pour la vengeance l'empêcha d'être bon politique, qualité sans laquelle on n'a jamais vu de conquérant. (Voltaire)

4. *Change all verbs in italics into the past definite or the imperfect as required:*

Lorsque la horde eut planté ses tentes sur la rive du fleuve, on apprêta le souper. Sur le gazon, les chevaux *errent* à l'aventure. Un ours apprivoisé *prend* son gîte auprès d'une tente . . . Les marteaux *font* résonner l'enclume de campagne. Mais bientôt sur la bande errante *s'étend* le silence du sommeil, et le calme de la steppe n'*est* plus troublé que par le hurlement des chiens et le hennissement des chevaux. Tout *repose;* les feux *s'éteignent,* la lune *brille* seule dans le lointain des cieux, versant sa lumière sur la horde endormie. Au point du jour, un vieillard, chef de la troupe, *sort* de sa tente: "Debout," *s'écrie-t-il,* "le soleil est levé!" Aussitôt la bande *s'épand* à grand bruit. On *plie* les tentes. On *s'ébranle* à la fois. (Mérimée)

5. *Give the 1st persons, singular and plural, past definite of:*

*acquérir	courir	écrire	mourir	prendre
asseoir	craindre	faire	mouvoir	savoir
battre	croire	fuir	naître	vaincre
conduire	croître	lire	plaire	venir
connaître	devoir	mettre	pouvoir	vivre

6. *Use the past definite whenever possible in the following sentences:*

1. He arrived too late to see her. 2. At that time his laziness prevented him from aiding the poor. 3. When he saw her in danger, he abandoned his companions and hastened to her side. 4. At five o'clock the battle started; it raged all through the night and ended in a victory for the Allies. 5. We were in the study hall when the supervisor entered.

7. *Change all verbs in the present indicative into the corresponding person of the past definite:*

Le soleil du matin s'échappant des replis d'un nuage d'or verse tout à coup sa lumière sur les bois, l'océan et les armées. La terre paraît embrasée du feu des casques et des

---

* See meaning of these words in the General Vocabulary.

lances, les instruments guerriers sonnent l'air antique de Jules César partant pour les Gaules. La rage s'empare de tous les cœurs, les yeux roulent du sang, la main frémit sur l'épée. Les chevaux se cabrent, creusent l'arène, secouent leurs crinières, frappent de leur bouche écumante leur poitrine enflammée, ou lèvent vers le ciel leurs naseaux brûlants, pour respirer les sons belliqueux.

(Chateaubriand)

8. *Translate into idiomatic French:*

1. Without any warning he returned home. 2. He sang loudly for more than an hour and now is exhausted. 3. Charles loves to gad about in fine weather. 4. I shall take pleasure in paying you a visit. 5. Every time he sees me he tries to teach me a lesson, but it's all the same to me.

I. THE PLUPERFECT AND PAST ANTERIOR —THEIR USE

1. VERB FORMS OF THE PLUPERFECT AND PAST ANTERIOR, pp. 19-20
2. USE OF THE PLUPERFECT AND PAST ANTERIOR OF THE INDICATIVE

THE PLUPERFECT.—The pluperfect has the function of indicating the anteriority of an action over another action likewise in the past. It shares this function with the past anterior.

Il avait déjà quitté la maison quand cinq heures sonnèrent.	He already had left the house when the clock struck five.
A peine fut-il parti que son ami arriva.	He had hardly left when his friend arrived.

According to certain grammarians, the past anterior seems to insinuate an immediate anteriority as regards another action also in the past, while the pluperfect appears to suggest an anteriority of lesser immediateness.

Nous partîmes quand nous nous fûmes réconciliés.	We left (immediately) after being reconciled.
Quand nous sommes partis nous nous étions réconciliés.	When we were leaving we were already reconciled.

Besides the above mentioned function, the pluperfect like the imperfect

1. Presents the state or action in the past as continuous, habitual, or repeated.

A Paris, quand nous avions déjeuné, nous allions nous promener.

In Paris, whenever we had had lunch we went out for a walk.

Nous avions toujours bu du vin à table quand arriva la prohibition.

We had been used to drinking wine at the table when prohibition came upon us.

Nous étions souvent allés au bord de la mer quand mourut mon père.

We had often gone to the seashore at the time my father died (= before my father's death).

2. Again like the imperfect, the pluperfect expresses possibility in the past.

Encore six jours de résistance et les assiégés avaient gagné leur liberté.

Six more days of resistance and the besieged would have won their freedom.

Deux mètres de plus et le cheval avait battu le record du monde.

Two more meters and the horse had beaten (= would have beaten) the world record.

3. The pluperfect sometimes denotes regret and blame.

Ah! si j'avais été là, je vous aurais secouru.

If only I had been there, I should have helped you.

Si seulement vous m'aviez écouté!

If you had only listened to me! (but you didn't).

4. The pluperfect, finally, establishes sometimes between the two actions expressed by the verbs in the sentence a relationship of cause and effect.

Les soldats gisaient à terre par milliers (*effect*); la mort les avait fauchés sans pitié (*cause*).

The soldiers were lying on the ground by the thousands: death had mowed them down without pity.

L'enfant s'endormait (*effect*); la mère l'avait bercé patiemment (*cause*).

The child fell asleep: her mother had lulled her to sleep patiently.

THE PAST ANTERIOR.—The past anterior is used either in simple or in compound sentences.

When used in *simple* sentences, the past anterior has the function of indicating:

1. That the action expressed by the verb is absolutely completed. It is then accompanied by such adverbs or adverbial phrases as denote the time within which the action in the past was accomplished.

En deux ans les ouvriers eurent terminé le palais.	In two years the workers were through building the palace.
En vingt bonds, il m'eut dépassé.	In twenty bounds he had bounced beyond me.
En moins d'une heure il eut achevé son poème.	In less than an hour he was through writing his poem.

2. That the action was accomplished with utmost rapidity. This is suggested by adverbs and adverbial phrases such as **aussitôt, bientôt, peu après, en moins de rien, en un moment, en un clin d'œil.**

Et le drôle eut lapé le tout en un moment.	And the queer one (dog) had lapped up everything in a minute.
Il eut bientôt fait d'écrire au maire.	It didn't take him long to write to the mayor.
La mort l'eut bien vite terrassé.	Death had crushed him quite rapidly.
En un clin d'œil, l'orateur eut suscité l'enthousiasme.	In a jiffy, the orator had stirred up enthusiasm.

When used in *compound* sentences, the past anterior is usually found in the subordinate clause and has the special function of denoting immediate anteriority over the verb in the main clause. The past anterior is then preceded by conjunctions like **dès que, après que, aussitôt que, quand, lorsque,** etc.

Quand il eut fini de manger, il vint me saluer.	When he had finished eating, he came to greet me.
Dès qu'il eut achevé son travail, il partit.	He left as soon as he had ended his work.
A peine furent-ils arrivés chez eux que l'orage éclata.	They had hardly arrived home when the storm broke out.

When the verb in the main clause is in the past indefinite, the past anterior in the subordinate clause is commonly replaced, especially in conversation, by a double-compound tense made up of the compound tense of the auxiliary + the past participle of the verb in question.

Quand il a eu fini (*instead of* quand il eut fini), il est venu me saluer.

When he was through eating, he came to greet me.

Dès qu'il a eu achevé (*instead of* dès qu'il eut achevé) son travail, il est parti.

As soon as he had finished his work, he left.

II. VERB REVIEW

1. Substitutions for the Passive Voice

The passive voice is not used as frequently in French as it is in English, but it is used.

When the passive voice is replaced, either the **on** + active voice construction or the reflexive verb may be used.

1. **On** + a verb in the active voice generally replaces a verb in the passive voice when the agent of the action expressed by the verb is anonymous.

On méprise d'ordinaire les menteurs.

Liars are ordinarily despised.

On aime et on admire les héros de son pays.

The heroes of one's own country are loved and admired.

In English it is permissible to make a prepositional or an indirect object the subject of a passive verb. This is not done in French; instead **on** or a noun + an active verb is required.

Mon meilleur ami se moque de moi.

I am laughed at by my best friend.

On leur a donné des crayons.

They were given pencils.

On m'a dit. . .

I was told. . .

On a dit à Paul de rester.

Paul was told to stay.

2. When the action expressed by the passive voice is viewed as being normal, habitual, possibly capable of materializing,' the reflexive form of the verb replaces the passive verb.

Cela se fait facilement.	This is easily done.
Les journaux se vendent tous les jours.	Papers are sold daily.
D'ordinaire ce travail ne se fait pas ainsi.	This work is not done this way usually.

2. IDIOMATIC USE OF valoir, *to be worth*, and penser, *to think*.

1. The verb VALOIR means

(a) *To be worth.*

Cette auto ne vaut rien.	This automobile isn't worth anything.
Cette propriété vaut beaucoup.	This estate is worth a great deal.

Note.—Notice expressions like valoir la peine, *to be worth while;* valoir le coup, *to be worth trying.*

(b) *To prefer, be preferable, be better.*

Il valait mieux le faire hier.	It was preferable to do it yesterday.
Il vaut mieux n'en rien dire.	It is better not to say a word about it.

Note.—Notice the meaning of se faire valoir, *to boast, praise one's self.*

2. The verb PENSER, *to think,* presents some difficulty to the student of French. Its meanings are the following:

(a) *To think* (intransitive verb).

Il y a toujours quelque chose à penser.	There is always matter for thought.
Il ne rêve pas, il pense.	He is not dreaming: he is thinking.

(b) *To think of* or *about, direct one's thought to.*

Je penserai à vous.	I shall think of you.
Veuillez ne pas y penser.	Please, don't think of it.

(c) *To think* (transitive verb) *something about someone* or *something.*

Que pensez-vous de cela?	What do you think about that?
Que pensiez-vous de Jean?	What did you think about John?

3. IRREGULAR VERBS

Present — *Principal Parts*

asseoir, *to seat* — asseoir, asseyant *or* assoyant, assis, assieds *or* assois, assis

assieds	asseyons *or* assois		assoyons
assieds	asseyez	assois	assoyez
assied	asseyent	assoit	assoient

écrire, *to write* — écrire, écrivant, écrit, écris, écrivis

écris	écrivons
écris	écrivez
écrit	écrivent

fuire, *to flee* — fuir, fuyant, fui, fuis, fuis

fuis	fuyons
fuis	fuyez
fuit	fuient

III. VOCABULARY

1. FRENCH-ENGLISH:

achever, to finish
agiter, to agitate, upset
l'avion *m.*, airplane
la bouche, mouth
campagne: aller à la —, to go to the country
au centuple, a hundredfold
le champ de blé, wheat field
le champ de course, race course
le cheval, horse
le conseil, advice
la corbeille, basket
croiser, to cross
se diriger, to head for

se disperser, to scatter
le domestique, servant
éclater, to start, burst (out)
s'effondrer, to collapse
l'émeute *f.*, outbreak, riot
entre: d' — eux, from among them
l'estrade, stage, platform
fort, -e, strong
la foule, crowd
la gelée, frost
s'habiller, to dress
hier, yesterday
longuement, a long time

lorsque, when
moins: en — de, in less than
où, when, where
*ouvrir, to open
peine: à —, hardly, scarcely
plus: de—, moreover, in
addition
la pomme, apple
rapporter, to yield

remporter, to carry off, win
réunir, to gather, unite
su (*p.p.* of *savoir*), known
le témoin, witness
tomber, to fall
la ville, town, city
vite, quickly
*vivre, to live, dwell

2. ENGLISH-FRENCH:

to boast, se vanter
future, l'avenir *m.*
to go on, continuer
homework, le devoir, les de-
voirs
to know, *savoir
to offer, *offrir
paper, le papier
picture, le tableau

to sit down, *s'asseoir
to succeed in, réussir à
to think, penser à or de
to touch, toucher
to walk, marcher
to write, *écrire
written, écrit, -e (*p.p.* of
*écrire)

IV. IDIOMATIC EXPRESSIONS

venir à bout de, to succeed
rien de beau, nothing beautiful
se servir de, to use, make use of
servir de, to serve as
prendre quelqu'un en grippe, to take a dislike to someone
s'en prendre à, to blame, lay the blame on
faire sa malle, to pack one's trunk
faire mal, to hurt, ache
à tantôt, Good bye! so long!
à l'avenir, in the future

V. EXERCISES

1. *Translate carefully:*

1. Il s'était présenté au palais au moment où le ministre
sortait. 2. L'orateur avait à peine ouvert la bouche qu'une
émeute éclata. 3. Aussitôt que les témoins furent arrivés.

on croisa les épées. 4. Les chevaux étaient arrivés et la foule des spectateurs s'est dirigée lentement vers le champ de courses. 5. N'avaient-ils donc rien entendu de cette explosion qui hier encore agitait la ville? 6. A peine eurent-ils fini leur conversation qu'ils se dispersèrent.

2. *Explain the use of the pluperfect in the following sentences:*

1. Nous étions souvent allés à la campagne quand mon oncle alla vivre à Paris. 2. Nous avions toujours eu des domestiques lorsque ma mère perdit sa fortune. 3. Un peu plus de persévérance, et ils avaient remporté une victoire glorieuse. 4. Deux minutes d'hésitation de plus et vous aviez perdu un régiment. 5. Si j'avais seulement su que vous étiez en ville, je n'aurais pas manqué de vous faire une visite. 6. Quel dommage! — Si vous aviez seulement suivi mes conseils! 7. Les pommes tombaient de l'arbre à pleines corbeilles; la gelée les avait touchées fortement. 8. Tout s'effondrait à Londres; des avions ennemis étaient venus visiter la ville. 9. Cette année-là les champs de blé rapportaient au centuple; on les avait fait valoir. 10. Georges savait sa leçon; il l'avait étudiée longuement.

3. *Explain the use of the past anterior and the double-compound past tense; then translate the sentences:*

1. En moins de trois ans les ingénieurs eurent achevé de construire le tunnel. 2. Ils eurent vite fait de s'habiller et d'aller jouer. 3. Peu après, les soldats eurent pris la ville sans perdre un seul d'entre eux. 4. Aussitôt que les députés se furent réunis, ils se déclarèrent tous contre la guerre. 5. Lorsqu'il a eu fini son discours, il est descendu de l'estrade. 6. Nous n'avons pas plus tôt eu achevé notre travail qu'on est venu nous dire de partir.

4. *Translate:*

1. Your homework isn't worth the paper on which it is written. 2. It is better to sit down a minute than to go on walking. 3. He does nothing but boast. 4. Does he think or is he dreaming? 5. Do you know what he is

thinking of? 6. What are you thinking of him? 7. Think of it, he never writes to his brother! 8. Think of what you are doing when you give alms to the poor. 9. He never thinks of his friends. 10. Is it worth the while to think of those who do not think of you?

5. *Translate into idiomatic French:*

1. Make use of your pen to write your homework. 2. There is nothing beautiful in this picture. 3. Why do you take a dislike to me?—Don't blame me if you did not succeed in your enterprise. 4. So you are packing, aren't you? So long! 5. Don't touch me; you hurt me. 6. In the future you shall serve me as my guide.

I. THE FUTURE AND FUTURE ANTERIOR —AND THEIR USE

The future time is expressed in French as it is in English by means of two future tenses, the future and the future anterior, the former being a primary tense, the latter a secondary tense.

1. VERB FORMS OF THE FUTURE AND FUTURE ANTERIOR, pp. 11 and 20
2. USE OF THE FUTURE AND FUTURE ANTERIOR

THE FUTURE.—The future expresses what will take place in future time without the exact time being intimated.*

Nous serons contents de le voir.	We shall be glad to see him.
Je ferai ce qui vous plaira.	I shall do what you like.
Vous viendrez me voir, n'est-ce pas?	You will come and see me, won't you?

The future assumes sometimes various functions. Thus, it is used to express

1. A generally admitted fact.

Les faibles seront toujours sacrifiés.	The weak will always be sacrificed.
La paresse sera toujours la mère de la pauvreté.	Laziness will always be the mother of poverty.

2. A probability or supposition (with the idea of an attenuated present tense).

Louis n'est pas ici; il sera malade.	Louis isn't here; he is probably sick.
Le pauvre garçon n'a pas mangé depuis hier, il aura sans doute faim.	The poor boy hasn't eaten since yesterday; no doubt he must be hungry.

*Note.—Contrary to the English, the future is used after **quand, lorsque,** *when,* **aussitôt que** and **dès que,** *as soon as,* when future time is implied: Je partirai quand il arrivera. *I shall leave when he arrives.*

3. An order.

Vous tâcherez d'arriver à temps.	Try to be here in time.
Tu finiras ce travail avant de t'en aller.	Do finish this work before leaving.
Voici ce que tu feras ce soir: . . .	Here is what you are going to do this evening . . .

4. A formal command or order.

Tes père et mère honoreras.	Honor your father and mother.

Note.—**Aller** in the present tense denotes an immediate future when it is followed by an infinitive.

Demain nous allons vous faire une visite.	Tomorrow we are going to pay you a visit.
Je vais aller me promener avec vous à l'instant.	I am going to take a walk with you presently.

THE FUTURE ANTERIOR.—The future anterior intimates that an action or event will be completed at a certain time in the future.

Je vous assure, tout sera fait ce soir.	I assure you, everything will be done by this evening.
Demain, nous serons arrivés à Paris.	Tomorrow we shall have arrived in Paris.
Dans un an, nous serons devenus riches.	In a year we shall have become rich.

Sometimes, the action or event intimated by the future anterior stands as fully completed in the future in relation to another action or event equally in the future.

Avant qu'il n'arrive (action in the future), nous aurons tout réglé (action in the future to be completed before the above mentioned action, also in the future).	We shall have settled everything before he arrives (= before his arrival).

According to the above examples, the future anterior has the double function of expressing both the completion of an action or event in the future, and the anteriority of that action or event over another also in the future.

At times, the future anterior intimates

1. Probability, or supposition.

Vous entendez ce bruit?— Louis se sera de nouveau battu.	Do you hear this noise?— In all probability, Louis has been fighting again.
On voit du sang partout. On aura tué quelqu'un.	Blood is seen everywhere. Somebody must have been killed.

2. Regret and indignation.

Je me serai sacrifié à ce point pour qu'un autre récolte ce que j'ai semé!	To think that I should have sacrificed myself so that someone else may reap what I have sown!
Les soldats auront donné leur vie pour la patrie et le général en recevra toute la gloire?	Will the soldiers have given their lives for their country so that the general will receive all the glory for it?

Note.—There is a *temps surcomposé* of the future anterior; it is, however, seldom used: Pourquoi vous en inquiéter?—J'aurai eu tout fini à temps. *Why worry about it?—Everything shall be finished in time.*

II. VERB REVIEW

1. IRREGULAR MODEL VERBS

Among the irregular verbs many can be classified according to definite types or model verbs. This classification simplifies considerably the study of French irregular verbs. The most usual model verbs and some of their affiliates are:

Principal Parts	*Affiliated Verbs*
recevoir, *to receive*	apercevoir, to see
recevant	concevoir, to conceive
reçu	décevoir, deceive
reçois	percevoir, perceive
reçus	devoir, owe
	redevoir, to owe a balance, etc.

partir, *to leave*	servir, to serve
partant	mentir, to lie
parti	sentir, to feel
pars	sortir, to go out
partis	se repentir, to repent
	dormir, to sleep, etc.
ouvrir, *to open*	offrir, to offer
ouvrant	couvrir, to cover
ouvert	souffrir, to suffer, etc.
ouvre	
ouvris	
connaître, *to know*	paraître, to appear
connaissant	repaître, to feed, etc.
connu	
connais	
connus	

2. IDIOMATIC USE OF tenir, *to hold*, AND mettre, *to put*.

1. The verb TENIR has various meanings according to its association with other words.

(a) Tenir, *to hold*.

Tenez-le bien, autrement il va tomber.	Hold it tight; otherwise it will fall.
Si vous le tenez, il ne s'en ira pas.	If you hold it, it won't run away.

(b) Tenir de, *to resemble*.

C'est étonnant comme il tient de son père.	It's surprising how he resembles his father.
Vous tenez de votre père et non pas de votre mère.	You resemble your father and not your mother.

(c) Tenir à, *to be eager, care*.

Il tient à vous faire plaisir.	He is eager to please you.
Tenez-vous à venir avec moi?	Do you care to come with me?

(d) **Tiens,** *well;* **tenez,** *to be sure,* used as interjection.

Tiens, c'est vous Paul!	Well, is that you, Paul!
Tenez, vous ne savez rien faire!	To be sure, you don't know how to do anything.

Note.—**Tenir** is found in expressions like n'y plus tenir,* *not to be able to bear it any longer;* tenir tête à, *to resist;* qu'à cela ne tienne, *never mind that;* s'il ne tient qu'à cela, *if that's all.*

2.   METTRE sometimes assumes the sense of

(a)   *To place, put:*

Mettez-vous là et tenez-vous tranquille.	Place yourself there and be quiet.
Vous mettrez tout cela sur la table.	You will put all that on the table.

(b)   *To put on:*

Mettez votre chapeau et sortons.	Put on your hat and let's go out.
Le temps change si vite qu'on ne sait que mettre.	The weather changes so quickly that one doesn't know what to put on.

Note.—**Mettre** is found in expressions like mettre à même de, *to enable;* mettre au courant de, *to inform of, acquaint with;* se mettre à, *to begin.*

3.   IRREGULAR VERBS

Present		*Principal Parts*
recevoir, *to receive*		recevoir, recevant, reçu, reçois, reçus
reçois	recevons	
reçois	recevez	
reçoit	reçoivent	
pourvoir, *to provide*		pourvoir, pourvoyant, pourvu, pourvois, pourvus
pourvois	pourvoyons	
pourvois	pourvoyez	
pourvoit	pourvoient	
vaincre, *to conquer*		vaincre, vainquant, vaincu, vaincs, vainquis
vaincs	vainquons	
vaincs	vainquez	
vainc	vainquent	

---

* In finite tenses *plus* follows *tenir:* je n'y tiens plus.

III. VOCABULARY

1. FRENCH-ENGLISH:

appel: répondre à l' —, to answer the roll
condamner, to condemn
la cour (de justice), court of justice
*détruire, to destroy
détruit, -e (*p.p.* of ***détruire**), destroyed
le devoir, duty
huer, to boo

loin: non —, not far
le monde, world; **tout le** —, everybody
oublier, to forget
le prisonnier, prisoner
répondre, to answer
sans, without
tout, -e, *pl. m.* **tous,** *f.* **toutes,** all, whole

2. ENGLISH-FRENCH:

advice, **le conseil**
age: for —s, **il y a des siècles**
also, **aussi**
to be angry, **être fâché, -e**
arm, **le bras;** with open —s, **à bras ouverts**
boy, **le garçon**
to call on, **faire (une) visite à**
cap, **la casquette**
to catch, **attraper;** to — a cold, **attraper un rhume**
China, **la Chine**
to come near, **approcher**
to cry, **pleurer**
to dare, **oser**
to despise, **mépriser**
even (adv.), **même**
event, **l'événement** *m.*
floor, **l'étage** *m.*
to follow, ***suivre**
haughty, **fier, -ère**
to honor, **honorer**
idleness, **l'oisiveté** *f.*

to keep informed, ***tenir au courant**
to live, ***vivre**
Monday, **(le) lundi**
mouth, **la bouche**
to notice, **remarquer**
once: at —, **de suite, tout de suite**
opinion, **l'opinion** *f.*
to order, **commander**
to pay, **payer;**—a visit, ***faire (une) visite**
play, **la pièce**
to please, ***plaire;** (if you) please, **s'il vous plaît**
to punish, **punir**
ready, **prêt, -e**
to resist, **résister**
room, **la chambre**
to say, ***dire**
to speak, **parler**
strange, **étrange**
study, **l'étude** *f.*
sum, **la somme**

surprising, **surprenant, -e**
to tell, ***dire**
tomorrow, **demain**
unfortunate, **malheureux,
-se**

want, **le besoin**
what: — about me, **et moi
donc**
when, **quand, lorsque**
with, **avec, à, de**

IV. IDIOMATIC EXPRESSIONS

à fleur de terre, even with the ground
à son gré, to his liking, his taste
être d'accord sur, to be agreed on, agree on
mourir d'envie, to long for
faire à sa tête, to have one's own way
avoir affaire à, to have to deal with
se douter de, to suspect
de temps à autre, from time to time
de la sorte, thus, so, in this manner
de long en large, up and down

V. EXERCISES

1. *Translate:*

1. They shall come and call on us tomorrow. 2. When you will be ready to go, call us. 3. They will always receive you with open arms and provide for all your wants. 4. I shall enable you to finish your studies. 5. Unfortunately, the poor will always be despised by the haughty. 6. Idleness will bring happiness to no one. 7. What I ordered hasn't been done; they (probably) have forgotten it. 8. He is crying, the poor boy; his father has (probably) punished him. 9. Louis hasn't paid me a visit for months; he must be angry at me. 10. Please do what I told you to do. 11. Honor your father and mother and you shall live long. 12. May I dare speak to you? 13. Tomorrow we are going to see that play of which you have so often spoken. 14. Are they going to leave by Monday?

2. *Translate carefully, paying special attention to the future tenses:*

1. Nos amis sont partis ce matin; ce soir ils seront sans doute arrivés chez eux. 2. Dans un an, si nous sommes

encore de ce monde, nous aurons parcouru tout le pays. **3.**
Avant qu'il n'ait le temps de se défendre, tout le monde
l'aura hué. **4.** Le prisonnier n'a pas encore paru en cour
et nous l'aurons déjà condamné. **5.** Voyez toutes ces
maisons détruites; une bombe sera tombée non loin d'ici.
6. Mes amis, le président de notre club n'est pas encore
ici, il aura été retenu. **7.** Personne ne répond à l'appel;
aura-t-on oublié le devoir de défendre son pays?

3. *Translate:*

1. You're too anxious to leave for Europe; don't you care
for your skin? 2. Did you notice how he resembles his
uncle? 3. Well, well, isn't that surprising! I haven't seen
you for ages and here you are! 4. Forward this sum to
your brother. 5. You say you can't bear it any longer;
what about me? 6. Put on your cap; do you care to
catch a cold? 7. Come near the table and tell me why you
came to see me. 8. Always keep me informed of the latest
events. 9. How dare you resist me? 10. If that's all,
you may leave at once.

4. *Translate into idiomatic French:*

1. I long for a trip to China; from time to time I dream of
going to strange countries. 2. He always has his own way
without even suspecting that other people may also have
opinions. 3. It's with you that I have to deal. 4. This
story is to his liking. 5. Follow my advice; in so doing
you and your friend will be agreed on this question. 6.
From time to time, he walked up and down his room. 7.
This wall is even with the ground.

I. PRESENT AND PERFECT CONDITIONAL —THEIR USE

The conditional mood denotes less the fact expressed by the verb than the eventuality of that fact, not what the subject is or was, but what it *would be* or *would have done* "if" a certain condition or conditions had materialized.

There are two tenses in the conditional, the present and the perfect.

1. VERB FORMS OF THE PRESENT AND PERFECT CONDITIONAL, pp. 20-21
2. USE OF THE PRESENT AND PERFECT CONDITIONAL

PRESENT CONDITIONAL.—The present of the conditional mood intimates either a possible action in the future or an action in the present that cannot materialize.

1. It intimates a possible action in the future, if the condition indispensable for its realization materializes.

Si vous vouliez me donner de l'argent, j'achèterais cette maison dès demain.	If you were to give some money (now), I should buy this house early to-morrow.
Si vous vous mettiez à étudier, vous seriez vite savant.	If you began to study, you would soon be a learned man.

2. It denotes an action that cannot materialize in the present because the condition in the present upon which depends its materialization is not realized.

Si je n'étais pas très occupé maintenant, je vous suivrais.	If I were not very busy just now, I would follow you.

133

Si nous étions en juillet maintenant, je partirais pour la France.	If now we were in July, I should leave for France.

The present conditional assumes various functions. Thus, it is often used:

1. To express a polite question, statement, a wish, or a desire.

Auriez-vous la bonté de faire cela pour moi?	Would you be kind enough to do that for me?
Je désirerais vous dire un mot.	I should like to have a word with you.
Comme je voudrais le voir!	How I should like to see him.

2. To express hypothetical statements or indignation.

Un petit garçon dit à son camarade: "Tu serais mon cheval, je te donnerais du sucre et de l'avoine, je monterais sur toi et tu trotterais du matin au soir."	A little boy said to his comrade: "Imagine that you are my horse, and that I should give you sugar and oats, and mount on you, and you would trot from morning till evening."
Je tendrais la main pour si peu!—Non, jamais!	I should extend my hand for so little!—Nay, not I.

3. To formulate statements without vouching for their accuracy.

Le général aurait des documents compromettants chez lui.	The general, allegedly, has compromising documents in his possession.
Au dire du maître, l'enfant refuserait d'obéir.	By what the teacher said, the child refuses to obey.

4. In exclamations.

Moi, j'oublierais ce que tu as dit!—Jamais!	*I* should forget what you have said!—Never!

PERFECT CONDITIONAL.—The perfect conditional intimates

an action in the past, the realization of which was depending upon a condition that never materialized.

Si (hier) j'avais eu un livre, je l'aurais lu.	If I had had a book (yesterday), I should have read it.
Si vous étiez venu à mon secours l'an dernier, je n'aurais pas tant souffert.	If last year you had come to my help, I shouldn't have suffered so much.

Then, the perfect conditional denotes sometimes an action which would be completed in the present, if a certain condition had materialized.

Si Louis n'était pas venu si tôt, j'aurais franchi la frontière française maintenant.	If Louis hadn't come so soon, I should have crossed the French frontier by now.

The perfect conditional is quite often used in simple sentences,

1. To soften an affirmation.

J'aurais voulu vous voir.	I should have liked to see you.
Ils auraient voulu vous avertir.	They would have liked to warn you.

2. To denote a hypothesis.

Le voleur aurait pris la fuite.	The thief must have taken to flight.
Le gendarme aurait été tué par le bandit.	The policeman was killed in all probability by the bandit.

3. To indicate a desire, a wish in the past.

Combien il aurait été heureux!	How happy he would have been!
Qu'il aurait voulu vous voir avant de mourir!	How he was longing to see you before dying!

II. VERB REVIEW

1. CONDITIONAL SENTENCES

Conditional sentences consist of two clauses, the *if* clause and the *result* clause.

The *if* clause is either in the present, imperfect, or pluperfect indicative and has as corresponding verb tenses in the result clause the future, present conditional, or perfect conditional.

"If" *Clause*	*Result Clause*
Si vous le voyez,	vous lui direz de venir me voir.
If you see him	you will tell him to come to see me.
Si vous le voyiez,	vous lui diriez de venir me voir.
If you were to see him	you would tell him to come to see me.
Si vous l'aviez vu,	vous lui auriez dit de venir me voir.
If you had seen him	you would have told him to come to see me.

Note.—In literary style, the pluperfect subjunctive* often takes the place of both the pluperfect indicative in the *if* clause and the perfect conditional in the result clause: S'il l'eût connu, il ne lui eût pas parlé ainsi. *Had he known him, he would not have spoken to him in this manner.*

2. IRREGULAR VERBS

Present		*Principal Parts*
luire, *to shine*		luire, luisant, lui, luis
luis	luisons	Note.—*Luire* has no past definite, no impera-
luis	luisez	tive, and no imperfect subjunctive.
luit	luisent	
maudire, *to curse*		maudire, maudissant, maudit, maudis, maudis
maudis	maudissons	
maudis	maudissez	
maudit	maudissent	
coudre, *to sew*		coudre, cousant, cousu, couds, cousis
couds	cousons	
couds	cousez	
coud	cousent	

* Cf. pp. 147–148.

III. VOCABULARY

1. FRENCH-ENGLISH:

l'amitié *f.*, friendship
l'astre du jour *m.*, sun
l'atelier *m.*, workroom
l'aube *f.*, dawn
colorer, to color
se coucher, to set (of sun)
devancer, to precede
éclairé, -e, lit up
élevé, -e, high
en (*prep.*), in, to
espérer, to hope
l'événement *m.*, event
fleurir, to blossom, bloom
le giron, bosom, lap
glaner, to glean
la goutte, drop
grâce; — à, thanks to
grimper, to climb
se hâter, to hasten
s'informer, to inquire
instruit, -e (*p.p.* of *instru-ire*), learned, educated

jouir de, to enjoy
la main, hand
la moisson, harvest
la montagne, mountain
pareil: sans —, peerless
le pas, step
le paysan, peasant
le pinceau, brush
précipiter, to hasten
la preuve, proof
se promener, to take a walk
la querelle, quarrel
le retour, return; être de —, to be back
la rosée, dew
la santé, health
souhaiter, to wish
*souvenir: offrir en —, to offer in remembrance
tremper, to dip
le troupeau, herd
uni, -e, united

2. ENGLISH-FRENCH:

along, le long de
back: to be—, *être de retour
enterprise, l'entreprise *f.*
to mention, mentionner
to pity, *plaindre
to promise, *promettre
proposition, la proposition
river, la rivière
to seem, sembler

to shine, briller, scintiller (stars)
South America, l'Amérique du Sud *f.*
star, l'étoile *f.*
trip, le voyage
walk: to take a —, se pro-mener
to worry, se tourmenter, se tracasser

IV. IDIOMATIC EXPRESSIONS

nulle part, nowhere
tant mieux, so much the better
tant pis, so much the worse
à la bonne heure! fine! well done!
d'ici un mois, a month from now, within a month
faire la sourde oreille, to turn a deaf ear
savoir (bon) gré à quelqu'un de quelque chose,
    to be thankful to someone for something

V. EXERCISES

1. *Translate:*

a. Que serait-ce si je lisais dans l'avenir? Je vous verrais
unis la main dans la main, oubliant vos querelles, frères non
pas de bouche mais de cœur, au giron de la France qui
ouvrirait ses grands bras pour embrasser le monde. Personne alors ne pourrait croire qu'il fut un temps où l'on
disputait le suffrage à l'ouvrier, au paysan, car grâce à leurs
mains cette terre "qui est la nôtre fleurirait de moissons sans
pareilles" où chacun de nous pourrait glaner, et l'industrie
y ferait des miracles.

(Edgar Quinet)

b. 1. Nelson aurait bien voulu, avant de mourir, jouir de
la victoire de Trafalgar. 2. Ceux qui auraient su profiter
du temps de leurs études seraient maintenant instruits. 3.
On ne serait pas parti de si bonne heure sans mon frère. 4.
Le vice-amiral français, Brueys, aurait pu éviter le désastre
d'Aboukir. 5. Nous pensions que vous auriez profité
d'une si belle journée pour aller voir vos amis.

2. *Explain the various uses of the conditional tenses:*

1. Me permettriez-vous de vous offrir ceci en souvenir de
notre amitié? 2. Louis est ici, papa; il voudrait s'informer
de ta santé. 3. Et quoi, je travaillerais dix heures par
jour pour un pareil salaire! 4. Il aurait désiré savoir le
prix de cette maison. 5. Comme j'aurais voulu vous
accompagner en Afrique! 6. Nous espérions tous que vous

seriez venus nous rejoindre pour célébrer cet heureux
événement. 7. J'aurais souhaité qu'un autre apporte ces
preuves. 8. Qu'il aurait voulu vous parler avant son
départ!

3. *Translate:*

1. Promise that you will never mention this to him, if you
should speak to him. 2. If the stars were shining, we
should take a walk along the river. 3. You would certainly
have pitied him if you had seen him. 4. If you had
followed my advice you would have succeeded in your enterprise. 5. We should not have been worrying so much if
our friends in Paris had written to us.

4. *Prefix the following selection with "Si j'étais peintre"; then,
accordingly, put all main verbs in the conditional and translate:*

Quitte ton atelier pour aller consulter la nature. Habite
les champs avec elle. Va voir le soleil se coucher et se lever,
le ciel se colorer de nuages. Promène-toi dans la prairie,
autour des troupeaux. Vois les herbes brillantes des
gouttes de la rosée. L'aube devance le retour du soleil.
Tourne tes regards vers les sommets des montagnes. Précipite tes pas; grimpe sur quelque colline élevée; et, de là,
découvre toute la scène de la nature éclairée de la lumière
de l'astre du jour. Hâte-toi de revenir. Prends le pinceau
que tu viens de tremper dans la lumière, dans les eaux, dans
les nuages. (Diderot)

5. *Translate into idiomatic French:*

1. I should be thankful to you for not having turned a deaf
ear to my proposition. 2. He seems to be nowhere. 3.
Fine! a month from now we should be back from our trip to
South America. 4. So much the better or so much the
worse, if you do not do what you are told. 5. What day
of the week is it today?—I don't know; maybe Friday. 6
In ten days from today, they shall come to pay us a visit.

I. THE SUBJUNCTIVE

1. Why a Subjunctive in French?

An action or state, besides being expressed simply and without limitation (*indicative mood*), or as dependent upon a condition for its realization (*conditional mood*), may also be viewed as dependent upon the idea expressed in the main clause. In this latter case, a dependence or logical subordination between the verb of the main clause and that of the dependent clause is brought about. The nature of the statement contained in the main clause will decide whether the verb in the dependent clause is to be in the indicative or in the subjunctive mood. Whenever that statement implies a fact, a probability, or a truth in the mind of the speaker, the indicative is used in the dependent clause.

Je sais qu'il est parti.	I know he left.
Il est probable qu'il est à la maison.	It is probable that he is at home.
Il est vrai que tous les hommes sont mortels.	It is true that all men are mortal.

But, when the statement expressed in the main clause suggests that the idea contained in the dependent clause is contrary to fact, or simply possible but not probable, or is uncertain, or contrary to truth, or at least doubtful, the subjunctive must be used in French. In this manner, a dependence or subordination, explanatory of the mental attitude of the speaker, is clearly established between the two clauses. Without the use of the subjunctive, the intimate connection of the two parts of the sentence would not be sufficiently emphasized.

Je ne crois pas qu'elle soit partie.	I don't believe she has left.
Il doute qu'elle vienne.	He doubts her coming.

Il faut qu'il écrive.	He must write.
Est-il possible que Louis soit ici?	Is it possible that Louis is here?

With verbs of emotion and sentiment, the subjunctive is used more particularly because the intimate psychological dependence between the statement or idea in the dependent clause and that of the main clause is brought out with greater emphasis.

Je désire qu'il vienne au plus tôt.	I wish him to come as early as possible.
Il veut qu'elle parte sans retard.	He wants her to leave without delay.
Nous défendons qu'on fasse cela.	We forbid anyone to do that.

2. WHERE SHOULD THE SUBJUNCTIVE MOOD BE USED?

The subjunctive mood is ordinarily found in the subordinate clause, but it also appears in the main clause (see p. 172).

Now a subordinate clause is either a noun, an adjectival, or an adverbial clause. In each of these sorts of clauses, the subjunctive is required when the main clause to which they are subordinate contains some expression of desire, necessity, doubt, etc

IN A NOUN CLAUSE

A noun clause takes the place of a noun. As a noun may be either the subject or the object of a sentence, a noun clause may exercise both of these functions. Thus,

Est-il certain *qu'il soit mort?*	= *Sa mort* est-elle certaine?
Is it certain that he died?	= Is his death certain?
Je désire *qu'il réussisse.*	= Je désire *son succès.*
I desire him to succeed.	= I desire his success.

Note.—Noun clauses are usually introduced by **que**.

Expressions of doubt, necessity, emotion, etc., occur in various verbal forms.

1. In the form of impersonal verbs; the most common ones are:

il est bon	it is good
il est temps	it is time

il vaut mieux il est préférable }	it is better
il faut il est nécessaire }	it is necessary
il importe il est important }	it is important
il convient il est convenable }	it is fitting, proper
il est possible il se peut }	it is possible
il est douteux	it is doubtful
il n'est pas certain	it is not certain
il est heureux	it is fortunate
il est dommage	it is a pity, it is too bad

Il est temps que vous vous en alliez.	It is time for you to go.
Il est possible qu'il nous surprenne ce soir.	It is possible for him to surprise us this evening.
Il est heureux qu'il ne soit pas parti.	It is fortunate that he didn't leave.

Note.—In familiar speech **il est** is often replaced by **c'est** in the expression: C'est dommage que vous ne soyez pas venu plus tôt. *It's a pity you didn't come sooner.*

2. In the form of personal verbal expressions or verbs:

Je suis content qu'il réussisse.	I am glad that he succeeds.
Il est fâché qu'elle soit arrivée en retard.	He is angry that she arrived late.
Nous regrettons que vous ne vouliez pas venir.	We regret that you don't want to come.

3. In the form of verbs or verbal expression in the negative or interrogative:

Je ne dis pas que vous soyez mécontents.	I am not saying that you are discontented.
Croyez-vous qu'elle soit heureuse?	Do you believe that she is happy?

In Adjectival Clauses

An adjectival clause limits like an adjective and is usually introduced by a relative pronoun.

An adjectival clause is in the subjunctive:

1. Whenever the verb in the main clause suggests a purpose not yet attained.

Je cherche un homme qui puisse m'aider.	I am looking for a man who can help me.

but:

J'ai trouvé un homme qui peut m'aider.	I have found a man who is able to help me.
Nous voulons une maison qui soit assez grande pour nous.	We want a house large enough (that would be large enough) for us.

but:

Nous avons acheté une maison qui est assez grande pour nous.	We have bought a house big enough (that is big enough) for us.

2. Whenever the verb in the main clause has a superlative as a predicate, a fact which may indicate possibility of doubt:

C'est le meilleur soldat que je connaisse.	This is the best soldier that I know.
Ce sont les seuls livres qu'il ait lus.	These are the only books that he has read.

However, when the superlative is followed by **des** + the predicate noun, the indicative mood is used because all uncertainty disappears from the main clause:

C'est le meilleur des soldats que je connais.	He is the best one of the soldiers that I know.
Ce sont les seuls des livres qu'il a lus.	These are the only ones of the books that he has read.

3. Whenever the compound relatives and the indefinite clauses have a concessive value:

Qui que vous soyez, parlez.	Whoever you may be, speak.
Quoi qu'on puisse dire, vous avez raison.	Whatever people may say, you are right.

Quels que soient vos talents, il faut travailler.	Whatever your talents may be, you must work.
Où que vous alliez, vous trouverez des difficultés.	Wherever you may go, you will find trouble.

In Adverbial Clauses

An adverbial clause, as suggested by its name, may exercise the functions of an adverb. It is then usually introduced by a conjunction which intimates some specific condition that requires the use of the subjunctive mood in the subordinate clause. Thus,

1. A conjunction of *time* may introduce an action as possible but not yet materialized and thereby may express uncertainty:

Il viendra me voir avant qu'il (ne) parte.	He is coming to see me before leaving.
Amusez-vous en attendant qu'il vienne.	Have a good time until he comes.

2. A conjunction of *purpose* may introduce an action or fact as intended and possible, but not yet realized, and may leave it uncertain:

Vous faites cela pour qu'il soit content.—Mais, le sera-t-il?	You do this in order that he may be happy.—But will he be happy?
Il faut étudier de manière que vous appreniez quelque chose.	You must so study that you may learn something.

3. A conjunction of *condition* or *assumption* may introduce an action or a fact as dependent in its fulfillment upon a restriction, a reservation, which suggests doubt:

Il partira demain, à moins qu'il ne soit malade.	He will leave tomorrow unless he is sick.
Je vous payerai, pourvu que vous ayez fini votre travail.	I shall pay you provided you are through with your work.

4. A conjunction of *concession* may introduce an action or a state as possible, although a concession is necessary for its realization:

J'ai fait mon devoir quoi-qu'il fût pénible.	I did my duty although it was painful.

5. A conjunction of *negation* may introduce an action or a fact as contrary to reality:

Je puis me tirer d'affaire sans que vous m'aidiez.	I can get along without your help.

Here are the main conjunctions

1.	of time:	avant que	before
		jusqu'à ce que	until
		en attendant que	until

2.	of purpose or result:	afin que	in order that
		pour que	so that, in order that
		de façon que	so that
		de sorte que	so that
		de crainte que	for fear that
		de peur que	for fear that

3.	of condition:	au cas où	in case that
		en cas que	in case that
		pourvu que	provided that
		supposé que	suppose that
		à moins que	unless

4.	of concession:	bien que	although
		quoique	although
		encore que	although
		malgré que	although, though
		soit que . . . soit que	whether . . . or

5.	of negation:	non que	not that
		non pas que	not that
		sans que	without
		loin que	far from + *pres. participle*

If the subject of the main clause is the same as that of the adverbial clause, a preposition followed by the infinitive must take the place of the conjunction + the verb in the subjunctive.

Je lui parlerai avant de partir.	I shall speak to him before leaving.
Il pense avant de parler.	He thinks before he speaks.

IN MAIN CLAUSES

The subjunctive mood, although less often than in subordinate clauses, also appears now and then in main clauses. Its functions are

1. To express a wish:

Vive la France!	Long live France!
C'est ainsi que parle Zoroastre, comprenne qui pourra.	Thus speaketh Zoroaster: let him understand who can.
Ainsi soit-il!	Be it so! (Amen!)

2. To denote a command, a prohibition, or an exhortation:

Qu'il sorte de suite!	Let him leave at once!
Surtout qu'il ne revienne jamais!	Above all, let him never come back!
Qui m'aime me suive!	Let those who love me follow me!

3. To intimate indignation, a supposition, or a concession:

Que j'obéisse, *moi* qui suis né pour commander!	*I* should obey, *I* a born commander!
Soit le triangle A B C . . .	Suppose the triangle A B C . . .
Advienne que pourra . . . Quoi qu'il advienne . . .	Come what may . . .

II. VERB REVIEW

1. FORMATION OF THE SUBJUNCTIVE TENSES

The subjunctive mood possesses four tenses: the present, the imperfect, the perfect, and the pluperfect. Two of these tenses are simple, the present and the imperfect, and two are compound, the perfect and pluperfect.

(a) The *present* subjunctive is usually derived from the third person plural present indicative. Drop -*ent* and add the endings of the present subjunctive, -*e*, -*es*, -*e*, -*ions*, -*iez*, and -*ent*, to the remaining part of the present indicative.

Present Subjunctive

(that) I may carry . . .	*(that) I may finish . . .*	*(that) I may sell . . .*
je porte	je finisse	je vende
tu portes	tu finisses	tu vendes
il porte	il finisse	il vende
nous portions	nous finissions	nous vendions
vous portiez	vous finissiez	vous vendiez
ils portent	ils finissent	ils vendent

The auxiliaries **avoir** and **être** have forms of their own.

(that) I may have . . .	*(that) I may be . . .*
j'aie	je sois
tu aies	tu sois
il ait	il soit
nous ayons	nous soyons
vous ayez	vous soyez
ils aient	ils soient

Note.—The present subjunctive is ordinarily translated by the English indicative.

(b) The *imperfect* subjunctive is usually derived from the second person singular of the past definite. After dropping -*s*, add -*sse*, -*sses*, -^*t*, -*ssions*, -*ssiez*, -*ssent*. There are no irregular forms in the imperfect subjunctive.

Imperfect Subjunctive

(that) I might carry . . .	*(that) I might finish . . .*	*(that) I might sell . . .*
je portasse	je finisse	je vendisse
tu portasses	tu finisses	tu vendisses
il portât	il finît	il vendît
nous portassions	nous finissions	nous vendissions
vous portassiez	vous finissiez	vous vendissiez
ils portassent	finissent	ils vendissent

(that)[1] *I might have . . .*	*(that) I might be . . .*
j'eusse	je fusse
tu eusses	tu fusses
il eût	il fût

[1] Usually, the subjunctive is preceded by the conjunction **que**, *that*. It should be noted that **que** is not a part of the subjunctive tense.

nous eussions
vous eussiez
ils eussent

nous fussions
vous fussiez
ils fussent

Note.—The imperfect subjunctive is often rendered either by the past indicative or by *should* or *would* + the verb, in addition to the above mentioned form.

(c) The *perfect* and *pluperfect*, being compound tenses, are formed with the present or imperfect subjunctive forms of **avoir** or **être** + the past participle which follows the general rules of agreement of participles. Cf. pp. 155-156.

Perfect Subjunctive

(*that*) *I may have carried* . . .
j'aie porté, etc.
nous ayons porté, etc.

(*that*) *I may have gone* . . .
je sois parti(e), etc.
nous soyons parti(e)s, etc.

Pluperfect Subjunctive

(*that*) *I might have finished* . . .
j'eusse fini, etc.
nous eussions fini, etc.

(*that*) *I might have left* . . .
je fusse parti(e), etc.
nous fussions parti(e)s, etc.

Note.—The imperfect and pluperfect, with the exception of the third person singular, are eliminated from informal speech. The present or perfect subjunctives are substituted for them. Often the whole sentence is recast to avoid these tenses.

2. IRREGULAR VERBS

Present

Principal Parts

valoir, *to be worth*

valoir, valant, valu, vaux, valus

vaux	valons
vaux	valez
vaut	valent

acquérir, *to acquire*

acquérir, acquérant, acquis, acquiers, acquis

acquiers	acquérons
acquiers	acquérez
acquiert	acquièrent

suffire, *to suffice*

suffire, suffisant, suffi, suffis, suffis

suffis	suffisons
suffis	suffisez
suffit	suffisent

III. VOCABULARY

1. French-English:

aider, to help
arranger, to arrange, fix
attendant: en—que, while, till
attendre, to await, wait for
aucun, -e, no one, no
se ***conduire,** to behave
*craindre, to fear
déranger, to disturb
dommage: c'est — , it's a pity
douter, to doubt
encore que, although
façon: de — que, so that
faux, fausse, false; **— pas,** slip, stumble, blunder
gagner, to earn
honnête, honest
le **jardinier,** gardener

jusqu'à ce que, until
malade, ill
même (*adv.*), even
moins: à — que, unless
pourvu que, provided that
prodigue, prodigal
régler, to settle
rencontrer, to meet, encounter
saluer, to greet
sauver, to save
sens: le bon —, common sense
sorte: de — que, so that
la **Suisse,** Switzerland
suite: tout de —, at once
tailler, to prune (trees)
tard, late

2. English-French:

to abide by, **obéir à**
climate, **le climat**
comfortably, **confortablement**
cook, **le chef, le cuisinier**
to cook, ***cuire, *faire la cuisine**
estate, **la propriété**
health, **la santé**
home: at —, **chez** (+ *disj. pron.*)
interested, **intéressé, -e**

law, **la loi**
to look after, **s'occuper de**
to look for, **chercher**
only one, **seul, -e**
to overexert, **se surmener**
painting, **le tableau, la peinture**
pleasure, **le plaisir**
skill, **l'habileté** *f.*, **le talent**
to spend, **passer**
toward, **envers, vers**
to travel, **voyager**

IV. IDIOMATIC EXPRESSIONS

il se fait avocat, he becomes a lawyer
être d'avis, to be of the opinion

il y va de, it is a question of, (it) is at stake[1]
aller à la rencontre de, to go and meet
aller au devant de, to go and meet
faire bonne chère, to eat well, live well
se faire à, to get accustomed to
faire un voyage, to take a trip
des gens comme il faut, well-bred people

V. EXERCISES

1. *Explain the use of the subjunctive mood in the following sentences:*

1. Il faut qu'il parte tout de suite; je crains même qu'il n'arrive trop tard. 2. Il ne veut pas qu'on le dérange quand il travaille. 3. Est-il sûr qu'il soit mort sur le champ de bataille? 4. Je doute que le médecin puisse le sauver. 5. Je ne dis pas qu'il soit indifférent à sa santé, mais il en est prodigue. 6. Ne croyez-vous pas que le bon sens décide de la solution de plus d'un problème? 7. Il est préférable qu'on s'en aille au lit tôt et qu'on se lève tôt. 8. Il est convenable qu'on salue ses amis quand on les rencontre. 9. C'est dommage qu'il ne sache pas mieux se conduire en société. 10. Il est regrettable qu'on fasse de pareils faux pas.

2. *Translate:*

1. I'm looking for a cook who is able to cook in the French manner. 2. Here is what I want; I want an estate where I can live comfortably. 3. He has a few good paintings at home, and these are the only ones in which he is interested. 4. He is (possibly) the best friend I ever had. 5. Whoever they may be, they ought to be polite toward everybody. 6. He has great skill; but whatever his skill may be, he must abide by the law. 7. Wherever you may be, you will make friends.

---

[1] In English the object of "de" usually becomes the subject: Il y va de votre santé, *Your health is at stake.*

3. *Justify the use of the subjunctive in the following sentences:*

1. En attendant que cette affaire soit réglée, allez vous reposer en Suisse. 2. Encore que mon travail soit difficile, je le finirai en temps voulu. 3. Il faut travailler de sorte que l'on puisse gagner honnêtement sa vie. 4. Tout est arrangé, nous partons demain matin à moins que Louis ne tombe de nouveau malade. 5. J'attendrai jusqu'à ce qu'elles reviennent du concert. 6. Tous les ans, mon jardinier taille les arbres afin qu'ils produisent de meilleurs fruits. 7. Il m'est impossible de lever cela sans que vous m'aidiez. 8. Il doit se conduire de façon qu'on n'ait aucun reproche à lui faire. 9. Pourvu que vous fassiez votre devoir tout ira bien. 10. Si vous faisiez un généreux effort, vous réussiriez dans vos études.

4. *Translate into idiomatic French:*

1. Do not overexert yourself; your health is at stake. 2 One must get accustomed to all climates if he wishes to spend his life traveling. 3. He should become a lawyer; at least that's my opinion (= I am of that opinion). 4. Why don't you go and meet these well-bred people? You must look after them. 5. To eat well has always been a habit and a pleasure with all classes in France.

I. THE TENSES OF THE SUBJUNCTIVE —THEIR USE

The subjunctive mood has four tenses, the present, imperfect, perfect, and pluperfect, of which the most important ones are the present and the perfect because they are more frequently used.

1. Verb Forms of the Subjunctive Tenses, pp 146-148
2. Use of the Subjunctive Tenses

The Present Subjunctive.—The present subjunctive has the tense value of a present or a future.

It usually follows a present tense verb in the main clause.

Je veux qu'il vienne.	I want him to come (*now*).
Il est possible qu'il ne vienne pas.	It is possible that he will not come (*tomorrow*).
Désirez-vous qu'il vienne dans huit jours?	Do you wish him to come in a week?

However, the present subjunctive in the dependent or subordinate clause is sometimes preceded by a past-tense verb in the main clause. This occurs when the present subjunctive expresses a general truth.

Je n'ai jamais pensé que la pauvreté soit un vice.	I never thought that poverty was a vice.
Je n'ai jamais dit que la paresse soit une vertu.	I never said that laziness was a virtue.

The Imperfect Subjunctive.—In the subjunctive sentence, the subordinate clause has its verb in the imperfect subjunctive whenever the verb in the main clause is in the past; that is, in the imperfect, past definite, perfect, or conditional present.

Je regardais sans que personne ne s'en aperçût.	I was looking without anybody noticing it.
Il cria pour qu'on ouvrît la porte.	He shouted so that someone might open the door.
Aimeriez-vous qu'il vînt?	Would you like him to come?

There is a tendency to eliminate the imperfect subjunctive (except perhaps the third person singular) because of its lack of euphony, and to replace it, where no ambiguity is feared, by the present subjunctive.

Je voulais que vous l'apportassiez.	I wanted you to bring it.

becomes

Je voulais que vous l'apportiez.	I wanted you to bring it.

The imperfect subjunctive is more often used in literary style to express a wish; the present subjunctive, in familiar speech.

Plût à Dieu que cela arrivât!	Would to God that that might happen!

THE PERFECT SUBJUNCTIVE.—This tense simply intimates a completed action, a "fait accompli" in the present or the future, without denoting any particular shade of thought.

Je regrette qu'il ne soit pas venu.	I regret he hasn't come.
Elle est heureuse que vous ayez acheté cette maison.	She is happy that you bought this house.

The perfect subjunctive expresses sometimes an order, a command with the connotation of a future anterior.

Que vous soyez couchés avant onze heures, n'est-ce pas?	You will be in bed before eleven o'clock, won't you?

THE PLUPERFECT SUBJUNCTIVE.—It expresses anteriority of a completed action over another equally completed.

Je ne pensais pas qu'il eût vendu sa maison avant son départ.	I didn't think he would have sold his house before his departure.

Qui n'espérait que vous eussiez échappé à l'accident.	Everybody had expected you to escape the accident.

Like the imperfect subjunctive, it is more and more discarded in familiar speech, except in the third person singular.

3. SEQUENCE OF SUBJUNCTIVE TENSES

The tense of the verb in the subjunctive clause is usually determined by the tense of the finite verb in the main clause.

When the verb of the main clause is in the present or future, the verb of the subjunctive or subordinate clause is either in the present or in the perfect subjunctive.

Je suis content que vous veniez me voir.	I am happy that you are coming to see me.
Il voudra que vous l'accompagniez.	He will want you to accompany him.
Je doute qu'il soit parti à temps.	I doubt that he left in time.
Il voudra que vous ayez fait cela ce soir.	He will want you to have done that by this evening.

In the first two examples, the time in both clauses is about the same, or is slightly later in the subjunctive clause.

In the last two examples, the action of the subjunctive clause is prior to that of the main clause.

When the verb in the main clause is a past tense of the indicative or conditional mood, the verb in the subordinate clause is in the imperfect or pluperfect subjunctive, unless, in familiar speech, it be replaced by the present or the perfect subjunctive.

Il était temps que vous arrivassiez.	It was time you arrived.
Nous regrettions qu'il fût parti.	We were sorry that he had left.

or

Il était temps que vous arriviez.	It was time that you arrived.
Nous regrettions qu'il soit parti.	We were sorry that he left.

II. VERB REVIEW

1. AGREEMENT OF PAST PARTICIPLES

The past participle agrees either with the subject or with the object in number and gender.

The past participle agrees with the subject under the following conditions:

1. When the verb is in the passive voice:

Vous êtes donc bien surprises de mon arrivée.	You are surprised indeed at my arrival.
Elle est honorée par le peuple.	She is honored by the people.
Nous sommes loués pour nos bonnes oeuvres.	We are praised for our good works.

2. When the verb is an intransitive verb of motion or change of condition:

Elle est morte.	She died.
Ils sont tombés de l'arbre.	They fell from the tree.
Nous sommes partis à cinq heures.	We left at five o'clock.

The past participle must agree with the direct object, placed before the verb.

1. When the verb is in the active voice:

Voici les pommes qu'il a achetées.	Here are the apples which he bought.
Combien de chaises avez-vous apportées?	How many chairs did you bring?
Laquelle avez-vous choisie?	Which one did you choose?
Quelle joie vos succès m'ont causée!	What joy your success has brought me!

2. When the verb is in the pronominal voice:

Elle s'est lavée.	She washed herself.
Les dames se sont saluées.	The ladies greeted one another.
Nous nous sommes dépêchées.	We made haste.

However, when the direct object of the pronominal verb in a compound tense follows the past participle there is no agreement possible:

Elle s'est lavé les mains.	She washed her hands.
Elles se sont écrit ces lettres.	They wrote these letters to each other.

Note.—Of course, when **se** represents an indirect object there is no agreement between the past participle and **se**. Elles se sont nui. (nuire à) *They harmed each other, one another.* Ils se sont parlé. (parler à) *They spoke to each other, to one another.*

Also, when a past participle is followed by an infinitive, no agreement is required[1] even though the direct object precedes the verb, unless lack of agreement might result in ambiguity:

Je les ai entendu parler.	I have heard them speak.
Nous les avons vu passer.	We have seen them pass.

but:

Louis l'a entendue gronder.	Louis heard her scold.
Il l'a entendue pleurer.	He heard her cry.

When the verb in a compound tense has as direct object a collective noun or a pronoun representing the same, the past participle that follows it may agree in number and gender with either the collective noun or the noun of the adjectival phrase that accompanies it, according to the idea to be emphasized.

La foule de garçons que j'ai vue.	The crowd of boys that I have seen.
La foule de jeunes filles que j'ai vue.	The crowd of girls that I have seen.

or:

La foule de garçons que j'ai vus.	The crowd of boys I have seen.
La foule de jeunes filles que j'ai vues.	The crowd of girls I have seen.

---

[1] Modern grammars such as *La pensée et la langue* by Ferdinand Brunot, 2nd edition (Masson, Paris), state that the direct object may or may not, at will, agree with the past participle.

2. IRREGULAR SUBJUNCTIVE FORMS

The present subjunctive may be derived either from the present participle or from the third person plural of the present indicative. As the first method of derivation does bring about a great many irregular subjunctives while the second reduces them to nine, it seems preferable to follow the latter form of derivation. The following are irregular subjunctive forms in the present:

aller	aille	ailles	aille	allions	alliez	aillent
avoir	aie	aies	ait	ayons	ayez	aient
être	sois	sois	soit	soyons	soyez	soient
falloir	(*impersonal*)		il faille	—	—	—
faire	fasse	fasses	fasse	fassions	fassiez	fassent
pouvoir	puisse	puisses	puisse	puissions	puissiez	puissent
savoir	sache	saches	sache	sachions	sachiez	sachent
valoir	vaille	vailles	vaille	valions	valiez	vaillent
vouloir	veuille	veuilles	veuille	voulions	vouliez	veuillent

III. VOCABULARY

1. FRENCH-ENGLISH:

accorder, to grant

le bourgeois, burgher, citizen

le cabaret, inn

casser, to break

confier, to confide

la côte, rib

*cueillir, to pick

la débâcle, defeat

l'examen *m.*, examination

le froid, cold

se garder de, to take care not to, be sure not to

juger: — à propos, to deem advisable, proper

*mettre à mort, to put to death

minuit *m.*, midnight

neiger, to snow

l'œil *m.*, eye

l'oisiveté *f.*, idleness

se parer, to adorn oneself

part: faire — de, to inform

peu: pour — que, if . . . ever so little, if only

le point d'appui, supporting basis

prêt, -e, ready

proprement, neatly

quoique, although

subir, to undergo

soulever, to lift, raise

supplier, to beg, entreat

le timbre, stamp

tonner, to thunder

tour: jouer un — à, to play someone a trick

le trouble, difficulty, pain

les yeux *m. pl.* (of œil *m.*), eyes

certainly, **certainement**

deal: a great —, **beaucoup**

to doubt, **douter**

hanger-on, sponger, **le para-site**

hunting: to go out—, ***aller à la chasse**

nice, **joli, -e**

weather, **le temps**

IV.   IDIOMATIC EXPRESSIONS

au grand jamais, no, never

cela coûte cher, it's expensive

mettre le couvert, to set the table

(le) mettre à la porte, to show (him) the door

grâce à Dieu, thank God

mon Dieu! goodness!

de bon cœur, willingly

à propos, by the way

il fait jour, it is light, dawning

à coup sûr, certainly

V.   EXERCISES

1. *Tell why the present subjunctive is used in the following sentences; then translate:*

(a)   1.   La douceur est le plus bel ornement dont la femme puisse se parer.   2.   Gardez-vous bien de croire qu'il faille admirer tout ce qui vous tombe sous les yeux.   3.   Il est tout seul dans ce monde, sans amis à qui il puisse confier ses chagrins.   4.   Ils l'ont voulu ainsi, qu'ils fassent maintenant ce qu'ils ont décidé que tous observent.   5.   Vous réussirez dans vos affaires pour peu que vous essayiez.   6. Qui a jamais pensé que l'oisiveté rende les hommes heureux!

(b)   1.   Nous voulons que ce travail soit fait proprement. 2.   Comme il désire que vous lui ayez fait visite avant votre départ!   3.   Il est fâché que Marie n'ait pas jugé à propos de lui faire part de son mariage.   4.   Qu'ils soient partis avant minuit.   5.   Tout le monde est content qu'elle ait réussi aux examens.

2. *Translate:*

(a) 1. Qu'il plût, qu'il tonnât, qu'il neigeât, rien n'arrêtait Napoléon et ses armées si ce n'était le froid. 2. Edouard III, roi d'Angleterre, voulut qu'on mît à mort six notables bourgeois de Calais; pour les sauver de la mort il fallut que la reine, sa femme, se jetât à ses pieds et le suppliât qu'il leur accordât la vie. 3. Corneille, dans ses tragédies, voudrait que les hommes missent toujours le devoir avant les plaisirs.

(b) 1. Nous ne croyions pas qu'elle eût pu finir son voyage en six semaines. 2. Je ne pensais pas que vous eussiez été capable de jouer ce tour à vos amis. 3. Personne ne semblait vouloir admettre qu'ils eussent été coupables. 4. Nous eussions été heureux de vous donner l'hospitalité si nous n'avions pas été absents. 5. La France n'eût jamais subi la débâcle de 1940 si elle eût été prête pour le "blitzkrieg." 6. Si j'eusse eu un point d'appui, disait Archimède, j'eusse soulevé le monde.

3. *Translate into French:*

1. We are very happy to have nice weather. 2. No doubt, you will want him to stay at home and to work. 3. I have my doubts that he will work a great deal. 4. He will have to (*falloir*) work. 5. Wouldn't you wish they had arrived? 6. Two minutes more and he would have left without having seen you.

4. *Point out all past participles in the following sentences and explain their agreement or lack of agreement:*

1. Elle est tombée de cet arbre; elle n'est pas morte, quoiqu'elle se soit cassé trois côtes. 2. Tout le monde l'a admirée, cette bonne fille qui a donné sa vie pour la patrie. 3. Quelles chaises avez-vous achetées? 4. Vous viendrez à table, quand vous vous serez lavés; n'oubliez pas, il faut que vous vous soyez lavé les mains. 5. Les pommes que vous avez cueillies hier sont vertes; je ne les ai pas trouvées bonnes. 6. Nous nous sommes souvent rencontrés au cabaret du Cheval Blanc. 7. Pourquoi ne se sont-elles

plus écrit? 8. Émile m'a dit qu'il l'a entendue chanter.
Quelle voix! 9. L'armée, que vous avez vue passer, part
pour le sud. 10. La collection des timbres que vous avez
vus s'est vendue trois mille dollars.

5. *Translate into idiomatic French:*

1. No, never shall I permit him to leave (= that he leave)
Paris. 2. Certainly that's expensive, but then, thank
God, we have the money to buy it. 3. Old Mary always
sets the table willingly, doesn't she? 4. Goodness! what
keeps you from showing this parasite the door? 5. By
the way, why don't we go out hunting now that it's dawning?

I. THE INFINITIVE MOOD AND ITS USE

1. The Infinitive Mood

The infinitive mood expresses the meaning of the verb in a general way without distinction of person or number.

The infinitive mood possesses two verbal forms, the present and the perfect infinitives. Like any finite verb, it may be modified by an adverb. **Ne pas,** *not*, precedes the infinitive.

The infinitive may be used as either a verbal noun, an adjective, or a verb.

Le manger est prêt.	Food is ready.
Voici une bonne machine à écrire.	Here is a good typewriter.
Sait-il nager?	Does he know how to swim?

When the infinitive completes the sense of a noun, an adjective, or a verb, it is either preceded by **de** or **à,** or, in the case of some verbs, connected directly with the verb without any intervening preposition.

Il cesse de travailler.	He stops working.
Il s'amuse à jouer aux cartes.	He has a good time playing cards.
Il veut aller à Paris.	He wishes to go to Paris.
Il est temps de travailler.	It is time to work.
Vous êtes habile à tromper.	You are skillful at deceiving.

1. There follows a list of *verbs* that take the preposition **de** before the following infinitive:

blâmer	blame (for)
cesser	cease
se charger	undertake
commander	command
commencer	begin
conseiller	advise
se contenter	be satisfied with

161

continuer	continue
convenir	agree
craindre	fear
décider	decide, resolve
défendre	forbid
défier	defy
demander	ask
se dépêcher	make haste
désespérer	despair (of)
dire	bid
dispenser	dispense
douter	hesitate
écrire	write
empêcher	prevent from
essayer	try
s'étonner	be astonished at
éviter	avoid
s'excuser	excuse (from)
faire bien	do well
se fatiguer	be tired of
se hâter	hasten
finir	finish
s'indigner	be indignant
jouir	enjoy
juger bon	think fit
offrir	offer
ordonner	order
oublier	forget
permettre	permit
prier	beg, pray
se presser	hasten
promettre	promise
refuser	refuse
regretter	regret
remercier	thank for

2. These take the preposition **à** before a following infinitive:

s'accoutumer	accustom
admettre	admit
aider	help

aimer	like
s'amuser	amuse (in, by)
s'appliquer	apply
apprendre	learn
s'apprêter	get ready
s'arrêter	stop
s'attacher	be intent (on)
avoir	have, must
chercher	seek, try
commencer	begin
se consacrer	devote
consentir	consent
continuer	continue
se décider	resolve
enseigner	teach
s'habituer	accustom
s'intéresser	interest (in)
laisser	leave
s'obliger	bind oneself
se mettre	begin, be about
s'obstiner	persist (in)
réussir	succeed (in)
songer	think (of)
suffire	suffice
travailler	work

3. These verbs take no intervening preposition before a following infinitive:

aimer autant	like as well
aimer mieux	prefer
aller	go
avoir beau	be in vain
avouer	avow
compter	intend
courir	run
croire	think
déclarer	declare
désirer	desire, wish
devoir	ought, be, etc.
écouter	listen to

entendre	hear, intend
envoyer	send
espérer	hope
faillir	be on the point of, to narrowly miss being (+ *past part.*)
faire	make, cause
falloir	be necessary
s'imaginer	fancy
laisser	let, allow
oser	dare
paraître	appear
penser	intend, be near, think
pouvoir	can, may
préférer	prefer
regarder	look at
savoir	know how to, can
sembler	seem
venir	come
voir	see
vouloir	will, wish

Some verbs take either **de** or **à** before a following infinitive without assuming a new meaning. Examples: commencer de, commencer à, *to begin;* continuer de, continuer à *to continue,* etc.

Other verbs change their meaning when they take, before the infinitive, the preposition **de** or **à**. Examples: Je suis obligé de partir, *I am obliged to go;* je l'obligerai à partir, *I shall force him to leave.*

When an *adjective* or a *noun* is followed by an infinitive, that infinitive is usually preceded by **de**.

Je suis content de vous voir.	I am glad to see you.
Comme vous êtes gentil d'être venu!	How nice of you to have come.
Il n'a aucune crainte de dire la vérité.	He is not afraid to say the truth.
Il a l'esprit de faire ce qui lui est avantageux.	He is smart enough to do what is advantageous to him.

However, the infinitive is sometimes preceded by **à**, in which case the adjective or the noun denotes fitness, purpose, tendency, etc.

C'est facile à faire.	This is easily done.
Il a une maison à vendre.	He has a house for sale.
Une civilisation à efféminer les hommes.	A civilization which tends to render men effeminate.

2. USE OF THE INFINITIVE

In certain cases the infinitive possesses a value of expression similar to that of other moods or tenses of the personal verbs. Thus,

1. The narrative infinitive exercises the functions of the historic present (= past definite).

Ainsi dit le renard et (les) flatteurs d'applaudir.	Thus spoke the fox and the flatterers applauded.
Et les soldats de crier, de protester . . .	And the soldiers (began) to shout and to protest . . .

2. Preceded by **à,** the infinitive may assume a conditional sense:

À vous voir si fatigué on vous prendrait pour un vieillard.	If one judged you by your tired looks, he would take you for an old man.
À vous regarder de près, on dirait que vous rajeunissez.	If one looked at you closely, he would say that you grow young again.

3. In its active form, the infinitive, preceded by **à,** renders sometimes a passive sense:

Voici un passage à recopier.	Here is a passage to be recopied.
Ce vin rouge est bon à boire.	This red wine is worth drinking.

4. The infinitive is also used to express a question, or an exclamation intimating anxiety, indignation, and suffering. It forms some sort of elliptic clause.

Que faire quand tout est perdu?	What is to be done, when all is lost?

Que dire?	What is to be said?
À qui m'adresser?	To whom should I speak?
Moi, lui pardonner!—Jamais!	*I*, forgive him?—Never!

5. The infinitive, finally, replaces an imperative.

Traduire en anglais les phrases suivantes.	Translate into English the following sentences.
Ne pas fumer ici.	Do not smoke here.

The perfect infinitive denotes anteriority and presents the action expressed by the verb as completed.

Il pense avoir fini son travail.	He thinks his work is done.
Il s'imagine être arrivé à son but.	He imagines he has reached his aim.
Il croyait être tombé de la lune.	He thought he had fallen from the moon.

II. VERB REVIEW

1. Verbal Syntax

Verbs in the personal moods must agree in person and number according to the following rules.

Verbs Must Agree in Person.—A verb is put in the first or second person singular or plural when its subject pronoun is of the first or second person singular or plural respectively.

Je pense, donc je suis.	I think; therefore I am.
Nous savons cela.	We know that.
Tu es donc malade.	So you are sick.
Vous travaillez toujours.	You are working all the time.
Et moi qui suis resté ici pour le voir!	And *I* have remained here to see him!

A verb is put in the third person singular or plural when its subject is a word other than a pronoun, or is a pronoun in the third person singular or plural.

Le garçon s'amuse.	The boy has a good time.
Les garçons s'amusent.	The boys have a good time.
Vouloir c'est pouvoir.	Where there's a will, there's a way.
Ils vivent heureux.	They live happily.
Elle se meurt, la pauvre!	She is dying, the poor thing!

Verbs Must Agree in Number.—A verb is in either the singular or the plural, according to the number of the subject.

1.   A subject in the plural always requires its verb in the plural.

Les enfants sont partis.	The children are gone.
Ces arbres sont magnifiques.	These trees are magnificent.

2.   A subject in the singular is either a common or a collective noun or a pronoun.

A common noun or a pronoun in the singular requires a verb in the singular.

Le livre est déchiré.	The book is torn.
La table est grande.	The table is large.
Elle est belle.	She is beautiful.

A collective noun is singular in form; hence its verb is in the singular.

Une foule l'assaille.	A crowd attacks him.
L'armée est partie.	The army is gone.

A collective noun, however, has its verb in the plural when the sense of the collective expression and its form are considered.

La moitié des pommes sont gâtées.	Half of the apples are spoiled.
Une infinité d'erreurs se sont glissées dans ce document.	An infinity of errors have crept into this document.

The use of the plural is common after expressions like:

force	many, numerous
quantité de	many
nombre de	a number of
la plupart de (+ *art.*)	most
le plus grand nombre de	the greater number
une infinité de	an infinity

Note.—**Tout le monde** and **le peu** take the verb in the singular.

3.   A compound subject may have its verb in the singular or the plural.

Ni mon père ni ma mère ne sont ici.	Neither my father nor my mother is here.
L'or ou l'argent achètera cela.	Either gold or money will buy it.

It has its verb in the singular when the action performed by each subject is isolated, when one subject acts at the exclusion of the other, or when one subject sums up all the others.

Louis ou Émile sera ici à l'heure.	Lewis or Emil shall be here in time.
Riches, pauvres, grands, personne ne s'échappera.	Rich, poor, or great, no one will escape.
Maisons, palais, châteaux, tout est en feu.	Houses, palaces, castles, everything is on fire.

It has its verb in the plural when the totality of the subjects is considered, and when their actions are added to one another.

Paul et Charles sont d'excellents étudiants.	Paul and Charles are excellent students.
Ni l'or ni l'argent seuls ne font le bonheur.	Neither gold nor silver alone makes up happiness.

2. IRREGULAR VERBS

Present | *Principal Parts*

assaillir, *to assail*

assaillir, assaillant, assailli, assaille, assaillis

assaille	assaillons
assailles	assaillez
assaille	assaillent

bouillir, *to boil*

bouillir, bouillant, bouilli, bous, bouillis

bous	bouillons
bous	bouillez
bout	bouillent

III. VOCABULARY

1. FRENCH-ENGLISH:

s'accoutumer, to get accustomed

applaudir, to applaud

*boire, to drink

le bord, bank, shore

se charger de, to take it upon oneself

*comprendre, to understand

corriger, to correct

crier, to shout

*dormir, to sleep

l'épreuve *f.*, proof

l'état *m.*, state

expédier, to send

feuilleter, to skim through
la gare, station
jusqu'à, until
le nord, north
***nuire,** to harm
le parler, language

reconnaissant, -e, grateful
se retirer, to retire
sage, wise
saisir, to seize
le tas, heap

2. ENGLISH-FRENCH:

addition: in —, **de plus**
calm, **calme**
chap: my old —, **mon vieux**
crowd, **la foule**
to help, **aider**
most, **la plupart de** (+ *art.*)
night, **la nuit;** at —, **la nuit**
pleasure: to be a — to, ***se faire un plaisir de**

secret, **le secret**
to sit up, **veiller**
spectator, **le spectateur**
to swear to, **certifier sous serment**
truth: to tell the —, ***dire la vérité**

IV. IDIOMATIC EXPRESSIONS

les mettre aux prises, to set them fighting
au premier abord, at first glance, on one's approach
pour de bon, for good
être plus fort que soi, not to be able to help it
faire du mieux qu'on peut, to do the best one can
raconter tout au long, to tell at length
passer un examen, to take an examination
à plus forte raison, all the more
il n'y a pas de quoi, never mind, don't mention it
par-dessus le marché, into the bargain, moreover

V. EXERCISES

1. *Study the use of the infinitive and its connecting preposition in the following sentences:*

1. Crier n'est pas avoir raison. **2.** Le parler provençal a des charmes qui lui viennent du soleil de Provence. **3.** Il est souvent préférable de se taire que de parler. **4.** Venez me dire demain si vous avez le temps de m'accompagner à la gare. **5.** Il se charge de vous défendre contre ceux qui vous assaillent. 6. Laissez-le s'exprimer et écoutez bien ce qu'il dit. 7. Il est difficile de s'accoutumer à vivre dans les climats chauds quand on vient du nord. 8. Désirez-vous lui parler maintenant ou voulez-vous attendre jusqu'à demain? 9. Je crains de la déranger, mais je lui serais fort reconnaissant d'être reçu maintenant. 10. Continuez à le servir, vous ne regretterez pas de l'avoir fait. 11. Je ne crains pas de vous dire combien je regrette de vous avoir confié cette affaire importante. 12. On nous a assuré qu'il était impossible de comprendre la situation européenne; je le veux bien, c'est un état de choses difficile à saisir.

2. *Translate and note the use of the prepositions before the infinitive in the following sentences:*

1. Nous irons nous promener (demain) sur les bords de l'Arno. 2. Il s'amuse toute la journée à feuilleter les journaux et il n'en est pas plus sage pour cela. 3. Encore hier il prétendait être malade. 4. Manger, boire, dormir, voilà l'idéal du paresseux. 5. Après avoir complété son travail, il se retira chez lui. 6. Ainsi parla le jeune patriote et le monde de huer ou d'applaudir. 7. À examiner ce diamant de plus près, on y trouve tous les signes d'authenticité. 8. Voilà un tas de travail à faire: des documents à lire et à relire, des lettres à écrire et à expédier, des épreuves à corriger. 9. À qui confier ce secret! 10. L'appeler "mon ami," lui qui ne cherche qu'à me nuire!—Jamais!

3. *Translate into idiomatic French:*

1. At first glance, the crowd of spectators seemed to be calm. 2. I cannot help it; I must tell you this secret. 3. Most people like to tell their stories at length. 4. Don't mention it; it always gives me pleasure to do my best when I help my friends. 5. My old chap, if you want to take examinations you will have to work for good and, in addition, sit up at night. 6. She always tells the truth, all the more when she swears to it.

I. THE IMPERATIVE AND PARTICIPIAL MOODS—THEIR USE

1. THE IMPERATIVE MOOD AND ITS USE

The imperative proper has three forms.   Cf. p. 66.

The specific function of the imperative mood is to express commands and prohibitions.   These commands and prohibitions may

1.   Intimate mere counsels.

Ne faites pas cela, je vous le conseille.	Don't do this, I advise you.
Rompez cette amitié, elle pourrait vous être funeste.	Break off this friendship; it might be harmful to you.

2.   Express a mere request.

Passez-moi ce livre, s'il vous plaît.	Please, hand this book over to me.
Lisez-moi cela.	(Please) read this to me.

3.   Denote simple recommendations or exhortations.

Aimez-vous les uns les autres.	Love one another.
Ne vous querellez donc pas.	Do not quarrel.

4.   Render a mere wish, a desire.

Portez-vous bien.	Enjoy the best of health.
Soyez heureuse!	Be happy!

5.   Express outright commands or prohibitions.

Allez-vous-en!	Be gone!
N'y touchez pas!	Do not touch it!

The imperative is sometimes expressed by the second person singular present indicative, by the future indicative, or by the present infinitive, more particularly in familiar speech.

Tu pars à l'instant et tu me rejoins à Paris.	Leave at once and join me at Paris.
Vous sortirez sans faute à quatre heures précises.	Go out sharply at four o'clock, without fail.
Ne pas se pencher par la fenêtre.	Don't lean out of the window.

The third persons singular and plural of the present subjunctive are also used to express commands:

Qu'il parte!	Let him go!
Qu'ils viennent!	Let them come!

2. THE PARTICIPIAL MOOD AND ITS USE

The participial mood is used to denote a state or action as continuing or incomplete, or as completed without regard to time.

The participial mood has two forms, the present and the perfect. Cf. pp. 203ff.

The present participle usually expresses an action simultaneous with the one expressed by the verb in the personal mood with which it is connected.

L'orateur parlant avec éloquence arrache des larmes.	L'orateur qui parle . . . arrache des larmes.
L'orateur parlant avec éloquence arracha des larmes.	L'orateur qui parla . . . arracha des larmes.
L'orateur parlant avec éloquence arrachera des larmes.	L'orateur qui parlera . . . arrachera des larmes.

The *present participle* represents three grammatical realities:

1. The present participle proper.

Il était assis, mangeant tranquillement son pain.	He was seated, eating quietly his bread.
Les nuages s'avancent couvrant le ciel.	The clouds move forward covering the sky.

2. An adjective.

Voici les lettres amusantes que j'ai reçues.	Here are amusing letters which I have received.
On loue les enfants obéissants.	Obedient children are praised.

Note.—There is sometimes a slight difference in the spelling of the present participle and the participial adjective.

Present Participles		*Participial Adjectives*	
convainquant	*convincing*	convaincant	*convincing*
fatiguant	*tiring*	fatigant	*tiresome*
suffoquant	*suffocating*	suffocant	*stifling*
adhérant	*adhering*	adhérent	*adherent*
affluant	*thronging*	affluent	*tributary*
différant	*differing*	différent	*different*
excellant	*excelling*	excellent	*excellent*

The participial adjective assumes a particular sense in fixed expressions like:

une rue passante	une rue où l'on passe
une soirée dansante	une soirée où l'on danse
une fête payante	une fête où l'on paie pour entrer

3. A gerundive which serves as an adverbial modifier of the main verb.

Georges mange en se promenant. (manner)	George eats while walking.
Il a fait fortune en travaillant. (means)	He made a fortune by working.

Note.—When the present participle follows **aller,** it often does not take the preposition **en**:

Il allait courant vers son ami.	*He went (steadily) running toward his friend.*

The *past participle* has in most cases a passive sense, and intimates

1. A sustained action.

Un riche, attaqué par des voleurs, ...	A rich man, attacked by thieves, ...
Une maison, ruinée par la pluie, ...	A house, ruined by rain, ...

2. A completed action.

Un palais, bâti de pierre . . .	A palace built with stones . . .
Une maison, vendue aux en-chères . . .	A house sold by auction . . .

Note.—A past participle used as a modifier is placed after the noun which it modifies: Un jeune homme marié . . . *A young married man* . . . Une maison incendiée . . . *A burnt down house* . . .

II. VERB REVIEW

1. SYNTAX OF THE PAST PARTICIPLE

The past participle, besides its verbal function, may also assume the function of an adjective, either as a modifier or a predicate. As an adjective, it must agree in gender and number with the noun it modifies or qualifies as a predicate.

C'est là une vie perdue.	This is a lost life.
Voilà des enfants gâtés.	These are spoiled children.
Cette femme est maltraitée.	This woman is mistreated.
Ces jeunes filles sont gâtées.	These girls are spoiled.

The following past participles, which are equivalents of prepositions, are invariable when placed in front of the noun and variable when put after.

attendu	*considering*	passé	*beyond*
y compris	*including*	non compris	*not included*
étant donné	*given*	ci-inclus	*enclosed*
excepté	*excepting*	ci-joint	*subjoint, herewith*
		supposé	*supposing*

Y compris la lettre . . .	The letter included . . .
Ces deux hommes exceptés . . .	Excepting these two men . . .
Les dames y comprises . . .	The ladies included . . .

2. IRREGULAR VERBS

Present		*Principal Parts*
conclure, *to conclude*		conclure, concluant, conclu, conclus, conclus
conclus	concluons	
conclus	concluez	
conclut	concluent	

conduire, *to lead*   conduire, conduisant, conduit, conduis, conduisis

conduis	conduisons
conduis	conduisez
conduit	conduisent

envoyer, *to send*   envoyer, envoyant, envoyé, envoie, envoyai

envoie	envoyons
envoies	envoyez
envoie	envoient

III. VOCABULARY

1. FRENCH-ENGLISH:

*apprendre, to learn

assis (*p.p.* of ***asseoir**), seated

la bise, north wind

le café dansant, dance café

chercher, to look for; ***aller —,** to fetch

la cigale, grasshopper, cicada

comble: au — de, at the height of

d'abord, at first

dépourvu, -e, destitute

dévoyé, -e, led astray

*être: ne plus y —, not to live there anymore, not to be there anymore

exceller, to excel

le fait, fact

le fauteuil, armchair

la force, strength

fumer, to smoke

incendié, -e, burnt down

jamais, ever

la lâcheté, cowardice

manquer, to be lacking

mépriser, to despise

paisible, peaceful

la phrase, sentence

se promener, to walk

spirituel, -le, witty

le vœu, wish

2. ENGLISH-FRENCH:

to act, **agir**

to excel, **exceller**

to hurry, **se hâter**

loser, **le perdant**

trade, **le métier**

wit, **l'esprit** *m.*

IV. IDIOMATIC EXPRESSIONS

prendre l'habitude de, to get into the habit of

à tort et à travers, at random

faire la grimace, to make faces

avoir un rendez-vous, to have an engagement

se mettre d'accord sur, to agree on
gagner sa vie, to earn one's living
se monter la tête, to get excited
faire la cuisine, to cook
avoir de l'esprit, to be witty
à la longue, in the long run

V. EXERCISES

1. *Put all imperatives of the following selection into the second person plural, making all changes required by the text:*

Travaille, sois fort, sois fier, sois indépendant, méprise les petites vexations attribuées à ton âge. Réserve ta force de résistance pour des actes et contre des faits qui vaudront la peine. Ces temps viendront. Si je n'y suis plus, pense à moi qui ai souffert et travaillé gaîment.

Garde en toi le trésor de la bonté. Sache donner sans hésitation, perdre sans regret, acquérir sans lâcheté. Sache mettre dans ton cœur le bonheur de ceux que tu aimes à la place de celui qui te manquera. (George Sand)

2. *Point out all imperatives and tell what they express:*

1. Vous voilà au comble de vos vœux; soyez tout à votre bonheur et que la vie vous soit douce. 2. Tu reviendras au plus tard à quatre heures et tu iras chercher ton frère. 3. Écrire les phrases suivantes dans votre cahier. 4. Ne pas toucher aux fleurs. 5. Qu'il fasse d'abord son devoir et ne se permette pas de s'amuser. 6. Qu'on s'amuse quand c'est le temps de s'amuser et qu'on travaille quand c'est le temps de travailler.

3. *Point out the use of the present and past participles in the following sentences:*

1. La cigale ayant chanté tout l'été se trouva fort dépourvue quand la bise fut venue. 2. Tous les soirs, je le voyais assis dans son grand fauteuil lisant son journal et fumant paisiblement sa vieille pipe. 3. Les lettres de Madame de Sévigné sont aussi charmantes que spirituelles; c'est en les lisant qu'on apprend à écrire. 4. Avez-vous

jamais vu un café dansant? 5. Excellant dans toutes les qualités morales et sociales, il s'est acquis une réputation excellente. 6. Il prépare toujours ses discours en se promenant. 7. Ils allaient cherchant le chien qu'ils avaient perdu. 8. Que de maisons incendiées pendant cette guerre! 9. Que de jeunes gens dévoyés par de fausses amitiés! 10. Voici un des fameux palais ruiné· par les bombes.

4. *Translate into idiomatic French:*

1. Do not get into the habit of making faces; it's no proof of wit. 2. Always act nobly; you will have every right to a good reputation. 3. Why get excited? In the long run he always is the loser. 4. To cook is a trade like any other trade; one easily earns a living when he excels in cooking. 5. Hurry and agree on the exact date when you will have your engagement.

I. THE ADVERB—ITS FORMATION AND POSITION—COMPARISON OF ADVERBS

The adverb is an invariable word primarily used to modify a verb, and occasionally an adjective or another adverb.

Il écrit rapidement.	He writes rapidly.
Il est très distingué.	He is very distinguished.
Il parle très vite.	He speaks very quickly.

1. FORMATION OF ADVERBS

In regard to their formation, adverbs are either primitive or derivative.

Primitive adverbs are those which are derived from no other words of the language, although they may be compounded etymologically.

désormais, *henceforth*, is formed from Latin *de ex hora magis*.
devant, *before*, is formed from Latin *de abante*.

Derivative adverbs are those which are derived from an adjective to which is added a suffix.

poliment is derived from poli + adverbial ending **-ment**.
pleinement is derived from the feminine of plein + adverbial ending **-ment**.

The derivative adverbs form the largest group of French adverbs. They are formed

1. By adding **-ment** to the masculine adjective that ends in a vowel:

difficile	*difficult*	difficilement	*with difficulty*
poli	*polite*	poliment	*politely*
absolu	*absolute*	absolument	*absolutely*

2. By adding **-ment** to the feminine of adjectives that end in a consonant:

vain	*vain*	vainement	*vainly*
gracieux	*gracious*	gracieusement	*graciously*
doux	*sweet*	doucement	*sweetly*

3. By replacing the endings **-ant** and **-ent** of the masculine adjectives with **-amment** and **-emment,** respectively.

constant	*constant*	constamment	*constantly*
puissant	*powerful*	puissamment	*powerfully*
prudent	*prudent*	prudemment	*prudently*
décent	*decent*	décemment	*decently*

EXCEPTIONS.—Among adjectives irregularly transformed into adverbs are the following:

1. The adjectives lent, *slow;* véhément, *vehement;* and présent, *present.*

lent	*slow*	lentement	*slowly*
véhément	*vehement*	véhémentement	*vehemently*
présent	*present*	présentement	*presently*

2. Some adjectives that end in -*e* mute and change -*e* mute to -*é* before adding **-ment:**

aveugle	*blind*	aveuglément	*blindly*
commode	*convenient*	commodément	*conveniently*
conforme	*conformable*	conformément	*conformably*
énorme	*enormous*	énormément	*enormously*
opiniâtre	*obstinate*	opiniâtrément	*obstinately*

3. Some adjectives that change the -*e* mute of their feminine to -*é* before taking the adverbial ending **-ment:**

commun, -e	*common*	communément	*commonly*
confus, -e	*confused*	confusément	*confusedly*
exprès, -esse	*express*	expressément	*expressly*

4. The following three **adjectives:**

gentil	*gentle*	gentiment	*gently*
bref	*brief*	brièvement	*briefly*
impuni	*unpunished*	impunément	*with impunity*

5. The corresponding adverbial forms of **bon** and **mauvais**:

bon	*good*	bien	*well*
mauvais	*bad*	mal	*badly*

Note.—A number of adjectives are used as adverbs without any change whatsoever in their adjectival form.

juste	Les soldats visaient juste.	The soldiers aimed *straight*.
clair	Voyez-vous clair?	Are you *able to* see?
ferme	Travaillez ferme.	Work *hard*.
haut	Pourquoi parler si haut?	Why speak so *loud?*
cher	Les livres coûtent cher.	Books are *expensive*.
court	Il s'arrête court.	He stops *short* (*suddenly*).
droit	Il va droit au but.	He goes *straight* to the point.
vrai	Nous disons vrai.	We tell the *truth*.
bon	Cette fleur sent bon.	This flower smells *good*.
fort	Ne criez pas si fort.	Don't shout so *loud*.
faux	Vous chantez faux.	You sing *out of tune*.
sec	Les gens de la noce buvaient sec.	The people at the wedding drank *hard*.
bas	Parlez bas!	Speak *low!*
mauvais	Ces fleurs sentent mauvais.	These flowers smell *bad*.
rouge	Il voit rouge.	He sees *red*.
serré	Ces messieurs jouent serré.	These gentlemen play *a cautious game*.
chaud, etc.	Il fait chaud.	It is *warm*.

2. POSITION OF ADVERBS

Adverbs modify verbs in simple and compound tenses.

In *simple* tenses, adverbs are usually placed after the verb which they modify.

Il écrit lisiblement.	He is writing legibly.
Vous parlez bien.	You speak well.

In *compound* tenses, adverbs are usually placed between the auxiliary verb and the past participle.

Il a beaucoup travaillé.	He has been working a great deal.
Elles sont vite parties.	They left rapidly.

However, adverbs of time and place follow the past participle, as well as long adverbs in **-ment**:

Ils sont partis hier.	They left yesterday.
On l'a trouvé là.	People found it there.
Il lui a parlé longuement.	He spoke to him for a long time.

Beaucoup, peu, trop, bien, mieux, mal, and also adverbs of negation, regularly precede infinitives:

On lui défend de trop travailler.	He is forbidden to work too much (they forbid him to work too much).
Il ne saurait mieux parler.	He couldn't speak better.
Je vous dis de ne jamais reparaître devant moi.	I tell you never to show up again in front of me.

When adverbs modify nouns, adjectives, or other adverbs, they generally precede these parts of speech.

Avez-vous assez de fleurs?	Do you have flowers enough?
Elles sont certainement assez chères.	They are certainly expensive enough.
Il vient bien à propos, n'est-ce pas?	He comes just in time, doesn't he?

COMPARISON OF ADVERBS

Adverbs, especially adverbs of manner, are compared like adjectives. Cf. pp. 28-29.

poliment	plus poliment	le plus poliment
	moins poliment	le moins poliment
gracieusement	plus gracieusement	le plus gracieusement
	moins gracieusement	le moins gracieusement

The following adverbs are compared irregularly:

bien	*well*	mieux	*better*	le mieux	*best*
beaucoup	*much*	plus	*more*	le plus	*most*
mal	*badly*	pis	*worse*	le pis	*worst*
		also: plus mal			

II. VERB REVIEW

1. TRANSLATION OF "HOW LONG"

In questions prefixed by *how long*, the tenses used in French usually differ from those used in English.

An action or state in the past continuing into the present is rendered in French by the present, preceded by **depuis quand,** in English by the present perfect, or the progressive perfect.

Depuis quand êtes-vous ici?	How long have you been here?
Depuis quand le faites-vous?	How long have you been doing it?
Depuis trois jours.	For three days.

An action or state begun in a more remote past and continuing in a more immediate past is rendered in French by the imperfect, preceded by **depuis quand,** in English by the past perfect.

Depuis quand étiez-vous ici, quand il est arrivé?	How long had you been here when he arrived?
Depuis trois jours.	For three days.

3.   When the duration of an action or state in the past or the future is expressed by the verb which follows *how long*, no reference being made to the present, *how long* is rendered by **combien de temps** and the verb is in the past indefinite or the future in French.   In English the imperfect or the future is used.

Combien de temps avez-vous fait cela?	How long were you doing that?
(Pendant) huit jours.	For a week.
Combien de temps serez-vous ici?	How long will you be here?
Je serai ici pour huit jours.	I'll be here for a week.

2.   IRREGULAR VERBS.

Present		*Principal Parts*
traire, *to milk*		traire, trayant, trait, trais, *none*
trais	trayons	
trais	trayez	
trait	traient	
moudre, *to grind*		moudre, moulant, moulu, mouds, moulus
mouds	moulons	
mouds	moulez	
moud	moulent	
résoudre, *to resolve*		résoudre, résolvant, résolu, résouds, résolus
résouds	résolvons	
résouds	résolvez	
résoud	résolvent	

III. VOCABULARY

1. FRENCH-ENGLISH:

arracher (de), to pull out (of)
le changement, change
le côté, side
le coup de poing, punch
se ***débattre,** to struggle
éclat: *faire un — de rire, to burst into a laughter, laugh loudly
enfermer, to shut in
étrange, strange
hors de, out of
la huée, hooting, booing
lâcher prise, to let go

le lendemain, next day
noir, -e, black
d'ordinaire, ordinarily
pain: au — sec et à l'eau, on bread and water
renverser sur, to knock down on
rester, to stay
tempêter, to rage, fume
traîner, to drag
vain: en —, in vain, uselessly

2. ENGLISH-FRENCH:

answer, **la réponse**
to assure, **assurer**
cautious, **prudent**
to come running, ***venir en courant**
delighted, **enchanté, -e**
disagreeable, **désagréable**
game, **le jeu**
hard, **fort** (*adv.*)
hasty, **précipité, -e, prompt, -e**
just, **donc**
to be lacking, **manquer**
lady, **la dame**
lazy, **paresseux, -se**

merely, **seulement**
mistake, **la faute**
perseverance, **la persévérance**
perturbed, **bouleversé, -e**
quickly, **vite**
riches, **la richesse**
rose, **la rose**
to smell, ***sentir**
soon, **bientôt**
in spite, **malgré**
to undertake, ***entreprendre**
valiant, **vaillant, -e**
to be wanting, **manquer de**

IV. IDIOMATIC EXPRESSIONS

quelle heure est-il? what time is it?
il est cinq heures et demie, it is half past five
il est cinq heures moins le quart, it is a quarter to five
il est cinq heures et quart, it is a quarter past five

il est une heure moins vingt-cinq, it is twenty-five minutes to one

cette chambre a dix mètres de large sur quinze mètres de long, this room is ten meters wide by fifteen meters long

lier connaissance, to become acquainted

il fait lourd, the weather is sultry

pas grand' chose, not much

il est de bonne politique, it is wise, good sense

V. EXERCISES

1. *Translate:*

   1. He works more than I; but I work harder when I am working. 2. He doesn't think as quickly as I. 3. These roses smell better than mine. 4. I assure you, it is better to speak low than loud. 5. I play a more cautious game than your friends. 6. So much the better for you. 7. Louis came running, but stopped short when he saw me. 8. This trip is rather expensive; don't you think so?

2. *Translate after pointing out all adverbs or adverbial locutions:*

   Le lendemain, je trouvai un étrange changement dans la maison: il fallut aller à la classe, il fallut subir un examen de mes talents, qui découvrit publiquement que je savais à peine lire; il s'éleva une huée générale, et un petit garçon de dix ans, qui était placé auprès de moi, fit un éclat de rire si impertinent que je n'hésitai pas à lui donner un coup de poing qui le renversa de l'autre côté sur son camarade. Aussitôt on me saisit, on m'arracha ignominieusement de ma place; on me traîna hors de la salle: je me débattais, je tempêtais, mais en vain. On me conduisit dans une chambre bien noire, on m'y enferma en me déclarant que j'y resterais huit jours au pain sec et à l'eau.

   (Mme. S.-F. de Genlis)

3. *Translate:*

   1. Has he as many friends as you? 2. There are many mistakes in this homework. 3. How valiantly they fight! 4. My sister is all perturbed over the present events. 5. In

spite of their riches, these ladies are not all happy.   6.   Just
think a bit more and you will find the answer.   7.   Only
lazy people always complain.   8.   He merely assured you
of his sympathy.   9.   Intelligence is not wanting; we have
only to study hard to succeed in our examinations.   10.
Most people lack perseverance when they undertake some
disagreeable work.

4.   *Translate the following sentences (a) and (b); then compare
them:*

1 (a)   *Tout à coup* la porte s'ouvrit.
   (b)   *Tout d'un coup* il lâcha prise et tomba de l'arbre.

2 (a)   Il a bien *plus* de talents que moi.
   (b)   Je vous assure que je travaille *davantage*.

3 (a)   Nous nous sommes levés *plus tôt* que d'ordinaire.
   (b)   *Plutôt* que de le voir souffrir, nous sommes partis.

4 (a)   Il peut nager deux heures *de suite* sans être fatigué.
   (b)   Quand il nage, il se fatigue *tout de suite*.

5 (a)   Nous discutions l'affaire *aussitôt* après son arrivée.
   (b)   *Aussitôt* les affaires réglées, nous sommes allés en pro-
         vince.

5.   *Translate into idiomatic French:*

1.   What time is it now?   2.   It is 9:25 or 9:30.—No, you're
wrong, it is 9:15.   3.   This house is 40 feet wide by 55 feet
long.   4.   I'm sure he will be delighted to become acquainted with Charles.   5.   It is wise not to be too hasty.
6.   The weather is sultry; it might rain soon.   7.   Nothing
new today?—No, not much.   8.   How long did the spectacle
last?   9.   How long has William been studying French?—
Two years.   10.   How long will you stay in Paris?—For
two days.   11.   How long had he been sick when Louis
arrived?   12.   How long have you had this book?—Three
days.

Lesson XXII

I. PREPOSITIONS AND CONJUNCTIONS

Among the parts of speech that are invariable in their form are the prepositions and the conjunctions.

1. PREPOSITIONS

A preposition is an invariable word which shows the relation between a noun, pronoun, infinitive, adjective, or adverb following it, and some other word in the sentence.

All prepositions (except **en,** which is followed by the present participle) require that the verb which they govern be in the infinitive.

L'amour de la justice . . .	Love of justice . . .
Il travaille pour moi.	He is working for me.
Il faut manger pour vivre.	One must eat to live.
Il a quelque chose de bon.	He has something good
Il s'instruit en s'amusant.	He improves his mind while having a good time.

A preposition without an object assumes the meaning of an adverb.

Est-elle dans la maison?— Non, elle est dehors.	Is she in the house?—No, she is outside.

Prepositions have the specific function of indicating a relationship of place, time, manner, cause, aim, purpose, or restrictions.

Il est chez mon oncle.	He is at my uncle's.
Il est ici depuis hier.	He has been here since yesterday.
Vous avez agi avec courage.	You acted with courage (= courageously).
Pour avoir été charitable, vous vous attirez une affaire.	For having been charitable, you are in a bad way.

186

Tout le monde va bien sauf Georges.

Everybody is well with the exception of George.

There are three classes of prepositions, the simple prepositions, the prepositional phrases, and the prepositions derived from adjectives or past participles. The simple prepositions are the more common ones. They are

à	*to, at*	jusque	*until*
après	*after*	malgré	*in spite of*
avant	*before*	moyennant	*by means of*
avant de + inf.	*before*	nonobstant	*notwithstanding*
avec	*with*	outre	*beyond*
chez	*at the home of*	par	*by, through*
contre	*against*	parmi	*among*
dans	*in*	pendant	*during*
de	*of, from*	pour	*for*
depuis	*since*	sans	*without*
derrière	*behind*	sauf	*save, except*
dès	*from . . . on*	selon	*according to*
devant	*before*	sous	*under*
durant	*during*	suivant	*according to*
en	*in*	sur	*on, upon*
entre	*between*	vers	*toward*
envers	*toward, to*	voici	*here is, are*
hormis	*except*	voilà	*there is, are*

Prepositional phrases and prepositions derived from adjectives are easily found in any good dictionary.

Some prepositions like **à, de, en, dans,** etc., deserve special treatment.

1. **À,** in its natural and obvious sense, denotes direction:

Il va à Londres.

He is going *to* London.

But the preposition **à** may also indicate
  (a) Cause:

À ne rien faire, on se fatigue.

One gets tired out, *doing nothing.*

Note.—Purpose is frequently intimated in phrases like **machine à coudre, verre à vin, bouteille à lait,** etc.

(b)   Result:

Il crie à s'égosiller.	He shouts *till* he is blue in the face (= *he shouts himself* hoarse).

(c)   Attribution:

Honneur aux vaincus!	All honor *to* the vanquished!

(d)   Possession:

Voici un chapeau à Jean.	Here is a hat *of John's*.

(e)   Manner, distance:

Il le punit à coups de bâton.	He punishes him *with* a stick.
À trois milles d'ici . . .	*Three miles (away)* from here . . .

(f)   Time:

Je le verrai à trois heures.	I'll see him *at* three o'clock.

(g)   Location:

Il est à table.	He is *at* the table.

(h)   Price:

Voici des places à trois francs.	Here are seats *at* three francs.

2.   **De,** in its natural sense, denotes

(a)   Origin:

Il vient de New York.	He comes *from* New York.

(b)   Duration:

Qu'avez-vous fait de la journée?	What have you been doing *all day long?*

(c)   Moment of action:

Le voilà qui se lève de bonne heure.	There he is getting up *early*.

Otherwise **de** may intimate

(a)   Cause:

Il meurt de soif.	He is dying *of* thirst.

(b)   Means, instrument:

Il frappe d'estoc et de taille.	He cuts and thrusts.
Ne le frappez pas de votre bâton.	Do not hit him *with* your stick.

(c)   Agent:

Vous me comblez de joie.	You fill me *with* joy.

(d)   Material and purpose:

Il a une table de marbre.	He has a *marble* table.
Voici une école de filles.	Here is a *girls'* school.

(e)   Origin, authorship:

Le fils de Louis est ici.	*Louis'* son is here.
Cette pièce est de Shakespeare.	This play is *by* Shakespeare.

(f)   Partitive:

Il me faut de l'encre	I need *ink*.

(g)   Possession:

Les livres de Marie sont sur la table.	Mary's books are *on* the table.

3.   **En** and **dans.**

En, with the exception of en l'honneur de, *in honor of;* en l'absence de, *in the absence of;* en l'an, *in the year;* and en l'air, *in the air*, is never used before a noun preceded by a definite article. It may denote:

(a)   Direction:

Il va en Russie.	He is going *to* Russia.
Je vais en France.	I am going *to* France.

(b)   Place:

Il demeure en Espagne.	He is living *in* Spain.
En Hollande, mai est le mois des tulipes.	*In* Holland May is the month of the tulips.

(c)   Duration:

En deux jours vous pouvez lire ce roman.	You can read this novel *in* two days.
Vous aurez fini ce travail en un jour, n'est-ce pas?	You will be through with this work *in* one day, won't you?

(d)   Manner:

Il agit toujours en galant homme.	He always acts *like* a gentleman.
C'est en travaillant qu'il a fait sa fortune.	It is *by* working that he made a fortune.

Dans expresses a determined moment of time or space:

Je viendrai dans trois jours.	I shall come *in* three days.
Vous paierez dans cinq mois.	You will pay *in* five months.
Je vous verrai dans l'après-midi.	I shall see you *during* the afternoon.
Elle se promène dans le jardin.	She is taking a walk *in* the garden.
L'ennemi est dans la ville.	The enemy is *within* the city.

4.   **Par** may denote

(a)   Agent:

Cette chanson a été composée par mon ami.	This song was composed *by* my friend.

(b)   Place:

L'oiseau entra par la fenêtre.	The bird entered *through* the window.

(c)   Cause:

C'est par méchanceté qu'il a fait cela.	He did it *through* nastiness.

(d)   Time:

Je le vois deux fois par jour, par semaine, par mois, etc.	I see him twice *a* day, *a* week, *a* month, etc.

5. **Sur** may denote

   (a)   Contact:

Le livre se trouve sur le pupitre.	The book is *on* the desk.

   (b)   Place:

Avez-vous de l'argent sur vous?	Have you some money *about* you?

   (c)   Superiority:

Les bleus l'emportent sur les rouges.	The blue win *over* the red.

   (d)   **Partitive** sense:

Payez sur vos économies.	Pay (for it) *out of* your savings.

2. CONJUNCTIONS

A conjunction is a word which connects words, phrases, or sentences.

Les pommes *et* les poires sont mûres.	The apples and pears are ripe.
Je pars, *mais* Louis reste.	I leave, but Louis stays.
Il travailla si fort *qu'*il en devint malade.	He worked so hard that he fell sick.

There are two kinds of conjunctions, co-ordinating and sub-ordinating conjunctions.

CO-ORDINATING CONJUNCTIONS.—Co-ordinating conjunctions establish a connection between words, groups of words, or phrases.

Co-ordinating conjunctions express a variety of relations:

1. Addition, expressed by conjunctions like **et, de même que, ainsi que, aussi bien que, comme, avec, non seulement . . . mais encore:**

Mon père ainsi que Paul sont partis pour la guerre.	My father as well as Paul left for the war.
Il est non seulement grand mais encore fort.	He is not only tall but also strong.

2. Negation, rendered by **ni**, *nor;* **ni . . . ni** (**ne**), *neither . . . nor:*

Il ne chante pas bien; ni moi non plus.	He doesn't sing well; nor I either.
Il n'a ni argent ni amis.	He has neither money nor friends.
Ni lui ni moi nous ne resterons ici.	Neither he nor I shall stay here.

3. An alternative, expressed by **ou**, *or;* **ou bien**, *or else;* **soit . . . soit**, *either . . . or;* **tantôt . . . tantôt**, *now . . . now:*

Il est grand ou petit.	He is either tall or small.
Vous êtes tantôt triste tantôt exubérant de gaîté.	Now you are sad, now overflowing with mirth.

4. Opposition or correction, intimated by conjunctions like **mais**, *but;* **cependant**, *however;* **pourtant**, *however;* **néanmoins**, *nevertheless;* **or**, *now;* **toutefois**, *yet;* **au surplus**, *besides;* **du reste**, *moreover;* and **au reste**, *besides:*

Vous êtes intelligent, mais sans éducation.	You are intelligent but without education.
Il est pauvre et pourtant il est généreux.	He is poor and yet he is generous.

5. Cause, intimated by **car**, *for;* **en effet**, *in fact:*

Louis est charmant car il est bien élevé.	Louis is a charming fellow for (because) he is well-mannered.

6. Consequence, expressed by **donc**, *therefore;* **c'est pourquoi**, *that's why;* **par conséquent**, *consequently;* **partant**, *therefore;* **aussi**, *so;* etc.

Vous êtes obéissant, donc vous méritez une récompense.	You are obedient, therefore you deserve a reward.

7. Conclusion, indicated by **enfin**, *finally;* **ainsi**, *so;* **aussi**, *so;* etc.

Louise a bien travaillé . . . aussi elle a fini son travail.	Louise did work hard . . . so she finished her work

Et is sometimes omitted in enumerations:

Femmes, moines, vieillards, tout était descendu. (La Fontaine)	Women, monks, old people, everybody came down.

SUBORDINATING CONJUNCTIONS.—The subordinating conjunctions join two clauses together and point out interdependence. These conjunctions introduce subordinate or dependent clauses.

The common subordinating conjunctions are **que,** *that;* **quand,** *when;* **comme,** *as;* **si,** *if.* There are numerous conjunctional expressions of subordination, which will be found in any good dictionary.

Que is used

1. To introduce a clause:

Que vous ayez perdu votre pari ne s'explique guère.	It can hardly be explained how you lost your bet.

2. To join a subordinate direct object clause to the main clause:

Il sent qu'il a perdu sa cause.	He feels that his cause is lost.

3. To unite the two terms of a comparison:

Il est plus riche que moi.	He is richer than I am.

4. To introduce an imperative:

Qu'elle parte et au plus vite!	Let her leave and as soon as possible!

5. To substitute for another conjunction:

Si elle vient, et qu'elle vous redise cela, ne l'écoutez pas.	If she comes and if she tells that again, refuse to listen to her.

Note.—**Que** is used to replace **si** in the second clause with the verb in the subjunctive.

Quand, derived from Latin *quando,* was introduced into French at an earlier date than **lorsque,** its synonym.

Quand les beaux jours seront passés, nous quitterons la campagne.	When the sunny days are gone, we shall leave the countryside.
Quand les oiseaux chanteront le matin, nous chanterons avec eux.	When the birds sing in the morning, we shall sing with them.

Comme, derived from the Latin *cum* or *quum*, expresses

1. Time (simultaneity):

Comme j'étais en ville, je l'entendis m'appeler.	As I was in town, I heard him call me.

2. Cause:

Comme j'étais fatigué, j'eus peine à arriver ici.	Because I was tired, I hardly was able to arrive here.

3. Restriction:

Tu ne travailles donc pas, comme je vois.	As I see, you are not working.

4. An attribute:

Tu seras employé comme secrétaire.	You will serve as secretary.

5. Comparison:

Tu mourras comme les autres humains.	You will die just like any other human being.

Si is used to express
1. A condition:

Il partira, si vous le commandez.	He will leave if you so order.

2. A supposition:

Si ce qu'il dit est vrai, il mérite des félicitations.	If what he says is true, he deserves congratulations.

3. A cause:

Si ce n'était mon rhumatisme, je t'accompagnerais.	Were it not for my rheumatism, I'd go with you.

4. Comparison (opposition):

Si vous êtes plus fort, moi je suis plus prudent.	If *you* are stronger, *I* am more careful.

II. VERB REVIEW

1. OMISSION OF pas

Ne alone is used

1. Chiefly in literary style, with **cesser, oser, pouvoir, savoir.**

Je ne cesse de le lui dire.	I do not stop telling him.
Il n'ose me le dire.	He doesn't dare tell me.
Tu ne peux me le dire?	You cannot tell me?
Je ne sais que dire.	I don't know what to say.
Il ne saurait vous le dire.	He cannot tell it to you.

2. Optionally in academic or literary style, with a rather vague negative connotation, after verbs of fear, **à moins que, de peur que, de crainte que,** and in comparisons.

J'ai peur qu'on ne me voie.	I'm afraid someone may see me.
Il craint que Louis ne prenne froid.	He is afraid Louis may catch cold.
Je prends mon manteau de crainte qu'il ne fasse froid.	I take my coat for fear it may be cold.
Prenez garde qu'on ne vous voie.	Take care not to be seen.
N'y allez pas à moins qu'on ne vous appelle.	Don't go, unless they call you.
Il est plus intelligent qu'il ne paraît.	He is more intelligent than he looks.

3. After a relative pronoun followed by a subjunctive.

Y a-t-il quelqu'un ici qui ne sache cela?	Is there anybody here who doesn't know that?

4. After **que,** *why,* pointing to a reproach and **que** in exclamations.

Que ne le faites-vous vous-même!	Why don't you do it yourself?
Que pareille conduite ne se répète à l'avenir!	Let no such behaviour happen again!

5. After **il y a** followed by a compound tense.

Il y a trois ans que je ne l'ai vue.	I haven't seen her for three years.

6. After certain indefinite pronouns such as **personne, rien, nul, aucun.** DO NOT SAY: Personne n'a pas frappé *or* Rien ne s'est pas passé.

Personne n'a frappé à la porte.	Nobody knocked at the door.
Nul ne s'est fait attraper.	No one was caught.
Rien ne s'est passé.	Nothing happened.
Aucun n'est venu.	Not one came.

2. Irregular Verbs

Present   *Principal Parts*

cueillir, *to pick*   cueillir, cueillant, cueilli, cueillis

cueille	cueillons
cueilles	cueillez
cueille	cueillent

tenir, *to hold*   tenir, tenant, tenu, tiens, tins

tiens	tenons
tiens	tenez
tient	tiennent

haïr, *to hate*   haïr, haïssant, haï, hais, haïs

hais	haïssons
hais	haïssez
hait	haïssent

III. VOCABULARY

1. French-English:

*abattre, to fell

la corde, rope; mourir par la —, to hang

dégénéré, -e, degenerate

dégrader, to degrade, lower

demander, to ask

le doigt, finger

le droit, right

envers, toward

s'épuiser, to exhaust oneself

la faim, hunger

la force, force, strength, might; la — prime le droit, might is right

le fusil, gun

l'intrus *m.*, intruder

au lieu de, instead (of)

manquer, to miss

le matin, morning; de si bon
   —, so early
le mépris, scorn
en patriote, like a patriot
   primer, to come before
puisque, since

se réunir, to gather
sauf, except
le secours, help
traverser, to cross
se tuer, to kill oneself

2. ENGLISH-FRENCH:

appearance, l'apparence *f.*;
   in —, en apparence
as, comme
to bathe, se baigner
breeze, la brise
closed, fermé, -e
delightful, délicieux, -se
to deteriorate, détériorer
disagreeable, désagréable
door, la porte
empty, vide
equally, également
ever so much, beaucoup
to feel, *sentir
foliage, le feuillage
gentle, doux, douce
lazy, paresseux, -se

neither . . . nor, ni . . . ni
   (ne, *before verb*)
now . . . now, tantôt . . .
   tantôt
owner, le propriétaire
rain, la pluie
ray, le rayon
rich-looking, avoir l'air (*m.*)
   riche
roof, le toit
to run through, traverser
spot, l'endroit *m.*
sun, le soleil
wall, le mur
as well as, aussi bien que
window, la fenêtre
yet: not —, pas encore

IV. IDIOMATIC EXPRESSIONS

par acquit de conscience, for conscience' sake
de grand matin, early in the morning
n'en pas revenir, not to be able to get over it
éventer la mèche, to let out a secret
passer une nuit blanche, to spend a sleepless night
pendant des semaines, for weeks
crier comme un perdu, to shout (or talk) as loudly as one can
dire à l'oreille, to whisper
d'arrache-pied, in earnest, steadily
avoir le cœur gros, to be heartbroken
courir par monts et par vaux, to be always on the move

V. EXERCISES

1. *Complete the following sentences by filling in the dashes with the proper prepositions:*

   1. L'été vient ——— le printemps. 2. Il faut être bon ——— les malheureux. 3. Il vous faudra traverser l'Océan Atlantique si vous voulez aller ——— France ——— Amérique. 4. L'intrépide Lorraine, Jeanne d'Arc, fut mise à mort ——— Rouen ——— les Anglais. 5. Les enfants aiment ——— grimper ——— les arbres. 6. Il a tout perdu ——— l'honneur. 7. Il est ici ——— huit jours. 8. Les Arabes habitent ——— des tentes. 9. Il va partir ——— demain. 10. ——— trois jours qu'elle est partie.

2. *Translate the following phrases:*

   *une bouteille à lait
   une machine à coudre
   un verre à boire
   une canne à épée
   un oiseau de proie
   pêcher à la ligne
   prendre de force
   travailler pour son compte
   travailler comme quatre
   à tant par tête

   montre en or
   chez le médecin
   œil pour œil
   courir au galop
   trembler de peur
   le long du mur
   derrière le jardin
   un livre de trente francs
   par monts et par vaux
   difficile à avaler

3. *Indicate the relationship between the preposition and its object* (Model: La porcelaine de Limoges est fameuse.—*Origin*):

   Voici un fusil à Jean.
   A vivre ainsi, on se tue.
   Il l'abat à coups de fusil.
   Honneur aux maîtres!
   On se réunira à minuit.
   Il ne parle jamais à son bureau.

   Il est mort de faim.
   Ne le tuez pas de votre sabre.
   Ce livre est d'Anatole France.
   On a dit cela de tout temps.
   Pourquoi se lever de si bon matin?
   Il ne parle pas de la journée.

---

* The meaning of these expressions or words will be found in the General Vocabulary.

Du vin à vingt francs la bouteille.

Il travaille à s'épuiser.

La fille de Charles est ici.

Allons en ville.

Il a fait cela en deux heures.

Ce n'est pas parler en patriote.

Est-il parti pour la France?

Pour vous faire plaisir?

Vêtements pour femmes.

On le montre du doigt.

Rien d'intéressant dans ce musée.

Il est mort par la corde.

Dans six mois il sera ici.

Avant cinq heures il sera devant votre maison.

Il court par monts et par vaux.

Sortir par ces temps de pluie?

Oui! Non!

4. *Translate with special emphasis on the conjunctions:*

1. Too much rain and too much sun are equally disagreeable. 2. As he entered the house he felt it was empty. 3. The windows as well as the doors were closed. 4. In appearance, it was not only rich-looking but also interesting. 5. Neither the roof nor the walls were deteriorated. 6. Now a gentle breeze ran through the trees; now the green foliage bathed lazily in the rays of the sun. 7. We liked this spot ever so much for it is a delightful place. 8. Its owner is sick; that's why no one had come as yet.

5. *Point out all conjunctions, co-ordinating and subordinating; then translate:*

1. Il partira seul aujourd'hui ou demain avec Paul. 2. Il veut travailler quoiqu'il soit malade. 3. Il n'est pas vrai que la force prime le droit. 4. Puisque vous sortez, prenez Georges et Lucie avec vous. 5. Venez au secours de vos amis sans qu'ils aient besoin de vous le demander; le soleil attend-il qu'on le prie pour faire part de sa lumière et de sa chaleur? 6. Il faut bien que tout le monde vive. 7. Alors même qu'il partirait, la perte ne serait pas grande. 8. Il me dit que vous avez manqué le train parce que vous vous êtes levé trop tard.

6. *Point out all prepositions and conjunctions in the following selection; then translate:*

L'âne.—L'âne n'est point un cheval dégénéré; il n'est ni étranger, ni intrus; il a comme tous les animaux, sa famille, son espèce et son rang, et quoique sa noblesse soit moins illustre, elle est tout aussi bonne et tout aussi ancienne que celle du cheval: pourquoi donc tant de mépris pour cet animal si bon, si patient, si sobre, si utile? On ne fait pas attention que l'âne serait par lui-même, et pour nous, le premier, le plus beau, le mieux fait, le plus distingué des animaux, si dans le monde il n'y avait pas de cheval. Il est le second au lieu d'être le premier, et par cela seul il semble n'être plus rien. C'est la comparaison qui le dégrade: on le voit, on le juge, non pas en lui-même, mais relativement au cheval: on oublie qu'il est âne, qu'il a toutes les qualités de sa nature, et on ne pense qu'à la figure et aux qualités du cheval, qui lui manquent et qu'il ne doit pas avoir.

Buffon

7. *Translate into idiomatic French:*

1. He is always on the move: he gets up early in the morning and, for weeks, spends sleepless nights. 2. To shout as loud as one can is no proof that one is right. 3. To satisfy himself, he works steadily all day long. 4. He always has something to whisper and more so when he is heartbroken. 5. They say that Louis committed a crime; knowing him as I do, I can't get over it.

APPENDIX

AUXILIARY VERBS

Avoir

INDICATIVE	CONDITIONAL	SUBJUNCTIVE
Present		*Present*
(*I*) *have* . . .		(*that I*) *may have*
ai		aie
as		aies
a		ait
avons		ayons
avez		ayez
ont		aient
Imperfect:		
(*I*) *had* . . .		
avais		
avais		
avait		
avions		
aviez		
avaient		
Past Definite		*Imperfect*
(*I*) *had* . . .		(*that I*) *might have* . . .
eus		eusse
eus		eusses
eut		eût
eûmes		eussions
eûtes		eussiez
eurent		eussent

INDICATIVE	CONDITIONAL	SUBJUNCTIVE
Future	*Present*	
(I) shall have ...	*(I) should have* ...	
aurai	aurais	
auras	aurais	
aura	aurait	
aurons	aurions	
aurez	auriez	
auront	auraient	
Perfect		*Perfect*
(I) have had ...		*(that I) may have had* ...
ai eu		aie eu
as eu		aies eu
a eu		ait eu
avons eu		ayons eu
avez eu		ayez eu
ont eu		aient eu
Pluperfect		
(I) had had ...		
avais eu		
avais eu		
avait eu		
avions eu		
aviez eu		
avaient eu		
Past Anterior		*Pluperfect*
(I) had had ...		*(that I) might have had* ...
eus eu		eusse eu
eus eu		eusses eu
eut eu		eût eu
eûmes eu		eussions eu
eûtes eu		eussiez eu
eurent eu		eussent eu

INDICATIVE	CONDITIONAL	SUBJUNCTIVE
Future Anterior	*Past* or *Perfect*	
(*I*) *shall have had* ...	(*I*) *should have had* ...	
aurai eu	aurais eu	
auras eu	aurais eu	
aura eu	aurait eu	
aurons eu	aurions eu	
aurez eu	auriez eu	
auront eu	auraient eu	

IMPERATIVE	INFINITIVE	PARTICIPLES
aie, *have*	*Present*	*Present*
	to have	*having*
	avoir	ayant
ayons *Let's have*	*Perfect*	*Perfect*
ayez *have*	*to have had*	*having had*
	avoir eu	ayant eu

Être

INDICATIVE	CONDITIONAL	SUBJUNCTIVE
Present		*Present*
(*I*) *am* ...		(*that I*) *may be* ...
suis		sois
es		sois
est		soit
sommes		soyons
êtes		soyez
sont		soient

Imperfect		
(*I*) *was* ...		
étais		
étais		
était		
étions		
étiez		
étaient		

INDICATIVE	CONDITIONAL	SUBJUNCTIVE
Past Definite		*Imperfect*
(*I*) *was* ...		(*that I*) *might be* ...
fus		fusse
fus		fusses
fut		fût
fûmes		fussions
fûtes		fussiez
furent		fussent
Future	*Present*	
(*I*) *shall be* ...	(*I*) *should be* ...	
serai	serais	
seras	serais	
sera	serait	
serons	serions	
serez	seriez	
seront	seraient	
Perfect		*Perfect*
(*I*) *have been* ...		(*that I*) *may have been* ...
ai été		aie été
as été		aies été
a été		ait été
avons été		ayons été
avez été		ayez été
ont été		aient été
Pluperfect		
(*I*) *had been* ...		
avais été		
avais été		
avait été		
avions été		
aviez été		
avaient été		

INDICATIVE	CONDITIONAL	SUBJUNCTIVE
Past Anterior		*Pluperfect*
(*I*) *had been* ...		(*that I*) *might have been* ...
eus été		eusse été
eus été		eusses été
eut été		eût été
eûmes été		eussions été
eûtes été		eussiez été
eurent été		eussent été
Future Anterior	*Past* or *Perfect*	
(*I*) *shall have been* ...	(*I*) *should have been* ...	
aurai été	aurais été	
auras été	aurais été	
aura été	aurait été	
aurons été	aurions été	
aurez été	auriez été	
auront été	auraient été	

IMPERATIVE	INFINITIVE	PARTICIPLES
sois, *be*	*Present*	*Present*
	to be	being
soyons, *let's be*	être	étant
	Perfect	*Perfect*
soyez, *be*	to have been	having been
	avoir été	ayant été

THREE REGULAR CONJUGATIONS

ACTIVE VOICE

INDICATIVE

I   II   III

Present

(I) carry, (I) am carrying, (I) do carry . . .	*(I) finish, (I) am finishing, (I) do finish* . . .	*(I) sell, (I) am selling, (I) do sell* . . .
porte	finis	vends
portes	finis	vends
porte	finit	vend
portons	finissons	vendons
portez	finissez	vendez
portent	finissent	vendent

Imperfect

(I) was carrying . . .	*(I) was finishing* . . .	*(I) was selling* . . .
portais	finissais	vendais
portais	finissais	vendais
portait	finissait	vendait
portions	finissions	vendions
portiez	finissiez	vendiez
portaient	finissaient	vendaient

Past Definite

(I) carried . . .	*(I) finished* . . .	*(I) sold* . . .
portai	finis	vendis
portas	finis	vendis
porta	finit	vendit

I	II	III
portâmes	finîmes	vendîmes
portâtes	finîtes	vendîtes
portèrent	finirent	vendirent

Future

(I) shall carry . . .	*(I) shall finish* . . .	*(I) shall sell* . . .
porterai	finirai	vendrai
porteras	finiras	vendras
portera	finira	vendra
porterons	finirons	vendrons
porterez	finirez	vendrez
porteront	finiront	vendront

Past Indefinite

(I) have carried . . .	*(I) have finished* . . .	*(I) have sold* . . .
ai porté	ai fini	ai vendu
as porté, etc.	as fini, etc.	as vendu, etc.

Pluperfect

(I) had carried . . .	*(I) had finished* . . .	*(I) had sold* . . .
avais porté	avais fini	avais vendu
avais porté, etc.	avais fini, etc.	avais vendu, etc.

Past Anterior

(I) had carried . . .	*(I) had finished* . . .	*(I) had sold* . . .
eus porté	eus fini	eus vendu
eus porté, etc.	eus fini, etc.	eus vendu, etc.

Future Anterior

(I) shall have carried . . .	*(I) shall have finished* . . .	*(I) shall have sold* . . .
aurai porté	aurai fini	aurai vendu
auras porté, etc.	auras fini, etc.	auras vendu, etc.

CONDITIONAL

I	II	III

Present

(*I*) *should carry* . . .	(*I*) *should finish* . . .	(*I*) *should sell* . . .
porterais	finirais	vendrais
porterais	finirais	vendrais
porterait	finirait	vendrait
porterions	finirions	vendrions
porteriez	finiriez	vendriez
porteraient	finiraient	vendraient

Past

(*I*) *should have carried* . .	(*I*) *should have finished* . . .	(*I*) *should have sold* . . .
aurais porté	aurais fini	aurais vendu
aurais porté, etc.	aurais fini, etc.	aurais vendu, etc.

SUBJUNCTIVE

Present

(*that I*) *may carry* . . .	(*that I*) *may finish* . . .	(*that I*) *may sell* . . .
porte	finisse	vende
portes	finisses	vendes
porte	finisse	vende
portions	finissions	vendions
portiez	finissiez	vendiez
portent	finissent	vendent

Imperfect

(*that I*) *might carry* . . .	(*that I*) *might finish* . . .	(*that I*) *might sell* . . .
portasse	finisse	vendisse
portasses	finisses	vendisses
portât	finît	vendît

I	II	III
portassions	finissions	vendissions
portassiez	finissiez	vendissiez
portassent	finissent	vendissent

Perfect

(that I) may have carried . . .	*(that I) may have finished . . .*	*(that I) may have sold . . .*
aie porté	aie fini	aie vendu
aies porté, etc.	aies fini, etc.	aies vendu, etc.

Pluperfect

(that I) might have carried . . .	*(that I) might have finished . . .*	*(that I) might have sold . . .*
eusse porté	eusse fini	eusse vendu
eusses porté, etc.	eusses fini, etc.	eusses vendu, etc.

IMPERATIVE

carry . . .	*finish . . .*	*sell . . .*
porte	finis	vends
portons	finissons	vendons
portez	finissez	vendez

INFINITIVES

Present

To carry	*To finish*	*To sell*
porter	finir	vendre

Perfect

To have carried	*To have finished*	*To have sold*
avoir porté	avoir fini	avoir vendu

PARTICIPLES

Present

Carrying	*Finishing*	*Selling*
portant	finissant	vendant

I	II	III

Perfect

Having carried	*Having finished*	*Having sold*
ayant porté	ayant fini	ayant vendu

PASSIVE VOICE

INDICATIVE

Present

(I) am (being) praised, etc.   . . . *cured*, etc.   . . . *caught*, etc.

suis ⎫		suis ⎫		suis ⎫	
es ⎬	loué(e)	es ⎬	guéri(e)	es ⎬	pris(e)
est ⎭		est ⎭		est ⎭	

sommes ⎫		sommes ⎫		somm ⎫	
êtes ⎬	loué(e)s	êtes ⎬	guéri(e)s	êtes ⎬	pris(e)s
sont ⎭		sont ⎭		sont ⎭	

Imperfect

(I) was praised, etc.   . . . *cured*, etc.   . . . *caught*, etc.

étais ⎫			
étais ⎬	loué(e)	guéri(e)	pris(e)
était ⎭			

étions ⎫			
étiez ⎬	loué(e)s	guéri(e)s	pris(e)s
étaient ⎭			

Past Definite

(I) was praised, etc.   . . . *cured*, etc.   . . . *caught*, etc.

fus ⎫			
fus ⎬	loué(e)	guéri(e)	pris(e)
fut ⎭			

fûmes ⎫			
fûtes ⎬	loué(e)s	guéri(e)s	pris(e)s
furent ⎭			

I	II	III

Future

(*I*) *shall be praised*, etc.	. . . *cured*, etc.	. . . *caught*, etc.
serai seras sera } loué(e)	guéri(e)	pris(e)
serons serez seront } loué(e)s	guéri(e)s	pris(e)s

Past Indefinite

(*I*) *have been praised*, etc.	. . . *cured*, etc.	. . . *caught*, etc.
ai été as été a été } loué(e)	guéri(e)	pris(e)
avons été avez été ont } loué(e)s	guéri(e)s	pris(e)s

Pluperfect

(*I*) *had been praised*, etc.	. . . *cured*, etc.	. . . *caught*, etc.
avais été avais été avait été } loué(e)	guéri(e)	pris(e)
avions été aviez été avaient été } loué(e)s	guéri(e)s	pris(e)s

Past Anterior

(*I*) *had been praised*, etc.	. . . *cured*, etc.	. . . *caught*, etc.
eus été eus été eut été } loué(e)	guéri(e)	pris(e)

	I	II	III

eûmes été ⎫
eûtes été ⎬ loué(e)s   guéri(e)s   pris(e)s
eurent été ⎭

Future Anterior

(*I*) *shall have been* . . . *cured*, etc.   . . . *caught*, etc.
praised, etc.

aurai été ⎫
auras été ⎬ loué(e)   guéri(e)   pris(e)
aura été ⎭

aurons été ⎫
aurez été ⎬ loué(e)s   guéri(e)s   pris(e)s
auront été ⎭

CONDITIONAL

Present

(*I*) *should be praised*, . . . *cured*, etc.   . . . *caught*, etc.
etc.

serais ⎫
serais ⎬   loué(e)   guéri(e)   pris(e)
serait ⎭

serions ⎫
seriez ⎬   loué(e)s   guéri(e)s   pris(e)s
seraient ⎭

Past

(*I*) *should have been* . . . *cured*, etc.   . . . *caught*, etc.
praised, etc.

aurais été ⎫
aurais été ⎬ loue(e)   guéri(e)   pris(e)
aurait été ⎭

aurions été ⎫
auriez été ⎬ loué(e)s   guéri(e)s   pris(e)s
auraient été ⎭

SUBJUNCTIVE

I	II	III

Present

(*That I*) *may be praised*, etc.	. . . *cured*, etc.	. . . *caught*, etc.
sois sois loué(e) soit	guéri(e)	pris(e)
soyons soyez loué(e)s soient	guéri(e)s	pris(e)s

Imperfect

(*That I*) *might be praised*, etc.	. . . *cured*, etc.	. . . *caught*, etc.
fusse fusses loué(e) fût	guéri(e)	pris(e)
fussions fussiez loué(e)s fussent	guéri(e)s	pris(e)s

Perfect

(*That I*) *may have been praised*, etc.	. . . *cured*, etc.	. . . *caught*, etc.
aie été aies été loué(e) ait été	guéri(e)	pris(e)
ayons été ayez été loué(e)s aient été	guéri(e)s	pris(e)s

Pluperfect

(*That I*) *might have been praised*, etc.	. . . *cured*, etc.	. . . *caught*, etc.
eusse été eusses été loué(e) eût été	guéri(e)	pris(e)

I	II	III
eussions été ⎱ eussiez été ⎰loué(e)s eussent été	guéri(e)s	pris(e)s

IMPERATIVE

Be praised, etc.	*Be cured*, etc.	*Be caught*, etc.
sois loué(e)	guéri(e)	pris(e)
soyons loué(e)s	guéri(e)s	pris(e)s
soyez loué(e)(s)	guéri(e)(s)	pris(e)(s)

INFINITIVES

To be praised être loué(e)(s)	*. . . cured* guéri(e)(s)	*. . . caught* pris(e)(s)

Perfect

To have been praised avoir été loué(e)(s)	*. . . cured* guéri(e)(s)	*. . . caught* pris(e)(s)

PARTICIPLES

Present

Being praised étant loué(e)(s)	*Being cured* étant guéri(e)(s)	*Being caught* étant pris(e)(s)

Perfect

Having been praised ayant été loué(e)(s)	*Having been cured* ayant été guéri(e)(s)	*Having been caught* ayant été pris(e)(s)

Pronominal Voice

INDICATIVE

Present *I wash myself . . .* je me lave tu te laves il se lave	*Past Indefinite* *I have washed myself . . .* je me suis lavé(e) tu t'es lavé(e) il s'est lavé

nous nous lavons

vous vous lavez

ils se lavent

nous nous sommes lavé(e)s

vous vous êtes lavé(e)s

ils se sont lavés

Imperfect

I was washing myself, I washed myself . . .

je me lavais, etc.

nous nous lavions, etc.

Pluperfect

I had washed myself . . .

je m'étais lavé(e), etc.

nous nous étions lavé(e)s, etc.

Past Definite

I washed myself . . .

je me lavai, etc.

nous nous lavâmes, etc.

Past Anterior

I had washed myself . . .

je me fus lavé(e), etc.

nous nous fûmes lavé(e)s, etc.

Future

I shall wash myself . . .

je me laverai, etc.

nous nous laverons, etc.

Future Anterior

I shall have washed myself . . .

je me serai lavé(e), etc.

nous nous serons lavé(e)s, etc.

CONDITIONAL

Present

I should wash myself . . .

je me laverais, etc.

nous nous laverions, etc.

Past

I should have washed myself . . .

je me serais lavé(e), etc.

nous nous serions lavé(e)s, etc.

SUBJUNCTIVE

Present

(That) I wash myself . . .

je me lave, etc.

nous nous lavions, etc.

Perfect

(That) I have washed myself . . .

je me sois lavé(e), etc.

nous nous soyons lavé(e)s, etc.

Imperfect

(That) I was washing myself, I washed myself . . .

je me lavasse, etc.

nous nous lavassions, etc.

Pluperfect

(That) I had washed myself . . .

je me fusse lavé(e), etc.

nous nous fussions lavé(e)s

IMPERATIVE

Wash yourself . . .

lave-toi

lavons-nous

lavez-vous

INFINITIVES

Present	Perfect
To wash oneself	To have washed oneself
se laver	s'être lavé(e)(s)

PARTICIPLES

Present	Perfect
Washing oneself	Having washed oneself
se lavant	s'étant lavé(e)(s)

PRINCIPAL PARTS OF IRREGULAR VERBS

This list comprises the principal parts[1] (the *infinitive, present participle, past participle, present indicative,* and *past definite*) of most irregular verbs. It also contains the irregular futures (*F.*) and subjunctive presents (*S. P.*)[2]. Irregular imperatives are already mentioned, p. 66.

1. acquérir, *to acquire*

acquérant	acquis	acquiers	acquérons	acquis
		acquiers	acquérez	
		acquiert	acquièrent	
		F. acquerrai		

2. aller, *to go*

allant	allé	vais	allons	allai
		vas	allez	
		va	vont	
		F. irai		*S.P.* aille

3. asseoir, *to seat*

asseyant	assis	assieds[3]	asseyons	assis
		assieds	asseyez	
		assied	asseyent	
		F. asseyerai, assiérai or assoirai		

---

[1] The full present indicative is given here although the first person alone is a part of the principal parts.

[2] Most subjunctive presents are *regularly* derived from the 3d person plural present indicative.

[3] *See also* **assois,** p. 121.

4. avoir, *to have*

ayant	eu	ai	avons	eus
		as	avez	
		a	ont	
		F. aurai		*S.P.* aie

5. battre, *to beat*

battant	battu	bats	battons	battis
		bats	battez	
		bat	battent	

6. boire, *to drink*

buvant	bu	bois	buvons	bus
		bois	buvez	
		boit	boivent	

7. bouillir, *to boil*

bouillant	bouilli	bous	bouillons	bouillis
		bous	bouillez	
		bout	bouillent	

8. conclure, *to conclude*

concluant	conclu	conclus	concluons	conclus
		conclus	concluez	
		conclut	concluent	

9. conduire, *to lead*

conduisant	conduit	conduis	conduisons	conduisis
		conduis	conduisez	
		conduit	conduisent	

10. connaître, *to be acquainted with*

connaissant	connu	connais	connaissons	connus
		connais	connaissez	
		connaît	connaissent	

11. coudre, *to sew*

cousant	cousu	couds	cousons	cousis
		couds	cousez	
		coud	cousent	

12. courir, *to run*

courant	couru	cours	courons	courus
		cours	courez	
		court	courent	

F. courrai

13. craindre, *to fear*

craignant	craint	crains	craignons	craignis
		crains	craignez	
		craint	craignent	

14. croire, *to believe*

croyant	cru	crois	croyons	crus
		crois	croyez	
		croit	croient	

15. Croître, *to grow*

croissant	crû	croîs	croissons	crûs
		croîs	croissez	
		croît	croissent	

16. cueillir, *to gather, pick*

cueillant	cueilli	cueille	cueillons	cueillis
		cueilles	cueillez	
		cueille	cueillent	

F. cueillerai

17. devoir, *to owe*

devant	dû	dois	devons	dus
		dois	devez	
		doit	doivent	

F. devrai

18. dire, *to say, tell*

disant	dit	dis	disons	dis
		dis	dites	
		dit	disent	

19. dormir, *to sleep*

dormant	dormi	dors	dormons	dormis
		dors	dormez	
		dort	dorment	

20. écrire, *to write*

écrivant	écrit	écris	écrivons	écrivis
		écris	écrivez	
		écrit	écrivent	

21. envoyer, *to send*

envoyant	envoyé	envoie	envoyons	envoyai
		envoies	envoyez	
		envoie	envoient	
		F. enverrai		

22. être, *to be*

étant	été	suis	sommes	fus
		es	êtes	
		est	sont	
		F. serai		*S.P.* sois

23. faillir, *to fail* (Little used except in *past def.*, *fut.*, and *compound tenses*.)

faillant	failli	faux	faillons	faillis
		faux	faillez	
		faut	faillent	
		F. faudrai *or* faillirai		

24. faire, *to do, make*

faisant	fait	fais	faisons	fis
		fais	faites	
		fait	font	
		F. ferai		*S.P.* fasse

25. falloir, *to be necessary*

(none)	fallu	il faut (impersonal)		il fallut
		F. il faudra		*S.P.* il faille

26. fuir, *to flee*

fuyant	fui	fuis	fuyons	fuis
		fuis	fuyez	
		fuit	fuient	

27. haïr, *to hate*

haïssant	haï	hais	haïssons	haïs
		hais	haïssez	
		hait	haïssent	

28. lire, *to read*

lisant	lu	lis	lisons	lus
		lis	lisez	
		lit	lisent	

29. luire, *to shine* (Has no *past def.*, *imper.*, or *impf. subj.*)

luisant	lui	luis	luisons	(none)
		luis	luisez	
		luit	luisent	

30. maudire, *to curse*

maudissant	maudit	maudis	maudissons	maudis
		maudis	maudissez	
		maudit	maudissent	

31. mettre, *to put*

mettant	mis	mets	mettons	mis
		mets	mettez	
		met	mettent	

32. moudre, *to grind*

moulant	moulu	mouds	moulons	moulus
		mouds	moulez	
		moud	moulent	

33. mourir, *to die*

mourant	mort	meurs	mourons	mourus
		meurs	mourez	
		meurt	meurent	
		F. mourrai		

34. mouvoir, *to move*

mouvant	mû	meus	mouvons	mus
		meus	mouvez	
		meut	meuvent	
		F. mouvrai		

35. naître, *to be born*

naissant	né	nais	naissons	naquis
		nais	naissez	
		nait	naissent	

36. offrir, *to offer*

offrant	offert	offre	offrons	offris
		offres	offrez	
		offre	offrent	

37. plaire, *to please*

plaisant	plu	plais	plaisons	plus
		plais	plaisez	
		plaît	plaisent	

38. pleuvoir, *to rain*

| pleuvant | plu | il pleut (*impersonal*) | il plut |
| | | *F.* il pleuvra | |

39. pouvoir, *to be able*

pouvant	pu	puis, peux	pouvons	pus
		peux	pouvez	
		peut	peuvent	
		F. pourrai	*S.P.* puisse

40. prendre, *to take*

prenant	pris	prends	prenons	pris
		prends	prenez	
		prend	prennent	

41. recevoir, *to receive*

recevant	reçu	reçois	recevons	reçus
		reçois	recevez	
		reçoit	reçoivent	
		F. recevrai	

42. résoudre, *to resolve*

résolvant	résolu	résous	résolvons	résolus
		résous	résolvez	
		résout	résolvent	

43. rire, *to laugh*

riant	ri	ris	rions	ris
		ris	riez	
		rit	rient	

44. savoir, *to know*

sachant	su	sais	savons	sus
		sais	savez	
		sait	savent	

F. saurai   *S.P.* sache

45. suffire, *to suffice*

suffisant	suffi	suffis	suffisons	suffis
		suffis	suffisez	
		suffit	suffisent	

46. suivre, *to follow*

suivant	suivi	suis	suivons	suivis
		suis	suivez	
		suit	suivent	

47. tenir, *to hold*

tenant	tenu	tiens	tenons	tins
		tiens	tenez	
		tient	tiennent	

F. tiendrai

48. traire, *to milk*

trayant	trait	trais	trayons	(none)
		trais	trayez	
		trait	traient	

49. vaincre, *to conquer*

vainquant	vaincu	vaincs	vainquons	vainquis
		vaincs	vainquez	
		vainc	vainquent	

50. valoir, *to be worth*

valant	valu	vaux	valons	valus
		vaux	valez	
		vaut	valent	

F. vaudrai   *S.P.* vaille

51. venir, *to come*

venant	venu	viens	venons	vins
		viens	venez	
		vient	viennent	

F. viendrai

52. vêtir, *to clothe*

vêtant	vêtu	vêts	vêtons	vêtis
		vêts	vêtez	
		vêt	vêtent	

53. vivre, *to live*

vivant	vécu	vis	vivons	vécus
		vis	vivez	
		vit	vivent	

54. voir, *to see*

voyant	vu	vois	voyons	vis
		vois	voyez	
		voit	voient	

F. verrai

55. vouloir, *to want*

voulant	voulu	veux	voulons	voulus
		veux	voulez	
		veut	veulent	

F. voudrai *S.P.* veuille

List of Idiomatic Expressions

A*

par acquit de conscience, XXII, for conscience' sake
  s'agir de, II, to be a question of
    aller à la rencontre de, XVII, to go and meet
    aller au devant de, XVII, to go and meet
    allons, IV, come; come, come
  d'arrache-pied, XXII, in earnest, steadily
    assister à, VII, to attend
  s'attendre à, VI, to expect
  d'aujourd'hui en huit, IX, a week from today
  à l'avenir, XIV, in the future
  à l'aventure, VI, at random, aimlessly
    avoir affaire à, XV, to have to deal with
    avoir beau, IV, in vain, to be useless to
    avoir besoin de, I, to need, be in need of
    avoir bonne mine, I, to look fine
    avoir coutume de, I, to be in the habit of
    avoir de l'esprit, XX, to be witty
    avoir envie, I, to have a mind to
    avoir faim, I, to be hungry
    avoir honte de, I, to be ashamed of
    avoir l'air de, IV, to appear, look like, have the appearance of
    avoir le cœur gros, XXII, to be heartbroken
    avoir lieu, I, to take place
    avoir mal à la tête, II, to have a headache
    avoir mauvaise mine, I, to look ill
    avoir peur, I, to be afraid, fear
    avoir raison, I, to be right
    avoir soif, I, to be thirsty
    avoir soin de, I, to take care of
    avoir sommeil, I, to be sleepy

---

* The Roman numbers refer to lessons.

avoir sujet de, I, to have cause for
avoir tort, I, to be wrong
avoir une occasion de, XI, to have an opportunity to
avoir un rendez-vous, XX, to have an engagement

B

au beau milieu, XI, in the very middle of
à la belle étoile, VI, in the open
à la belle saison, XIII, in the summer, in fine weather
bien entendu, II, of course
de bon cœur, XVIII, willingly
bon marché, XI, cheap, inexpensive
de bonne heure, XI, early
à la bonne heure! XVI, fine! well done!
au bout de, X, at the end of

C

cela coûte cher, XVIII, it's expensive
cela ne me fait ni froid ni chaud, XIII, it's all the same
    to me
c'est-à-dire, III, that is to say
c'est aujourd'hui le 27 septembre, IX, today is September 27
c'est entendu, IV, agreed, very well
c'est une question de, II, it is a question, matter of
cette chambre a dix mètres de large sur quinze mètres
    de long, XXI, this room is ten meters wide by fifteen
    meters long
chanter à pleine gorge, XIII, to sing loudly, at the top of
    one's voice
le combien sommes-nous? IX, what day of the month is it?
comme il vous plaira, XII, please yourself, as you like it
au contraire, IV, on the contrary
contre toute attente, XIII, without any warning, con-
    trary to all expectation
à côté de, III, beside, next to
du côté de, III, in the direction of
à coup sûr, XVIII, certainly
courir la prétentaine, XIII, to gad about, run around
courir le risque de, I, to run the risk

courir par monts et par vaux, XXII, to be always on
the move

crier comme un perdu, XXII, to shout (or talk) as loudly
as one can

D

d'ici un mois, XVI, a month from now, within a month

à Dieu ne plaise (que), XII, God forbid (that)

dire à l'oreille, XXII, to whisper

donner sur, VIII, to face, look out upon

se douter de, XV, to suspect

E

l'échapper belle, VI, to have a narrow escape

en effet, III, indeed, in fact

en faire autant, XI, to do likewise

n'en pas revenir, XXII, not to be able to get over it

en plein air, VIII, in the open, outdoors

en somme, III, in short

entendre dire, VIII, to hear (it) said

entendre parler de, X, to hear about

s'en tirer, X, to get along

envoyer chercher, III, to send for

et ainsi de suite, XI, and so on

être à même de, X, to be in a position to, able to

être bien aise (de), IX, to be glad to

être d'accord sur, XV, to be agreed on

être d'avis, XVII, to be of the opinion

être des nôtres, X, to be one of the party

être de retour, VIII, to be back

être en train de (+ inf.), IV, to be busy, be in the act of

être plus fort que soi, XIX, not to be able to help it

éventer la mèche, XXII, to let out a secret

F

se faire à, XVII, to get accustomed to

faire à sa tête, XV, to have one's own way

se faire attendre, X, to make people wait for oneself

faire beau, V, to be fine weather
faire bonne chère, XVII, to eat well
faire de son mieux, VI, to do one's best
faire du mieux qu'on peut, XIX, to do the best one can
faire grand cas de, X, to attach great importance to
faire la connaissance de, VII, to become acquainted with
faire la cuisine, XX, to cook
faire la grimace, XX, to make faces
faire la lecon, XIII, to teach a lesson
faire la sourde oreille, XVI, to turn a deaf ear
faire le malade, V, to pretend to be sick
faire mal, XIV, to hurt, ache
faire mauvais, V, to be bad weather
faire mention de, IX, to mention
faire mine de ne pas comprendre, V, to pretend not to
    understand
faire partie de, VII, to belong
faire sa malle, XIV, to pack one's trunk
faire semblant de, V, to pretend to
se faire un plaisir de, XIII, to take pleasure in
faire un voyage, XVII, to take a trip
il fait jour, XVIII, it is dawning
il fait lourd, XXI, the weather is sultry
il se fait avocat, XVII, he becomes a lawyer
il se fait tard, VII, it is late, it is getting late
finir par (+ *inf.*), VIII, finally, to end up by
à fleur de terre, XV, even with the ground

G

gagner sa vie, XX, to earn one's living
des gens comme il faut, XVII, well-bred people
grâce à Dieu, XVIII, thank God
au grand jamais, XVIII, no, never
de grand matin, XXII, early in the morning
à son gré, XV, to his liking, his taste

I

il est cinq heures et demie, XXI, it is half past five
il est cinq heures et quart, XXI, it is a quarter past five

il est cinq heures moins le quart, XXI, it is quarter to
    five

il est de bonne politique, XXI, it is wise, good sense

il est une heure moins vingt-cinq, XXI, it is twenty-five
    minutes to one.

il n'y a pas de quoi, XIX, don't mention it, never mind

il y a, II, ago

il y a, III, there is, there are

il y a une semaine, IX, a week ago

il y va de, XVII, it is a question of, (it) is at stake

L

lier connaissance, XXI, to become acquainted

de long en large, XV, up and down

à la longue, XX, in the long run

M

manquer de, VI, to come near + *pres. part.*, almost

se mettre à, V, to begin, start

(le) mettre à la porte, XVIII, to show (him) the door

les mettre aux prises, XIX, to set them fighting

se mettre d'accord sur, XX, to agree on

mettre le couvert, XVIII, to set the table

au moins, II, at least

du moins, II, at least

mon Dieu, XVIII, heavens! goodness!

se monter la tête, XX, to get excited

se moquer de, IX, to make fun of

mourir d'envie, XV, to long for

N

nulle part, XVI, nowhere

je n'y puis rien, VII, I can't help it

O

obéir à, VIII, to obey, to abide by

s'occuper de, XI, to look after

P

par-dessus le marché, XIX, into the bargain, moreover
de parti pris, VII, deliberately
à partir de, VIII, beginning from, from . . . on
pas grand' chose, XXI, not much
pas que je sache, VII, not that I know of
se passer de, VI, to do without
passer une nuit blanche, XXII, to spend a sleepless night
passer un examen, XIX, to take an examination
à peine, III, hardly, scarcely
pendant des semaines, XXII, for weeks
penser à, VIII, to think of, direct one's thought to
penser de, VIII, to think (have an opinion) of
y perdre son latin, VII, not to be able to make head or tail of it
peu importe, VI, little matters, it matters little
à peu près, IV, nearly, almost
plaît-il, XII, I beg your pardon, what did you say?
pleuvoir à verse, IX, to be pouring
à plus forte raison, XIX, all the more
pour de bon, XIX, in earnest, for good
n'en pouvoir plus, XIII, to be exhausted
au premier abord, XIX, at first glance, sight, on one's approach
s'en prendre à, XIV, to blame, lay the blame on
prendre l'habitude de, XX, to get into the habit of
prendre quelqu'un en grippe, XIV, to take a dislike to someone
prendre son courage à deux mains, XI, to summon one's courage
prendre un parti, VII, to make up one's mind
à propos, XVIII, by the way

Q

quant à, III, as for, as to, as regards
qu'avez-vous? III, what's the matter with you?

quel jour du mois est-ce? IX, what day of the month
   is it?

quelle date sommes-nous? IX, what day of the month
   is it?

quelle heure est-il? XXI, what time is it?

à qui le dites-vous? X, don't I know?

à quoi bon? VI, what's the use? what for?

R

raconter tout au long, XIX, to tell at length

rebrousser chemin, VII, to turn back

rendre visite, XIII, to call on, pay a visit

rentrer chez soi, XIII, to go (back) home

rien de beau, XIV, nothing beautiful

S

sauter aux yeux, IX, to be obvious, evident

savoir bon gré à quelqu'un de, XI, to be thankful to
   someone for

servir de, XIV, to serve as

se servir de, XIV, to use, make use of

s'il vous plait, XII, (if you) please

de la sorte, XV, thus, so, in this manner

sur-le-champ, XI, at once

T

tant mieux, XVI, so much the better

tant pis, XVI, so much the worse

à tantôt, XIV, good-bye for the present, so long

de temps à autre, XV, from time to time

tenir à, II, to be anxious to, to care for

tiens! IV, well!

se tirer d'affaire, X, to get along, to manage

tirer parti de, X, to profit by

à tort et à travers, XX, at random

tous les deux, tous deux, IX, both
tout à fait, II, altogether
tout à l'heure, II, IV, in a little while
tout de même, X, all the same, just the same
tout de suite, II, at once
à toute heure, IV, at any time
à toute vitesse, IX, at full speed

V

venir à bout de, XIV, to succeed
venir de (+ *inf.*), II, to have just
veuillez, XII, please
en vouloir à, VI, to have a grudge against, be offended at
vouloir bien, V, to be willing, like to
s'en vouloir de, XII, not to forgive oneself for
vouloir dire, V, to mean
vouloir du mal, XII, to bear ill will to
voyons! IV, surely; come! come!

VOCABULARIES

Irregular verbs are preceded by an asterisk(*). See list of irregular verbs and their principal parts, pp. 218–225.

"H" aspirate is indicated by a cross (†).

A

*abattre [abatr], to fell

abbaye [abeji] *f.*, monastery

abdomen [abdɔmɛn] *m.*, abdomen

abîme [abiːm] *m.*, abyss

aboi [abwa] *m.*, (a dog's) bark

aboyer [abwaje], to bark

abricot [abriko] *m.*, apricot

abruti [abryti] *m.*, sot, fool

absolu, -e [apsɔly], absolute

*absoudre [apsudr], to absolve; to forgive

accent [aksã] *m.*, accent

acclamer [aklɑme], to acclaim

accord [akɔːr] *m.*, accord, settlement

accorder [akɔrde], to grant

*accourir [akuriːr], to come in a hurry

s'accoutumer [sakutyme], to get accustomed

accru [akry] *m.*, sucker (*gardening*)

acheter [aʃte], to buy

achever [aʃve], to finish, end

acier [asje] *m.*, steel

*acquérir [akeriːr], to acquire

acteur [aktœːr] *m.*, actor

actrice [aktris] *f.*, actress

Adam [adã] *m.*, Adam

admirable [admirabl], admirable

aérer [aere], to air

agenda [aʒēda] *m.*, memorandum book

agiter [aʒite], to agitate, upset

agrandir [agrãdiːr], to enlarge

aide de camp [ɛdəkã] *m.*, aide-de-camp

aider [ɛde], to help

aïeul [ajœl], *pl.* aïeux [ajø] *m.*, ancestor

aigu, -ë [egy], sharp, pointed

aiguiser [egize], to sharpen; to stimulate

aimable [ɛmabl], amiable

aimer [ɛme], to love, like

ainsi [ēsi], thus, so

air [ɛːr] *m.*, air, tune

album [albɔm] *m.*, album

alcool [alkɔl] *m.*, alcohol

Allemagne [almaɲ] *f.*, Germany

allemand, -e [almã, -ɪd], *adj.*, German

235

*aller [ale], to go
*s'en aller [sãnale], to go away, leave
allumer [alyme], to light
alun [alœ̃] *m.*, alum
amant [amɑ̃] *m.*, lover
ambiguité [ãbigɥite] *f.*, ambiguity
âme [ɑːm] *f.*, soul, spirit
amen [amɛn] *interjection and n. m.*, amen
amener [amne], to bring along
ami [ami] *m.*, friend; amie [ami] *f.*, friend
amitié [amitje] *f.*, friendship
ample [ãːpl], ample, spacious
Amsterdam [amstɛrdam] *f.*, Amsterdam
s'amuser [samyze], to have a good time
an [ã] *m.*, year
analyser [analize], to analyze
ancien, -ne [ãsjɛ̃, -ɛn], ancient, former, old
âne [ɑːn] *m.*, donkey
Anglais [ãglɛ] *m.*, Englishman
anglais, -e [ãglɛ, -ɪz] *adj.*, English
Angleterre [ãglətɛːr] *f.*, England
année [ane] *f.*, year
août [u] *m.*, August
apaiser [apɛze], to appease
*apercevoir [apɛrsəvwaːr], to perceive, see
*appartenir [apartəniːr], to belong
appel [apɛl] *m.*, call; répondre à l'— [repɔ̃ːdral—], to answer the call *or* roll
appeler [aple], to call

appendice [apẽdis] *m.*, appendix
applaudir [aplodiːr], to applaud
apporter [apɔrte], to bring
*apprendre [aprãːdr], to learn
apprêter [aprɛte], to get ready
apprivoisé, -e [aprivwaze], tame
approche [aprɔʃ] *f.*, drawing near
approfondir [aprɔfɔ̃dːir], to go deep into
appuyer [apɥije], to support
aquatique [akwatik], aquatic
aquilon [akilɔ̃] *m.*, north wind
arbre [arbr] *m.*, tree
arc-en-ciel [arkãsjɛl] *m.*, rainbow
argent [arʒã] *m.*, money, silver; *faire de l'— [fɛːrdəlarʒã], to make money
arome [arom] *m.*, aroma, perfume
arracher [araʃe], to pull out
arranger [arãʒe], to arrange; to regulate
arrêt [arɛ] *m.*, stop
s'arrêter [sarɛte], to stop
arriver [arive], to arrive
arroser [aroze], to water
*assaillir [asajiːr], to assail
*asseoir [aswaːr], to seat
*s'asseoir [saswaːr], to sit (down)
assez (de) [ase (də)], enough (of)
assis, -e [asi, -ɪz], seated
astre du jour [astrdyʒuːr] *m.*, sun
atelier [atəlje] *m.*, workroom
*atteindre [atẽːdr], to reach, attain
en attendant que [ãnatãdãkə], until, till, while

attendre [atãːdr], to wait for

attraper [atrape], to catch

aube [oːb] *f.*, dawn

auberge [obɛrʒ] *f.*, inn, tavern

aucun, -e [okœ̃, -yn] *pron.*, no one; *adj.* no, any (with negation understood or expressed)

audace [odas] *f.*, audacity, boldness

aujourd'hui [oʒurdɥi], today

auprès de [oprɛdə], near

auréole [ɔreɔl] *f.*, aureole, halo

aurore [ɔrɔːr] *f.*, dawn

aussi [osi], so, also, too

aussitôt [osito], at once

autant [otã], as much, as many; — de, so much, so many

automne [otɔn] *m. or f.*, fall, autumn

autour (de) [otuːr (də)], around

autrui [otrɥi], other people, others

avaler [avale], to swallow

avant [avã] *adv.*, before; — de (+ *infinitive*), before

avant-bras [avãbra] *m.*, forearm

avare [avaːr] *m.*, miser

avec [avɛk], with

avenir [avniːr] *m.*, future

aventure [avãtyːr] *f.*, adventure; à l'—, at random

aventurier [avãtyrje] *m.*, adventurer

avion [avjɔ̃] *m.*, airplane

avis [avi] *m.*, advice, opinion

*avoir [avwaːr], to have, to feel (pain, hunger, etc.); *avoir raison, to be right; qu'avez-vous, what is the matter?

avril [avril] *m.*, April

B

bague [bag] *f.*, ring

bail [baːj] *m.*, lease

bâiller [baje], to yawn

balayer [balɛje], to sweep

ban [bã] *m.*, ban, announcement

bas [bɑ] *m.*, stocking

bas, -se [bɑ, -is], low

basse-cour [bɑskuːr] *f.*, poultry yard

bataille [batɑːj *or* -aːj] *f.*, battle

batelier [batəlje] *m.*, boatman, ferryman

bâtir [bɑtiːr], to build

*battre [batr], to beat

*se battre [səbatr], to fight

beau, bel, belle [bo, bɛl], beautiful

beaucoup [boku] much, many; — de (+ *noun*), much, many

bébé [bebe] *m.*, baby

berger [bɛrʒe] *m.*, shepherd

bergère [bɛrʒɛːr] *f.*, shepherdess

bête [bɛːt] *f.*, animal

Bethléem [bɛtleɛm] *f.*, Bethlehem

bêtise [betiːz] *f.*, stupidity

beurrer [bœre], to butter (bread, etc.)

bicyclette [bisiklɛt] *f.*, bicycle

bien [bjɛ̃], well; — de (+ *noun*), much, many; eh — [e—], well, now then

bille [biːj] *f.*, billiard ball

bise [biːz] *f.*, north wind

blague [blag] *f.*, hoax, joke

blanc, blanche [blã, -iʃ], white

blé [ble] *m.*, wheat

blesser [blɛse], to wound

bleu [blø], blue

bœuf [bœf], *pl.* **bœufs** [bø] *m.*,
ox, beef

*****boire** [bwaːr], to drink

bois [bwɑ] *m.*, wood, woods

boisson [bwasɔ̃] *f.*, beverage

boîte [bwat] *f.*, box

bon, -ne [bɔ̃, -ɔn], good

bonheur [bɔnœːr] *m.*, happiness,
good fortune

bonifier [bɔnifje], to better, im-
prove

bonté [bɔ̃te] *f.*, kindness

bord [bɔːr] *m.*, shore, bank

borner [bɔrne], to bound, limit

bouche [buʃ] *f.*, mouth

boucher [buʃe] *m.*, butcher

*****bouillir** [bujiːr], to boil

boulanger [bulɑ̃ʒe] *m.*, baker

bourgeois [burʒwa] *m.*, burgher,
citizen, commoner

bourrer [bure], to stuff (a chair)

bout [bu] *m.*, end

bouteille [butɛːj] *f.*, bottle

boxe [bɔks] *f.*, boxing

bras [brɑ] *m.*, arm

brave [braːv], worthy, brave

bravo [bravo] *interjection and
n. m.*, bravo

briller [brije], to shine

brouillard [brujaːr] *m.*, fog

bru [bry] *f.*, daughter-in-law

bruit [brɥi] *m.*, noise

brûler [bryle], to burn

brumeux, -se [brymø, -ɪz],
foggy

brun, -e [brœ̃, -yn], brown

bûche [byʃ] *f.*, log; (*fig.*) block-
head

bureau [byro] *m.*, desk, office

C

cabaret [kabarɛ] *m.*, inn, tavern

câble [kɑːbl] *m.*, cable

se cabrer [səkabre], to rear

cacher [kaʃe], to hide

cadet, -te [kadɛ, -t], the young-
est (of a family), younger

cadre [kɑːdr] *m.*, frame, outline

café-dansant, *pl.* **cafés-dan-
sants** [kafedɑ̃sɑ̃] *m.*, café pro-
viding dancing

cage [kaːʒ] *f.*, cage; coop (for
fowls)

cahier [kaje] *m.*, notebook

caillou, *pl.* **cailloux** [kaju] *m.*,
pebble

calme [kalm] *m.*, calmness

camarade [kamarad] *m.*, comrade

campagne [kɑ̃paɲ] *f.*, country,
countryside; *****aller à la —, to
go to the country

camper [kɑ̃pe], to encamp

canaille [kanɑːj] *f.*, rabble;
scoundrel

canaliser [kanalize], to intersect
with canals

canne [kan] *f.*, cane; **— à épée**
[— aepe], swordstick

cantique [kɑ̃tik] *m.*, hymn

capitaine [kapitɛn] *m.*, captain

car [kaːr], for, because

caractère [karaktɛːr] *m.*, character (of alphabet); nature, dis-
position

carré [kɑre] *m.*, square

cas [kɑ] *m.*, case, instance

casque [kask] *m.*, helmet

casser [kɑse], to break

causer [koze], to cause, bring about; to chat, talk

caution [kosjõ] *f.*, bail; pledge

cave [kaːv] *f.*, cellar

ceci [səsi], this

*ceindre [sɛ̃ːdr], to encircle, wreathe

cela [səla, sla], that

célébrer [selebre], to celebrate

cendre [sãːdr] *f.*, ash(es)

centenier [sãtənje] *m.*, centurion

centuple [sãtypl] *m.*, hundred-fold; **au —**, a hundredfold

cercueil [sɛrkœːj] *m.*, coffin

cerfeuil [sɛrfœːj] *m.*, chervil (herb)

cesse [sɛs] *f.*, ceasing; **sans —** [sãsɛs], ceaselessly

chacun, -e [ʃakœ̃, -yn] *pron.*, each, everyone

chagrin [ʃagrɛ̃] *m.*, grief, pain

chaise [ʃɛːz] *f.*, chair

chaleur [ʃalœːr] *f.*, heat, warmth

chambre [ʃãːbr] *f.*, room

champ [ʃã] *m.*, field; **— de blé,** wheat field; **— de courses,** racecourse

chanceler [ʃãsle], to stagger

chandelier [ʃãdəlje] *m.*, candle-stick

changement [ʃãʒmã] *m.*, change

chant [ʃã] *m.*, song

chanteur [ʃãtœːr] *m.*, singer

chapeau [ʃapo] *m.*, hat

chaque [ʃak] *adj.*, each

se charger de [sə ʃarʒe də], to take care of, take upon one-self to

charmant,-e [ʃarmã, -ɪt], charming

charrue [ʃary] *f.*, plough

chartreuse [ʃartrøːz] *f.*, char-treuse (liqueur)

chasse [ʃɑs] *f.*, hunt

chat [ʃa] *m.*, cat

chaud [ʃo], hot, warm

chaume [ʃoːm] *m.*, thatch

chef-d'œuvre [ʃɛdœːvr] *m.*, masterpiece

chemin [ʃmɛ̃] *m.*, way, path, road

chêne [ʃɛːn] *m.*, oak

cher, chère [ʃɛːr], dear, expen-sive

chercher [ʃɛrʃe], to seek, look for; ***aller —,** to fetch

cheval [ʃəval] *m.*, horse

chez [ʃe], at the house of; **— moi** (**— mwa**), at my house, home

chien [ʃjɛ̃] *m.*, dog

chiffon [ʃifõ] *m.*, rag

chinois, -e [ʃinwa, -z], Chinese

choc [ʃɔk] *m.*, shock, collision

chœur [kœːr] *m.*, choir

choisir [ʃwaziːr], to choose, se-lect

cholérique [kɔlerik], choleric

chose [ʃoːz] *f.*, thing

chou, *pl.* **choux** [ʃu] *m.*, cabbage

chou-fleur [ʃuflœːr] *m.*, cauli-flower

chrétien, -ne [kretjɛ̃, -ɛn], Christian

chuchoter [ʃyʃɔte], to whisper

chute [ʃyt] *f.*, fall; failure

ciel [sjɛl], *pl.* **cieux** [sjø] *m.*, sky, heaven

cigale [sigal] *f.*, cicada, cricket

ciguë [sigy] *f.*, hemlock

cinq [sɛ̃ːk], five

cirage [sira:ʒ] *m.*, waxing, wax (for floors, leather)

citoyen [sitwajɛ̃] *m.*, citizen

clair, -e [klɛːr], clear

clef [kle] *f.*, key

climat [klimɑ] *m.*, climate

cloison [klwazɔ̃] *f.*, partition

clos, -e [klo, -iz], closed, shut; finished

clouage [kluaːʒ] *m.*, nailing

cœur [kœːr] *m.*, heart

coffre-fort [kɔfrfɔːr] *m.*, safe

coin [kwɛ̃] *m.*, corner

colère [kɔlɛːr] *f.*, anger

colline [kɔlin] *f.*, hill

colonel [kɔlɔnɛl] *m.*, colonel

colorer [kɔlɔre], to color

colosse [kɔlɔs] *m.*, colossus

***combattre** [kɔ̃batr], to fight

au comble de [okɔ̃bldə], at the height of

commande [kɔmɑ̃ːd] *f.*, order

comme [kɔm], as, like; how (*exclam.*)

commère [kɔmɛːr] *f.*, gossip

commun, -e [kɔmœ̃, -yn], common; vulgar

compagnon [kɔ̃paɲɔ̃] *m.*, companion, fellow

compère [kɔ̃pɛːr] *m.*, comrade

***comprendre** [kɔ̃prɑ̃ːdr], to understand, comprise

compte: pour son — [puːrsɔ̃kɔ̃ːt], on his own account

comte [kɔ̃ːt] *m.*, count

***conclure** [kɔ̃klyːr], to conclude

condamner [kɔ̃dɑne], to condemn

***conduire** [kɔ̃dɥiːr], to lead

***se conduire** [səkɔ̃dɥiːr], to behave

confier [kɔ̃fje], to confide; **se — à**, to confide in

***connaître** [kɔnɛitr], to know, be acquainted with; **se — à**, to be a judge of: **je m'y connais,** I am a good judge of it; **se — en** (+ *noun*): **je me connais en art,** I am a good judge of art

conquérant [kɔ̃kerɑ̃] *m.*, conqueror

conseil [kɔ̃sɛij] *m.*, advice

conserver [kɔ̃sɛrve], to keep

constamment [kɔ̃stamɑ̃], constantly

conte [kɔ̃ːt] *m.*, short story

content, -e [kɔ̃tɑ̃, -it], happy, contented, satisfied

continuer [kɔ̃tinɥe], to continue

contre [kɔ̃ːtr], against

contrée [kɔ̃tre] *f.*, countryside, region

coq [kɔk] *m.*, rooster

cor [kɔːr] *m.*, horn

corbeille [kɔrbɛij] *f.*, basket; **à pleines —s,** in basketfuls

corde [kɔrd] *f.*, rope; ***mourir par la —,** to hang, be hanged

corps [kɔːr] *m.*, body; matter

corriger [kɔriʒe], to correct

côte [koːt] *f.*, slope; rib

côté [kote] *m.*, side

coton [kɔtɔ̃] *m.*, cotton

couard [kwaːr] *m.*, coward

coucher [kuʃe], to put to bed; **se coucher,** to go to bed, lie down; to set (sun)

coucou [kuku] *m.*, cuckoo

*coudre [kuːdr], to sew; **une machine à —**, a sewing machine

couenne [kwan] *f.*, crackling (of pork)

couler [kule], to flow

coup [ku] *m.*, blow, strike; **à —s redoublés**, repeatedly; **— de poing** [—dpwɛ̃], punch

coupable [kupabl], guilty

cour [kuːr] *f.*, court (of justice)

*courir [kuriːr], to run; **— par monts et par vaux** [— par mɔ̃zeparvo], to be always on the move

cours [kuːr] *m.*, course; **— d'eau** [— do], brook

course [kurs] *f.*, race; **— de taureaux,** bull fight

court, -e [kuːr, -t], short

couteau [kuto] *m.*, knife

coûter [kute], to cost

couvert, -e [kuvɛɪr, -t], *p.p. of* *couvrir, covered

*couvrir [kuvriːr], to cover

craie [krɛ] *f.*, chalk

*craindre [krɛ̃ːdr], to fear

crampe [krɑ̃ːp] *f.*, cramp

cravate [kravat] *f.*, tie

crayon [krɛjɔ̃] *m.*, pencil

créer [kree], to create

crêpe [krɛːp] *m.*, crape; *f.*, pancake

cresson [krəsɔ̃] *m.*, water cress

creuser [krøze], to dig, hollow out

creux, -se [krø, -ɪz], hollow, empty

cri [kri] *m.*, shout, cry

crier [krie], to shout, cry out

crinière [krinjɛɪr] *f.*, mane

*croire [krwaɪr], to believe

croiser [krwaze], to cross

*croître [krwaːtr], to grow

croix [krwa] *f.*, cross

cruauté [kryote] *f.*, cruelty

*cueillir [kœjiːr], to gather, pick

cuisinier [kɥizinje] *m.*, cook

curer [kyre], to cleanse

cycle [sikl] *m.*, cycle

cygne [siɲ] *m.*, swan

cynique [sinik], cynical

D

d'abord [dabɔːr], at first, first

dame [dam] *f.*, lady

davantage [davɑ̃taːʒ] *adv.*, more

débâcle [debɑːkl] *f.*, defeat

*débattre [debatr], to struggle, debate

debout [dəbu], standing, up

début [deby] *m.*, beginning

*décevoir [desəvwaɪr], to deceive

déchirer [deʃire], to tear

*découvrir [dekuvriːr], to discover

dedans [dədɑ̃], inside, within, in (it, them)

*défaire [defɛɪr], undo; *se défaire (de), to get rid (of)

défaut [defo] *m.*, fault, defect

défunt, -e [defœ̃, -ɪt], deceased, defunct

dégénéré, -e [deʒenere], degenerate

dégrader [degrade], to degrade, lower

déjeuner [deʒœne] *m.*, lunch; **petit —,** breakfast

déjeuner [deʒœne], to lunch

délices (*pl.*) [delis] *f.*, delight(s)

demain [dəmɛ̃], tomorrow

demander [dəmɑ̃de], to ask

demeure [dəmœːr] *f.*, dwelling

demeurer [dəmœre], to live (dwell), stay

denier [dənje] *m.*, penny, mite; interest

dent [dɑ̃] *f.*, tooth

départ [depaːr] *m.*, departure

dépense [depɑ̃ːs] *f.*, expense

dépensier, -ère [depɑ̃sje, -ɛr], extravagant

***déplaire** [deplɛːr], to displease

dépourvu, -e [depurvy], destitute

de profundis [deprɔfɔ̃dis], out of the depths

depuis [dəpɥi], since

déranger [derɑ̃ʒe], to disturb

dernier, -ère [dɛrnje, -ɛːr], last, past

derrière [dɛrjɛːr], behind

désirer [dezire], to desire, wish

désolé, -e [dezɔle], desolate

dessécher [deseʃe], to dry (up)

dessous [dəsu], beneath, under

dessus [dəsy] *m.*, top; lid

désunion [dezynjɔ̃] *f.*, disunion

***détruire** [detrɥiːr], to destroy

deux [dø], two, both

devancer [dəvɑ̃se], to precede, get ahead of

devant [dəvɑ̃], before (*location*)

***devenir** [dəvniːr], to become

devoir [dəvwaːr] *m.*, duty

***devoir** [dəvwaːr], to owe; to have to

dévoyé, -e [devwaje], led astray

dicter [dikte], to dictate

Dieu [djø] *m.*, God

difficile [difisil], difficult

digne [diɲ], deserving; dignified

diplôme [diploːm] *m.*, diploma

***dire** [diːr], to say, tell

se diriger [sədiriʒe], to betake oneself, head for

discuter [diskyte], to discuss

se disperser [sədispɛrse], to scatter

dispute [dispyt] *f.*, dispute, quarrel

disputer [dispyte], to quarrel

distrait, -e [distrɛ, -t], distracted

dix [dis], ten

do [do] *m.*, do (*music*)

doigt [dwa] *m.*, finger

dom [dɔ̃] *m.*, dom (title)

domestique [dɔmɛstik] *m. and f.*, servant

domination [dɔminɑsjɔ̃] *f.*, domination

domino [dɔmino] *m.*, domino

dommage [dɔmaːʒ] *m.*, damage; **c'est —**, it is a pity

don [dɔ̃] *m.*, gift

donc [dɔ̃k], therefore, then

donner [dɔne], to give

dorénavant [dɔrenavɑ̃], henceforth

***dormir** [dɔrmiːr], to sleep

dos [do] *m.*, back

doucement [dusmɑ̃], softly, cautiously, slowly

douceur [dusœːr] *f.*, sweetness, gentleness

douleur [dulœːr] *f.*, pain, grief, suffering

doute [dut] *m.*, doubt; **sans —,** without doubt

douter [dute], to doubt; **— de,** to question

se douter de [sədute də], to suspect

doux, -ce [du, -s], sweet, soft

douzaine [duzɛn] *f.*, dozen

drap [dra] *m.*, cloth

drapeau [drapo] *m.*, flag

droit [drwa] *m.*, right, law

drôle [droɪl], droll; curious

duel [dɥɛl] *m.*, duel, struggle

Dunkerque [dœ̃kɛrk] *m.*, Dunkirk

E

eau [o] *f.*, water

*s'ébattre [sebatr], to gambol, play

s'ébranler [sebrɑ̃le], to start, get under way; to stagger

s'échapper [seʃape], to escape

écho [eko] *m.*, echo

éclairer [eklɛre], to light up

s'éclairer [seklɛre], to enlighten oneself

éclat [ekla] *m.*, burst (of laughter); **partir d'un — de rire,** to burst out laughing

éclatant, -e [eklatɑ̃, -ɪt], resplendent, shining

éclater [eklate], to burst out, explode

écolier [ekɔlje] *m.*, pupil, student, schoolboy

économie: par — [parekɔnɔmi], through thrift

écouter [ekute], to listen to

*écrire [ekriɪr], to write

écrivain [ekrivɛ̃] *m.*, writer

écueil [ekœɪj] *m.*, reef, rock

écumant, -e [ekymɑ̃, -ɪt], foaming

écuyer [ekɥije] *m.*, squire; circus rider

s'effondrer [sefɔ̃dre], to collapse

égal, -e [egal], equal, (all the) same

s'élancer [selɑ̃se], to dash

élève [elɛɪv] *m. and f.*, pupil

élevé, -e [elve], high

s'élever [selve], to arise, rise

embarrasser [ɑ̃barase], to embarrass

embaumer [ɑ̃bome], to perfume; to embalm

embrasé, -e [ɑ̃brɑze], flaming, fiery, blazing

embrasser [ɑ̃brase], to embrace; to include

émeute [emøɪt] *f.*, outbreak, riot

emmancher [ɑ̃mɑ̃ʃe], to put a handle to; to manage

emménager [ɑ̃menaʒe], to move in

emmener [ɑ̃mne], to take away

émotion [emosjɔ̃] *f.*, emotion

s'emparer (de) [sɑ̃pare (də)], seize, take hold of

empêcher [ɑ̃pɛʃe], to prevent, hinder, impede

emporter [ɑ̃pɔrte], to carry away

emprunt [ɑ̃prœ̃] *m.*, loan

emprunter [ɑ̃prœ̃te], to borrow

en [ɑ̃] *prep.*, in, to

en [ɑ̃] *pron.*, of it, of them, from it, from them

enclume [ɑ̃klym] *f.*, anvil

encore [ãkɔːr], still, yet, again

encore que [ãkɔːrkə], although, even though

encre [ãːkr] *f.*, ink

endormi, -e [ãdɔrmi], *p.p. of* **s'endormir*, asleep

*endormir [ãdɔrmiːr], to put to sleep

énergie [enɛrʒi] *f.*, energy, strength

enfant [ãfã] *m. and f.*, child

enfermer [ãfɛrme], to shut in

enfin [ãfɛ̃], finally

enflammé, -e [ãflame], inflamed, fiery

enfouir [ãfwiːr], to bury; to hide

*s'enfuir [sãfɥiːr], to flee

enivrer [ãnivre], to intoxicate

ennemi [ɛnmi] *m.*, enemy

ennui [ãnɥi] *m.*, worry, boredom

ennuyer [ãnɥije], to worry, annoy, bore

énorme [enɔrm], enormous

enseigne [ãsɛɲ] *m.*, ensign; *f.*, sign

ensemble [ãsãːbl], together

ensevelir [ãsəvliːr], to shroud; to engulf

ensuite [ãsɥit], after, then

entendre [ãtãːdr], to hear, understand

en-tête [ãtɛit] *m.*, heading (of a letter)

entre [ãːtr], between; **d'— eux** [dãːtrø], from among them

*entretenir [ãtrətniːr], to entertain, keep; **s'— de,** to converse about

envahir [ãvaiːr], to invade

envers [ãvɛːr], toward

envie [ãvi] *f.*, envy, desire; ***avoir — de,** to want, have a mind to

*envoyer [ãvwaje], to send

s'épandre [sepãːdr], to spread, scatter

s'épanouir [sepanwiːr], to open out, bloom, broaden

épaule [epoːl] *f.*, shoulder

épée [epe] *f.*, sword

épeuré, -e [epœre], frightened

épi [epi] *m.*, ear (of wheat)

épreuve [eprœːv] *f.*, trial, affliction, proof, test

épuisé, -e [epɥize], exhausted

s'épuiser [sepɥize], to become exhausted

errer [ɛre], to err; to wander about; to go astray

Esaü [ezay] *m.*, Esau

esclave [ɛsklɑːv] *m.*, slave

escrime [ɛskrim] *f.*, fencing

espérer [ɛspere], to hope

espion [ɛspjɔ̃] *m.*, spy

espoir [ɛspwaːr] *m.*, hope

esprit [ɛspri] *m.*, spirit; wit

essayer [esɛje], to try

essence [ɛsãːs] *f.*, gasoline

estrade [ɛstrad] *f.*, platform, stage

estuaire [ɛstɥɛːr] *m.*, estuary

état [eta] *m.*, state

Etats-Unis (*pl.*) [etazyni] *m.*, the United States

été [ete] *m.*, summer

été [ete] *p.p. of* **être*, been

*s'éteindre [setɛ̃ːdr], to go out, die out

s'étendre [setãːdr], to spread, extend

étendue [etãdy] *f.*, stretch, range, area

étoile [etwal] *f.*, star

étoilé, -e [etwale], starry

étrange [etrã:ʒ], strange

étranger, -ère [etrãʒe, -ɛɪr], foreign

étranger [etrãʒe] *m.*, foreigner, stranger

*être [ɛɪtr], to be; ne plus y —, not to be (live) there any more, any longer; to be confused

étroit, -e [etrwa, -t], narrow

étudier [etydje], to study

Euclide [øklid] *m.*, Euclid

Eugénie [øʒeni] *f.*, Eugenia

euphonique [øfɔnik], euphonic

Euphrate [øfrat] *m.*, Euphrates

Europe [ørɔp] *f.*, Europe

européen, -ne [ørɔpeẽ, -ɛn], European

éveil [evɛɪj] *m.*, awakening; alarm

événement [evɛnmã] *m.*, event

éviter [evite], to avoid

exact, -e [ɛgzakt], exact; precise; punctual

examen [ɛgzamẽ] *m.*, examination

exceller [ɛksɛle], to excel

expédier [ɛkspedje], to send, expedite

exprimer [ɛksprime], to express

extrême [ɛkstrɛɪm], extreme

F

fâché, -e [faʃe], angry; *être —, to regret

façon [fasõ] *f.*, fashion, manner, way; de — que, so that

*faillir [fajiːr], to fail; — tomber [— tõbe], to come near falling

faim [fẽ] *f.*, hunger

*faire [fɛɪr], to make, do; *avoir vite fait, to be quick about, to do in no time

faiseur [fəzœɪr] *m.*, maker

fait [fɛ] *p. p. of* *faire, done, made

fait [fɛ *or* fɛt] *m.*, fact

*falloir [falwaːr], to be necessary, have to

fanfare [fãfaɪr] *f.*, band (of musicians)

fangeux, -se [fãʒø, -ɪz], muddy

fardeau [fardo] *m.*, burden

fatigué, -e [fatige], tired

faute [foːt] *f.*, mistake, fault

fauteuil [fotœɪj] *m.*, armchair

faux, -sse [fo, -ɪs], false; — pas *m.*, blunder

femme [fam] *f.*, woman, wife

fenêtre [fənɛɪtr] *f.*, window

fer [fɛɪr] *m.*, iron

ferme [fɛrm], firm; strong; resolute

fermeté [fɛrməte] *f.*, firmness

fermier [fɛrmje] *m.*, farmer

fête [fɛɪt] *f.*, feast, holiday

feu [fø] *m.*, fire

feuille [fœɪj] *f.*, leaf; sheet (of paper)

feuilleter [fœjəte], to skim through (a book); to turn over

fiacre [fjakr] *m.*, cab; hack

fier, fière [fjɛɪr], proud, haughty

fille [fiːj] *f.*, girl, daughter

fils [fis] *m.*, son

fin [fɛ̃] *f.*, end

finir [finiːr], to finish

flatter [flate], to stroke; to please; to flatter

flatteur [flatœːr] *m.*, flatterer

flatteur, -se [flatœːr, -øːz], flattering

fleur [flœːr] *f.*, flower

fleurir [flœriːr], to blossom, bloom

fleuve [flœːv] *m.*, river, stream

flûte [flyːt] *f.*, flute

foi [fwa] *f.*, faith, loyalty

fois [fwa] *f.*, time; **à la —**, at the same time, both; **une —**, once

folio [fɔljo] *m.*, folio

fondre [fɔ̃ːdr], to dissolve; **— en larmes,** to burst into tears

fonte [fɔ̃ːt] *f.*, smelting

force [fɔrs] *f.*, strength, force; **la — prime le droit** [lafors primlədrwa], might is right; **de —**, violently; **à — de**, by dint of

forêt [fɔrɛ] *f.*, forest

fort, -e [fɔːr, fɔrt], strong

fort [fɔːr] *adv.*, very

fosse [foːs] *f.*, pit, grave

fou, fol, folle [fu, fɔl], insane, crazy, lighthearted

foule [ful] *f.*, crowd

foyer [fwaje] *m.*, hearth

frais, fraîche [frɛ, -ʃ], fresh

franc [frã] *m.*, franc

franc, franche [frã, -ıʃ], frank

Français, Française [frãsɛ, -ız], Frenchman, Frenchwoman

français [frãsɛ] *m.*, French (language)

français, -e [frãsɛ, -ız], French

France [frãːs] *f.*, France

franco [frãko], free of charge

frapper [frape], to strike

frelon [frəlɔ̃] *m.*, hornet

frémir [fremiːr], to tremble with fear

frère [frɛːr] *m.*, brother

froid, -e [frwa, -d], cold

froideur [frwɑdœːr] *f.*, coldness; indifference

fromage [frɔmaːʒ] *m.*, cheese

fruit [frɥi] *m.*, fruit

*fuir [fɥiːr], to flee

fumer [fyme], to smoke

fureur [fyrœːr] *f.*, rage; violence

fusil [fyzi] *m.*, gun, rifle

G

gagner [gaɲe], to win, earn, gain

gai, -e [ge], gay

gaîment, gaiement [gemã], gaily, merrily

gaîté, gaieté [gete *or* gɛte] *f.*, gaiety, mirth

galop [galo] *m.*, gallop

gamin [gamɛ̃] *m.*, urchin, youngster

gant [gã] *m.*, glove

garçon [garsɔ̃] *m.*, boy, waiter

garde [gard] *m.*, keeper; *f.*, guard

garder [garde], to keep, watch over; **se — de**, to take care not to, be sure not to

gare [gaːr] *f.*, station

gâteau [gɑto] *m.*, cake

gaz [gɑːz] *m.*, gas

gazer [gɑze], to cover with gauze

gazon [gɑzɔ̃] *m.*, lawn

*geindre [ʒɛ̃ːdr], to moan; to complain

gelée [ʒəle] *f.*, frost

geler [ʒəle], to freeze

gémir [ʒemiːr], to groan; to grieve

gendre [ʒɑ̃ːdr] *m.*, son-in-law

genou, *pl.* genoux [ʒənu] *m.*, knee

gens (*pl.*) [ʒɑ̃] *m. and f.*, people, folk

gentil, -le [ʒɑ̃ti, -tiːj], gentle, nice

gérer [ʒere], to manage

gilet [ʒilɛ] *m.*, vest

girafe [ʒiraf] *m.*, giraffe

giron [ʒirɔ̃] *m.*, lap

gîte [ʒit] *m.*, lodging, home, lair

glaner [glane], to glean

gloire [glwaːr] *f.*, glory

glouglou [gluglu] *m.*, gurgling; gobble (of turkeys)

goût [gu] *m.*, taste

goûter [gute], to taste, enjoy

goutte [gut] *f.*, drop; gout

grâce à [grɑːs a], thanks to

grand, -e [grɑ̃, -ɪd], tall, large; famous (*when placed before noun*)

gras, -se [grɑ, -ɪs], fat; greasy; indecent

gratis [grɑtis], gratis

grimper [grɛ̃pe], to climb

gros, -se [gro, -ɪs], stout

guêpe [gɛɪp] *f.*, wasp

ne . . . guère [nə . . . gɛɪr], hardly, scarcely

guérir [geriːr], to cure

guerre [gɛɪr] *f.*, war

gueule [gœl] *f.*, mouth (of some animals)

guitare [gitaːr] *f.*, guitar

gymnase [ʒimnɑɪz] *m.*, gymnasium

gypseux, -se [ʒipsø, -ɪz], gypseous, made of plaster of Paris

H

habile [abil], skillful, smart

s'habiller [sabije], to dress oneself

habit [abi] *m.*, dress, suit of clothes; *pl.* clothes

habiter [abite], to inhabit, dwell

habitude [abityd] *f.*, habit

†*haïr [aiːr], to hate

se †hâter [səɑte], to hasten

†haut, -e [o, -t], high

†hautain, -e [otɛ̃, -ɛn], proud, haughty

†havre [ɑɪvr] *m.*, haven

hélas [elɑːs], alas!

†hennissement [anismɑ̃] *m.*, neighing

herbe [ɛrb] *f.*, grass

héroïque [erɔik], heroic

†héros [ero] *m.*, hero

heure [œɪr] *f.*, hour, time, o'clock

heureux, -se [œrø, -ɪz], happy

†hibou, *pl.* hiboux [ibu] *m.*, owl

hier [jɛɪr], yesterday

histoire [istwaːr] *f.*, history, story

hiver [ivɛɪr] *m.*, winter

homme [ɔm] *m.*, man

honnête [ɔnɛɪt], honest

†**horde** [ɔrd] *f.*, horde
†**hors de** [ɔrdə], out of
†**huée** [ɥe] *f.*, hooting, booing
†**huer** [ɥe], to hoot, boo
huile [ɥil] *f.*, oil
†**huitaine** [ɥitɛin] *f.*, eight days, week
†**Humbert** [œ̃bɛir] *m.*, Humbert
humble [œ̃ibl], humble
†**hurlement** [yrləmɑ̃] *m.*, howling

I

ïambe [jɑ̃ib] *m.*, iambus
ici [isi], here
ici-bas [isibɑ], here below, on earth, in this world
idée [ide] *f.*, idea
idole [idɔl] *f.*, idol
ignominieux, -se [iɲɔminjø, -iz], shameful, disgraceful, unceremonious
île [il] *f.*, island
illicite [illisit], illicit
imaginer [imaʒine], to imagine
imbécile [ɛ̃besil], imbecile
immortel, -le [imɔrtɛl], immortal
impératrice [ɛ̃peratris] *f.*, empress
impie [ɛ̃pi], impious, irreligious
importer [ɛ̃pɔrte], to import; to be of importance
importun, -e [ɛ̃pɔrtœ̃, -yn], importunate
impossible [ɛ̃pɔsibl], impossible
impromptu, -e [ɛ̃prɔ̃pty], impromptu
incendié, -e [ɛ̃sɑ̃dje], burnt down
incertain, -e [ɛ̃sɛrtɛ̃, -ɛn], uncertain

indéfini, -e [ɛ̃defini], indefinite
indescriptible [ɛ̃dɛskriptibl], indescribable
infect, -e [ɛ̃fɛkt], foul, stinking
infini, -e [ɛ̃fini], infinite
s'informer de [sɛ̃fɔrme də], to inquire about
inquiet, -ète [ɛ̃kjɛ, -t], uneasy
***s'instruire** [sɛ̃strɥiir], to learn, to educate oneself
instruit, -e [ɛ̃strɥi, -t], educated
insupportable [ɛ̃sypɔrtabl], unbearable
intéressant, -e [ɛ̃terɛsɑ̃, -it], interesting
intéressé, -e [ɛ̃terɛse], interested
s'intéresser à [sɛ̃terɛse a], to be interested in
intérêt [ɛ̃terɛ] *m.*, interest
intime [ɛ̃tim], intimate
intrus [ɛ̃try] *m.*, intruder
ionique [jɔnik], Ionic
iota [jota] *m.*, iota
s'irriter [sirite], to get angry
issu, -e [isy], born, descended
italien, -ne [italjɛ̃, -ɛn], Italian

J

jamais [ʒamɛ], ever; **ne . . . jamais,** never; **jamais!** (*standing alone*), never!
janvier [ʒɑ̃vje] *m.*, January
jardin [ʒardɛ̃] *m.*, garden
jardinier [ʒardinje] *m.*, gardener
jaune [ʒoin], yellow
jersey [ʒɛrzɛ] *m.*, jersey (cloth)
jet [ʒɛ] *m.*, jet, throw
jeter [ʒəte], to throw; — **les hauts cris** [leocri], to raise

an outcry, cry out, give vent to one's indignation

jeu [ʒø] *m.*, game, play

jeudi [ʒødi] *m.*, Thursday

à jeun [aʒœ̃], on an empty stomach

jeune [ʒœn], young

jeûne [ʒøːn] *m.*, fast, abstinence

jeûner [ʒøne], to fast

jeunesse [ʒœnɛs] *f.*, youth

jockey [ʒɔkɛ] *m.*, jockey

joie [ʒwɑ] *f.*, joy

*joindre [ʒwɛ̃dr], to join

joli, -e [ʒɔli], pretty

jouer [ʒwe], to play

jouet [ʒwɛ] *m.*, toy

jouir de [ʒwiːr də], to enjoy

joujou [ʒuʒu] *m.*, toy

jour [ʒuːr] *m.*, day

journée [ʒurne] *f.*, day; **de la —,** all day long

joyeux, -se [ʒwajø, -ɪz], cheerful, gay, joyful

juger [ʒyʒe], to judge; **— à propos** [aprɔpo], to deem it advisable, proper

juillet [ʒɥijɛ] *m.*, July

juin [ʒɥɛ̃] *m.*, June

jumeau [ʒymo] *m.*, twin

junte [ʒɔ̃ːt] *f.*, junta (Spanish council)

jurer [ʒyre], to swear

jusqu'à [ʒyska], until

jusqu'à ce que [ʒyskaskə] *conj.*, until

juste [ʒyst], right, fair

K

kilo [kilo] *m.*, kilogram (about 2⅕ lbs.)

kilomètre [kilomɛɪtr] *m.*, kilometer (about ⅝ mi.)

L

là [la], there; **de —,** hence, therefrom

là-bas [labɑ], yonder

laborieux, -se [labɔrjø, -ɪz], laborious, industrious

laboureur [laburœɪr] *m.*, farm hand

lâcher [lɑʃe], to let go; **— prise** [— priːz], to let go one's hold

lâcheté [lɑʃte] *f.*, cowardice

laine [lɛn] *f.*, wool

lampe [lɑ̃ːp] *f.*, lamp

lance [lɑ̃s] *f.*, spear

langage [lɑ̃gaːʒ] *m.*, language

larme [larm] *f.*, tear; **fondre en larmes,** to burst into tears

larynx [larɛ̃ks] *m.*, larynx

Laure [lɔɪr] *f.*, Laura

laver [lave], to wash

se laver [səlave], to wash, to wash oneself

léger, -ère [leʒe, -ɛɪr], light; **à la légère,** lightly

légume [legym] *m.*, vegetable

lendemain [lɑ̃dmɛ̃] *m.*, next day

lent, -e [lɑ̃, -ɪt], slow

lettre [lɛtr] *f.*, letter

lever [ləve], to lift, raise

se lever [sələve], to arise, get up

lèvre [lɛɪvr] *f.*, lip

lien [ljɛ̃] *m.*, link, tie

lieu, *pl.* **lieux** [ljø] *m.*, place; **au — de,** instead of

ligne [liɲ] *f.*, line

lilas [lilɑ] *m.*, lilac

limite [limit] *f.*, boundary
lingual, -e [lɛ̃gwal], lingual
linguiste [lɛ̃gɥist] *m. or f.*, linguist
linguistique [lɛ̃gɥistik] *f.*, linguistics
lionceau [ljɔ̃so] *m.*, lion's cub
***lire** [liːr], to read
lit [li] *m.*, bed
livre [liːvr] *m.*, book
livre [liːvr] *f.*, pound
loi [lwa] *f.*, law
loin [lwɛ̃], far; **non — de,** not far from
lointain, -e [lwɛ̃tɛ̃, -ɛn], distant, far away
lointain [lwɛ̃tɛ̃] *m.*, distance
long, -ue [lɔ̃, -ɪg], long; **le — de,** along
longuement [lɔ̃gmã], a long time, at length
lors [lɔːr], then, at that time
lorsque [lɔrskə], when
lot [lo] *m.*, prize (at a lottery); **le gros —,** first prize
lotion [losjɔ̃] *f.*, lotion
Louis [lui, lwi] *m.*, Louis, Lewis
loup [lu] *m.*, wolf
lourd, -e [luːr, lurd], heavy
loyal, -e [lwajal], loyal
***luire** [lɥiːr], to shine
lumbago [lɔ̃bago] *m.*, lumbago
lumière [lymjɛːr] *f.*, light
lundi [lœ̃di] *m.*, Monday
lune [lyn] *f.*, moon
lutter [lyte], to wrestle

M

machine à coudre [maʃinakuːdr] *f.*, sewing machine

mai [mɛ] *m.*, May
main [mɛ̃] *f.*, hand
maintenant [mɛ̃tnã], now
maintien [mɛ̃tjɛ̃] *m.*, upholding, bearing
maison [mɛzɔ̃] *f.*, house
maître [mɛːtr] *m.*, master
mal, *pl.* **maux** [mal, mo] *m.*, evil
mal [mal] *adv.*, badly, ill
malade [malad], sick, ill
mâle [mɑːl] *m.*, male
malfaisant [malfəzã], evil, harmful
malheur [malœːr] *m.*, misfortune
malheureux, -se [malhœrø, -ɪz], unhappy, unfortunate
manche [mãʃ] *m.*, handle; *f.*, sleeve
manger [mãʒe], to eat
manquer [mãke], to be lacking
marais [marɛ] *m.*, marshland
marcher [marʃe], to walk, march
marquer [marke], to stamp, mark, indicate
marquis [marki] *m.*, marquis
marquise [markiːz] *f.*, marchioness
marraine [marɛn] *f.*, godmother
mars [mars] *m.*, March
marteau [marto] *m.*, hammer
masse [mas] *f.*, mass
mât [mɑ] *m.*, mast
matelas [matlɑ] *m.*, mattress
matin [matɛ̃] *m.*, morning; **de si bon —,** so early
matinée [matine] *f.*, (the whole) morning
***maudire** [modiːr], to curse
mauvais, -e [mɔvɛ, -ɪz], bad

maximum [maksimɔm] *m.*, maximum

méchant, -e [meʃɑ̃, -ɪt], wicked

médecin [metsɛ̃] *m.*, physician; **chez le —**, at the doctor's

méditerranéen, -ne [meditɛranɛɛ̃, -ɛn], Mediterranean

meilleur, -e [mɛjœːr] (*comparative of* **bon**), better

même [mɛɪm] *adj.*, same; *adv.*, even, very; **pas —**, not even

mener [məne], to lead

mensonge [mɑ̃sɔ̃ɪʒ] *m.*, lie

mention: *faire — de [fɛɪrmɑ̃sjɔ̃ də], to mention

mépris [mepri] *m.*, disdain, scorn

mépriser [meprize], to scorn

mer [mɛɪr] *f.*, sea

mère [mɛɪr] *f.*, mother

mériter [merite], to deserve; **— de,** to deserve well of

merveille [mɛrvɛɪj] *f.*, marvel

mésaventure [mezavɑ̃tyɪr] *f.*, mischance

mesure [məzyɪr] *f.*, measure; **n'est pas —**, is no measure at all

*mettre [mɛtr], to put; **se — à,** to begin; **— à mort,** to put to death

Meung [mœ̃], Jean de Meung, author of second part of *Roman de la Rose*

meunier [mønje] *m.*, miller

meurtre [mœrtr] *m.*, murder

meute [møɪt] *f.*, pack (of hounds)

mil [mil], thousand (in dates)

milieu [miljø] *m.*, middle; **au — de,** in the middle of

mille [mil], (a) thousand

mille [mil] *m.*, mile

minimum [minimɔm] *m.*, minimum

minuit [minɥi] *m.*, midnight

mitiger [mitiʒe], to mitigate

mode [mɔd] *m.*, manner, mood; *f.*, style, fashion

modérer [mɔdere], to moderate

moelle [mwal] *f.*, pith, marrow

moins [mwɛ̃], **à — de,** less; **à — que,** unless; **en — de,** in less than

mois [mwɑ] *m.*, month

moisson [mwasɔ̃] *f.*, harvest

moitié [mwatje] *f.*, half

monde [mɔ̃ɪd] *m.*, world; **tout le —,** everybody

monsieur [məsjø] *m.*, Mr., sir

monstrueux, -se [mɔ̃stryø, -ɪz], prodigious

montagne [mɔ̃taɲ] *f.*, mountain

montre [mɔ̃ɪtr] *f.*, watch; **— en or,** gold watch

se moquer de [səmɔke də], to mock, make fun of

s'en moquer [sɑ̃mɔke], not to care

morne [mɔrn], morose

mort, -e [mɔɪr, mɔrt], dead

mort [mɔɪr] *f.*, death

mortel, -le [mɔrtɛl], mortal

mortel [mɔrtɛl] *m.*, mortal

mot [mo] *m.*, word

mou, mol, molle [mu, mɔl], soft

*moudre [mudr], to grind

*mourir [muriɪr], to die

se *mourir [səmuriɪr], to be dying

*mouvoir [muvwaɪr], to move
moyen [mwajɛ̃] *m.*, means
mur [myɪr] *m.*, wall
mûr, -e [myɪr], ripe
mystique [mistik], mystical

N

nager [naʒe], to swim
naguère [nagɛɪr], lately
*naître [nɛɪtr], to be born; to spring up
naseau [nazo] *m.*, nostril (of animals)
nation [nɑsjɔ̃] *f.*, nation
natte [nat] *f.*, mat
naturel, -le [natyrɛl], natural
n'est-ce pas? [nɛspɑ], isn't it so? don't you?
neige [nɛɪʒ] *f.*, snow
neiger [nɛʒe], to snow
net, -te [nɛt], neat
neuf [nœf], nine
neuf, -ve [nœf, -ɪv], new
neutre [nøɪtr], neutral, neuter
neveu [nəvø] *m.*, nephew
nez [ne] *m.*, nose
Noël [nɔɛl] *m.*, Christmas
nœud [nø] *m.*, knot
noir, -e [nwaɪr], black
noix [nwɑ] *f.*, nut
nom [nɔ̃] *m.*, name
nord [nɔɪr] *m.*, north
normand, -e [nɔrmɑ̃, -ɪd], Norman
Normand [nɔrmɑ̃] *m.*, Norman
note [nɔt] *f.*, note
notion [nosjɔ̃] *f.*, notion
nourrissant, -e [nurisɑ̃, -ɪt], nourishing
nourrir [nuriɪr], to feed, nourish

nouveau, nouvel, nouvelle [nuvo, nuvɛl], new
de nouveau [dənuvo], anew, again
noyer [nwaje], to drown
nu, -e [ny], naked
nuage [nɥaɪʒ] *m.*, cloud
nuée [nɥe] *f.*, cloud
*nuire [nɥiɪr], to harm
nuisible [nɥizibl], harmful
nuit [nɥi] *f.*, night
numéro [nymero] *m.*, number
nymphe [nɛ̃ɪf] *f.*, nymph

O

objet [ɔbʒɛ] *m.*, object
obligeant, -e [ɔbliʒɑ̃, -ɪt], obliging
obscur, -e [ɔpskyɪr], dark
observer [ɔpsɛrve], to notice
obstacle [ɔpstakl] *m.*, obstacle
obstiné, -e [ɔpstine], obstinate
*obtenir [ɔptəniɪr], to obtain
occasion [ɔkazjɔ̃] *f.*, opportunity
occlusion [ɔklyzjɔ̃] *f.*, closing
occuper [ɔkype], to occupy
œil [œɪj], *pl.* yeux [jø] *m.*, eye;
— pour —, an eye for an eye
œillet [œjɛ] *m.*, pink (flower)
œuf [œf], *pl.* œufs [ø], *m.*, egg
œuvre [œɪvr] *f.*, work
office [ɔfis] *m.*, office; duty; *f.*, pantry
officier [ɔfisje] *m.*, officer
*offrir [ɔfriɪr], to offer
oie [wa] *f.*, goose
oiseau [wazo] *m.*, bird
oisiveté [wazivte] *f.*, idleness
ombre [ɔ̃ɪbr] *f.*, shadow, shade
onze [ɔ̃ɪz], eleven

opiniâtre [ɔpinjɑːtr], obstinate

opium [ɔpjɔm] *m.*, opium

opportun, -e [ɔpɔrtœ̃, -yn], opportune

opposé, -e [ɔpoze], opposed, opposite

or [ɔːr] *m.*, gold

oracle [ɔrɑːkl] *m.*, oracle

d'ordinaire [dɔrdinɛːr], ordinarily

orgueil [ɔrgœːj] *m.*, pride

orgueilleux, -se [ɔrgœjø, -ːz], proud

oser [oze], to dare

ou [u], or

où [u], where, when (time)

ouaille [wɑːj] *f.*, flock (biblical)

ouate [wat] *f.*, cotton batting

oublier [ublie], to forget

ouest [wɛst] *m.*, west

*ouïr [wiːr], to hear

ours [urs] *m.*, bear

outrage [utrɑːʒ] *m.*, outrage

ouverture [uvɛrtyːr] *f.*, opening

ouvrage [uvrɑːʒ] *m.*, work

ouvrier [uvrie] *m.*, worker

*ouvrir [uvriːr], to open

ozone [ɔzon] *m.*, ozone

P

page [pɑːʒ] *m.*, page (boy); *f.*, page (of book)

païen, -ne [pajɛ̃, -ɛn] *m.*, pagan

paillasse [pajas] *m.*, clown; *f.*, straw mattress

paimpolais, -e [pɛ̃pɔlɛ, -z] *m. and f.*, citizen of Paimpol (*See* Loti, *Pêcheur d'Islande.*)

pain [pɛ̃] *m.*, bread; mettre au — sec et à l'eau [mɛtropɛ̃sɛk ealo], to put on bread and water; petit pain, roll

paisible [pɛzibl], peaceful

palais [palɛ] *m.*, palace

pâle [pɑːl], pale

panier [panje] *m.*, basket

papier [papje] *m.*, paper

par [par], by, through

paragraphe [paragraf] *m.*, paragraph

*paraître [parɛːtr], to appear, seem

*parcourir [parkuriːr], to go over

par delà [pardəla], beyond

pardonner [pardɔne], to pardon

pareil, -le [parɛːj], like, similar, such a; sans —, peerless

parent [parɑ̃] *m.*, relative

parents (*pl.*) [parɑ̃] *m.*, parents

se parer [səpare], to adorn oneself

paresseux, -se [parɛsø, -ːz], lazy

parfait, -e [parfɛ, -t], perfect

parfum [parfœ̃] *m.*, perfume

parier [parje], to bet

parler [parle], to speak

parler [parle] *m.*, speech

parleur [parlœːr] *m.*, talker

parole [parɔl] *f.*, word

parrain [parɛ̃] *m.*, godfather

part [paːr] *f.*, share, part, participation; *faire — de, to inform

*partir [partiːr], to leave, depart

partout [partu], everywhere

pas [pɑ] *m.*, step

pas [pɑ]: non — [nɔ̃pɑ], not so; — du tout [pɑdytu], not at all; ne . . . pas, not

passe-partout [pɑspartu] *m.*, master key

passer [pɑse], to pass; **en passant,** by the way, casually

passion [pɑsjɔ̃] *f.*, passion

pâte [pɑːt] *f.*, paste

pâtir [pɑtiːr], to suffer

pâtre [pɑːtr] *m.*, herdsman

patriote [patriɔt] *m.*, patriot; **en —,** like a patriot

patron [patrɔ̃] *m.*, boss

patronne [patrɔn] *f.*, boss, proprietress

patte [pat] *f.*, paw

Paul [pɔl] *m.*, Paul

pauvre [poːvr], poor, pitiable

pauvre [poːvr] *m.*, poor person

payer [pɛje], to pay (for)

pays [pe(j)i] *m.*, country

paysage [peizɑːʒ] *m.*, landscape

paysan [peizɑ̃] *m.*, peasant

peau [po] *f.*, skin

pêche: — à la ligne [pɛʃalaliɲ] *f.*, angling

***peindre** [pɛ̃ːdr], to paint, depict

peine [pɛn *or* pɛin] *f.*, pain, sorrow; **à —,** hardly; ***valoir la —** [valwaːrla —], to be worth the trouble

peintre [pɛ̃ːtr] *m.*, painter

peinture [pɛ̃tyːr] *f.*, painting

pelouse [pluːz] *f.*, lawn

pendant [pɑ̃dɑ̃], during

pendant que [pɑ̃dɑ̃kə], while

pendule [pɑ̃dyl] *m.*, pendulum; *f.*, timepiece

pénétrant, -e [penetrɑ̃, -ɪt], penetrating, piercing

pénible [penibl], painful

penser [pɑ̃se], to think; **— à,** to think of, about; **j'y pense,** I think of it

pensum [pɛ̃sɔm] *m.*, extra task (at school), imposition

Pensylvanie [pɛ̃silvani] *f.*, Pennsylvania

pente [pɑ̃ːt] *f.*, slope

perdre [pɛrdr], to lose

père [pɛr] *m.*, father

perfidie [pɛrfidi] *f.*, treachery

perle [pɛrl] *f.*, pearl

***permettre** [pɛrmɛtr], to permit

personne [pɛrsɔn] *f.*, person

ne . . . personne [nə . . . pɛrsɔn], nobody, no one

peser [pəze], to weigh

petiot, -e [pətjo, -ɔt], tiny

petit, -e [pəti, -t], small; **—s pains,** rolls; **—s pois,** green peas

peu [pø] *adv.*, little; **— de,** few, little of; **en — de mots,** in a few words; **pour — que** *conj.*, if only, if ever

à peu près [apøprɛ], nearly, almost

peur [pœːr] *f.*, fear; **de — de,** for fear of; **de — que** *conj.*, for fear that; ***faire —,** to frighten; ***prendre —,** to get frightened

peut-être [pətɛːtr], perhaps

philosophe [filɔzɔf] *m.*, philosopher

phrase [frɑːz] *f.*, sentence

pied [pje] *m.*, foot

pied-à-terre [pjɛtatɛːr] *m.*, small temporary lodging

piège [pjɛːʒ] *m.*, trap
pierre [pjɛːr] *f.*, stone
pieu [pjø] *m.*, stake
pinceau [pɛ̃so] *m.*, brush (for painting)
pinte [pɛ̃ːt] *f.*, pint
pionnier [pjɔnje] *m.*, pioneer
pipe [pip] *f.*, pipe
piquer [pike], to prick, sting
pire [piːr] *adj.*, worse
pis [pi] *adv.*, worse
plaie [plɛ] *f.*, wound, sore
plaine [plɛn] *f.*, plain
*plaire [plɛːr], to please
plaisir [plɛziːr] *m.*, pleasure
plan [plɑ̃] *m.*, plan
planche [plɑ̃ːʃ] *f.*, board
plein, -e [plɛ̃, -ɛn], full
pleutre [pløːtr] *m.*, cad
*pleuvoir [plœvwaːr], to rain
plier [plie], to fold
plomb [plɔ̃] *m.*, lead (metal)
ployer [plwaje], to bend
pluie [plɥi] *f.*, rain
plus [ply], more; de —, moreover, in addition; ne . . . plus, no longer; de — en —, more and more
plusieurs [plyzjœːr], several
plus tôt [plyto], earlier
plutôt [plyto], rather
poêle [pwal] *m.*, stove; *f.*, frying pan
poids [pwɑ] *m.*, weight
poing [pwɛ̃] *m.*, fist
point [pwɛ̃] *m.*, point; — d'appui, supporting basis; au — que, so much so that; au — du jour, at dawn
ne . . . point [nə . . . pwɛ̃],

(*emphatic*) not; **point du tout,** not at all
poire [pwaːr] *f.*, pear
poitrine [pwatrin] *f.*, chest
pôle [poːl] *m.*, pole
poli, -e [pɔli], polite
politique [pɔlitik] *m.*, politician; *f.*, politics
pomme [pɔm] *f.*, apple
pompe [pɔ̃ːp] *f.*, pump
port [pɔːr] *m.*, port
porte [pɔrt] *f.*, door
porter [pɔrte], to carry, wear
portier [pɔrtje] *m.*, doorman
pose [poːz] *f.*, pose
poser [poze], to put, place
poste [pɔst] *m.*, post, station; *f.*, post office
pot [po] *m.*, jug
pot-au-feu [pɔtofø] *m.*, boiled beef and vegetables
potion [posjɔ̃] *f.*, potion
pou, *pl.* poux [pu] *m.*, louse
pour [puːr], for, in order to (*before infinitive*), as to
pour que [purkə] *conj.*, in order that, so that
pourquoi [purkwa], why
*poursuivre [pursɥiːvr], to pursue
*pourvoir [purvwaːr], to provide
pourvu que [purvykə], provided that
pousser [puse], to push forward, grow
*pouvoir [puvwaːr], to be able
prairie [prɛri] *f.*, meadow
pratiquer [pratike], to practice
pré [pre] *m.*, meadow

précipiter [presipite], to precip-
itate, hurry, hasten
se précipiter (sur) [səpresipite
(syr)], to dash (at)
préférer [prefere], to prefer
***prendre** [prãːdr], to take;
— **garde à,** to pay attention to
près [prɛ], near; **de —,** close,
closely
présage [prezaːʒ] *m.*, omen
***pressentir** [presãtiːr], to have
a presentiment of
présumer [prezyme], to presume
prêt, -e [prɛ, -t], ready
prétendu, -e [pretãdy], pretended, so called
prêter [prete], to lend
preuve [prœːv] *f.*, proof
primer [prime], to excel, come
before
prince [prɛ̃s] *m.*, prince
printemps [prɛ̃tã] *m.*, spring
prisonnier [prizɔnje] *m.*, prisoner
prix [pri] *m.*, price; prize
prodigue [prɔdig], prodigal, extravagant
profiter de [prɔfite də], to profit
by
profond, -e [prɔfɔ̃, -ɪd], deep
proie [prwa *or* prwɑ] *f.*, prey;
en — à, a prey to; **oiseau
de —,** bird of prey
se promener [səprɔmne], to take
a walk
promesse [prɔmɛs] *f.*, promise
prompt, -e [prɔ̃, -ɪt], prompt
pronom [prɔnɔ̃] *m.*, pronoun
proposer [prɔpoze], to propose
propre [prɔpr], own, clean

proprement [prɔprmã], properly, neatly
propriété [prɔpriete] *f.*, property
proue [pru] *f.*, prow
prouesse [pruɛs] *f.*, prowess
provençal, -e [prɔvãsal], Provençal
prudemment [prydamã], pru-
dently
prudent, -e [prydã, -ɪt], prudent
puis [pɥi], then, next
puisque [pɥiskə] *conj.*, since
puits [pɥi] *m.*, well
punch [pɔ̃ːʃ] *m.*, punch (drink)
pur, -e [pyːr], pure

Q

quadrupède [kwadrypɛd] *m.*,
quadruped
quai [ke] *m.*, quay; track, platform (railroad)
quand [kã], when
quant à [kãta], as for
quelque chose [kɛlkəʃoːz, *col-
loquially:* kɛkʃoːz], something
quelquefois [kɛlkəfwa, *collo-
quially:* kɛkfwa], sometimes
querelle [kərɛl] *f.*, quarrel
quiconque [kikɔ̃ːk], whoever
quitter [kite], to quit, leave
quoique [kwak(ə)], although

R

raconter [rakɔ̃te], to tell (a
story)
rage [raːʒ] *f.*, madness (in dogs)
ramasser [ramase], to pick up,
gather
Raphaël [rafaɛl] *m.*, Raphael
rapide [rapid], fast

rapporter [raporte], to bring back, yield, report

rare [raːr], rare

raser [raze], to shave

rassurer [rasyre], to reassure

rat [ra] *m.*, rat

ration [rasjɔ̃] *f.*, ration

Raymond [rɛmɔ̃] *m.*, Raymond

rayon [rejɔ̃] *m.*, ray; bookshelf

récemment [resamɑ̃], recently

*recevoir [rəsəvwaːr], to receive

récolter [rekɔlte], to harvest

recommencer [rəkɔmɑ̃se], to begin again

récompenser [rekɔ̃pɑ̃se], to reward

reconnaissance [rəkɔnɛsɑ̃ːs] *f.*, gratitude

reconnaissant, -e [rəkɔnɛsɑ̃, -ɪt], thankful, grateful

*redire [rədiːr], to repeat; trouver à —, to criticize

redoubler [rəduble], to increase, redouble

se réfugier [sərefyʒje], to take refuge, shelter

regard [rəgaːr] *m.*, look

regarder [rəgarde], to look at

régler [regle], to settle

règne [rɛɲ] *m.*, reign

regret [rəgrɛ] *m.*, regret

regretter [rəgrɛte], to regret

Reims (Rheims) [rɛ̃s] *m.*, Rheims

rein [rɛ̃] *m.*, kidney

reine [rɛn] *f.*, queen

*rejoindre [rəʒwɛ̃ːdr], to join

rembrunir [rɑ̃bryniːr], to make darker

*remettre [rəmɛtr], to put back

remplir [rɑ̃pliːr], to fill

remporter [rɑ̃pɔrte], to carry off, win

remuer [rəmɥe], to move

rencontrer [rɑ̃kɔ̃tre], to meet, encounter

rendre [rɑ̃ːdr], to give back

se rendre [sərɑ̃ːdr], to surrender, betake oneself, head for

renoncer à [rənɔ̃se a], to renounce

rentrer [rɑ̃tre], to re-enter, return home

renverser [rɑ̃vɛrse], to upset, throw over

se renverser (sur) [sərɑ̃vɛrse (syr)], to fall over, overturn, turn over on

*renvoyer [rɑ̃vwaje], to send back, send away, dismiss

répéter [repete], to repeat

repli [rəpli] *m.*, fold

répondre [repɔ̃ːdr], to answer

reposer [rəpoze], to rest

se reposer [sərəpoze], to rest; — sur, to rely upon

*reprendre [rəprɑ̃ːdr], to scold

réservoir [rezɛrvwaːr] *m.*, reservoir

résister (à) [reziste (a)], to resist

résonner [rezɔne], to resound

*résoudre [rezuːdr], to resolve

respirer [rɛspire], to breathe

*ressentir [rəsɑ̃tiːr], to feel (emotion)

ressort [rəsɔːr] *m.*, spring (mechanical)

*ressortir [rəsɔrtiːr], to go out again

rester [rɛste], to stay, remain

en retard [ɑ̃rətaːr], late; ***être —**, to be late

*retenir [rətniːr], to hold back, remember, keep

se retirer [sərətire], to retire

retour [rətuːr] *m.*, return; ***être de —**, to be back

réunir [reyniːr], to gather, reunite

se réunir [səreyniːr], to gather

réussir [reysiːr], to succeed; **— aux examens** [ozegzamɛ̃], to pass examinations

rêve [rɛːv] *m.*, dream

réveil [revɛːj] *m.*, awakening

réveiller [revɛje], to awaken

*revenir [rəvniːr], to come back

revers [rəvɛːr] *m.*, reverse

Rhin [rɛ̃] *m.*, Rhine

rhum [rɔm] *m.*, rum

rien [rjɛ̃], anything, nothing; **ne . . . —**, nothing

rigide [riʒid], stiff

*rire [riːr], to laugh

rituel, -le [rituɛl], ritual

rival [rival] *m.*, rival

rive [riːv] *f.*, bank, shore

rocher [rɔʃe] *m.*, rock

rôder [rode], to prowl

roi [rwa] *m.*, king

rôle [roːl] *m.*, role; list

rond, -e [rɔ̃, -ːd], round

rose [roːz] *f.*, rose

rosée [roze] *f.*, dew

rosier [rozje] *m.*, rose bush

rossignol [rɔsiɲɔl] *m.*, nightingale

roue [ru] *f.*, wheel

rouge [ruːʒ], red

rougir [ruʒiːr], to blush, become red

rouler [rule], to roll; **les yeux roulent du sang**, his (*or* her) eyes are bloodshot

roux, rousse [ru, -s], red, reddish

rude [ryd], rough

rue [ry] *f.*, street

ruisseau [ruiso] *m.*, brook, creek, stream

ruse [ryːz] *f.*, trick

S

sable [saːbl] *m.*, sand

sabot [sabo] *m.*, hoof

sabre [saːbr] *m.*, saber

sage [saːʒ], wise

sain, -e [sɛ̃, sɛn], sane, healthy

saint, -e [sɛ̃, -ːt], holy

saisir [seziːr], to seize, understand

saison [sɛzɔ̃] *f.*, season

salaire [salɛːr] *m.*, salary

salle à manger [salamɑ̃ʒe] *f.*, dining room

saluer [salue], to greet; **se —**, to greet each other, one another

sang [sɑ̃] *m.*, blood

sans [sɑ̃], without

santé [sɑ̃te] *f.*, health

sauf, -ve [sof, soːv] *adj.*, safe

sauf [sof] *prep.*, except

saut [so] *m.*, leap

sauter [sote], to jump

sauver [sove], to save

se sauver [səsove], to run away, escape

*savoir [savwaːr], to know (how)

sceau [so] *m.*, seal
scène [sɛn] *f.*, scene
schéma [ʃema, skema] *m.*, scheme, diagram
schématique [ʃematik, skematik], diagrammatic
schismatique [ʃismatik], schismatic
schisme [ʃism] *m.*, schism
schiste [ʃist] *m.*, shale
scier [sje],to saw
scintiller [sɛ̃tije], to shine, scintillate
sciure [sjyir] *f.*, sawdust
scythe [sit], Scythian
secouer [səkwe, skwe], to shake
secours [səkuir, skuir] *m.*, help
secundo [səgɔ̃do], secondly
séduisant, -e [sedɥizɑ̃, -it], tempting, seductive, seducing, attractive
sein [sɛ̃] *m.*, bosom
sel [sɛl] *m.*, salt
semaine [səmɛn, smɛn] *f.*, week
sembler [sɑ̃ble], to seem, appear
semer [səme], to sow
sens [sɑ̃s] *m.*, sense; bon —, common sense
série [seri] *f.*, series
serrer [sɛre], to press, clasp
service [sɛrvis] *m.*, service
*servir [sɛrviir], to serve
se *servir de [səsɛrviir də] to make use of, help oneself to
serviteur [sɛrvitœir] *m.*, servant
seul, -e [sœl], alone, only
seulement [sœlmɑ̃], only
sexe [sɛks] *m.*, sex
si [si], if
signaler [siɲale], to signal

signe [siɲ] *m.*, sign; *faire —, to signal, motion, beckon
sillon [sijɔ̃] *m.*, furrow
singe [sɛ̃ʒ] *m.*, monkey
situer [sitɥe], to situate
six [sis], six
sœur [sœir] *f.*, sister
soie [swa] *f.*, silk
soif [swaf] *f.*, thirst
soin [swɛ̃] *m.*, care
soir [swair] *m.*, evening
soixante [swasɑ̃t], sixty
soldat [sɔlda] *m.*, soldier
soleil [sɔlɛij] *m.*, sun
solennel, -le [sɔlanɛl], solemn
somme [sɔm] *m.*, nap; *f.*, sum
sommeil [sɔmɛij] *m.*, sleep; *avoir —, to be sleepy
sommet [sɔmɛ] *m.*, summit
son [sɔ̃] *m.*, sound
sonner [sɔne], to ring, sound
sorte [sɔrt] *f.*, kind, sort; de — que, so that
sortie [sɔrti] *f.*, exit
*sortir [sɔrtiir], to go out; — de, to spring from
sot, -te [so, sɔt], foolish, silly
sottise [sɔtiiz] *f.*, silliness, foolishness, foolish thing; *dire une —, to say a silly thing
sou [su] *m.*, sou (small French coin)
souche [suʃ] *f.*, stump (of a tree)
soucoupe [sukup] *f.*, saucer
soudain [sudɛ̃], suddenly
souffrance [sufrɑ̃s] *f.*, suffering, pain
souhait [swɛ] *m.*, wish
souhaiter [swɛte], to wish
soulever [sulve], to lift, raise

soulier [sulje] *m.*, shoe

sourd, -e [suːr, -d], deaf

sourire *or* **souris** (*poetic*) [suriːr, suri] *m.*, smile

souris [suri] *f.*, mouse

se *souvenir de [səsuvniːr də], to remember

souvenir [suvniːr] *m.*, remembrance, souvenir; ***offrir en —**, to offer in remembrance

souvent [suvã], often

spécimen [spesimɛn] *m.*, specimen

spirituel, -le [spiritɥɛl], spiritual, witty

steppe [stɛp] *m. or f.*, steppe

su, -e [sy], *p.p. of* ***savoir**, known

suave [sɥaːv], sweet, mild

subir [sybiːr], to undergo

subit, -e [sybi, -t], sudden

sucre [sykr] *m.*, sugar

sud [syd] *m.*, south

suède [sɥɛd] *m.*, suède (leather)

Suède [sɥɛd] *f.*, Sweden

*suffire [syfiːr], to suffice

Suisse [sɥis] *f.*, Switzerland

de suite [dəsɥit], at once; **tout —**, immediately, at once

*suivre [sɥiːvr], to follow

sujet [syʒɛ] *m.*, subject

superflu [sypɛrfly] *m.*, superfluity

superflu, -e [sypɛrfly], superfluous

supplier [syplie], to entreat, beg

supprimer [syprime], to suppress

sur [syr], on, upon

sûr, -e [syːr], sure

surlendemain [syrlãdmɛ̃], day after tomorrow

surpris, -e [syrpri, -ːz], *p.p. of* ***surprendre**, surprised

synthèse [sɛ̃tɛːz] *f.*, synthesis

T

tabac [taba] *m.*, tobacco

table [tabl] *f.*, table

tableau [tablo] *m.*, painting, picture; **— de maître**, masterpiece

taille [taːj *or* tɑːj] *f.*, measure, stature, height (*of persons*)

tailler [taje *or* tɑje], to prune (trees)

tant [tã], so much

tant soit peu [tãswapø], ever so little, somewhat

tant y a que [tãtijakə], the fact remains that

tante [tãːt] *f.*, aunt

tantôt [tãto], a little while ago

tard [taːr], late

tas [tɑ] *m.*, heap

tasse [tɑːs] *f.*, cup

taureau [tɔro] *m.*, ox, bull

teint [tɛ̃] *m.*, complexion

tel [tɛl], such a

témoin [temwɛ̃] *m.*, witness

tempête [tãpɛːt] *f.*, tempest

tempêter [tãpɛte], to rage, fume

temple [tãːpl] *m.*, temple

temps [tã] *m.*, time, weather; **de — en —**, now and again

*tenir [təniːr], to hold

tente [tãːt] *f.*, tent

terre [tɛːr] *f.*, earth, soil, ground

tertre [tɛrtr] *m.*, mound

tête [tɛːt] *f.*, head; **tant par —**, so much a head

thé [te] *m.*, tea

thème [tɛm] *m.*, topic

thermomètre [tɛrmɔmɛtr] *m.*, thermometer

thym [tẽ] *m.*, thyme

tiers [tjɛɪr] *m.*, third part; — état [tjɛrzeta], the third estate

timbre [tẽɪbr] *m.*, stamp

timbre-poste [tẽbrpɔst] *m.*, postage-stamp

tirer [tire], to pull out

tissu [tisy] *m.*, tissue

tomber [tõbe], to fall

tombola [tõbɔla] *f.*, tombola, lottery

tome [toɪm] *m.*, volume

tonner [tɔne], to thunder

tort [tɔɪr] *m.*, wrong

tortueux, -se [tɔrtɥø, -ɪz], winding

tôt [to], early, soon

toucher [tuʃe], to touch

toujours [tuʒuɪr], always

tour [tuɪr] *m.*, round; trick; jouer un —, to play a trick

tour [tuɪr] *f.*, tower

tourner [turne], to turn

tousser [tuse], to cough

tout, -e, *pl. m.* tous, *f.* toutes [tu, tut, tu, tut], whole, all; tout à coup [tutaku], suddenly; tout à fait [tutafɛ], altogether; tout à l'heure [tutalœɪr], in a little while, presently; tout de suite [tutsɥit], at once; tout d'un coup [tudẽku], all at once; tout près [tuprɛ], nearby; tout ce que [tuskə], all that which

tracas [traka] *m.*, turmoil; worry

tracer [trase], to trace

traîner [trɛne], to pull, drag

*traire [trɛɪr], to milk

tranquille [trãkil], quiet

transalpin, -e [trãzalpẽ, -in], transalpine

transiger [trãziʒe], to compromise

transit [trãzit] *m.*, transit

travail [travaɪj] *m.*, work

travailler [travaje], to work; — comme quatre, to work like a horse

traverser [travɛrse], to cross

trembler [trãble], to tremble; — de peur, to tremble with fear

tremper [trãpe], to soak, dip

trésor [trezɔɪr] *m.*, treasure

tribun [tribœ̃] *m.*, tribune

trois [trwɑ], three

tromper [trõpe], to deceive

trompeur, -se [trõpœɪr, -øɪz] *adj.*, deceptive; *n. m.*, deceiver

trop [tro], too much, too many; de —, too much, too many; en —, too much, too many

trouble [trubl] *m.*, difficulty, pain

troublé, -e [truble], troubled, disquieted

troupeau [trupo] *m.*, herd

trouver [truve], to find

se trouver [sətruve], to be, find oneself

truite [trɥit] *f.*, trout

tuer [tɥe], to kill

se tuer [sətɥe] to commit suicide, kill oneself

tumeur [tymœɪr] *f.*, tumor
tunique [tynik] *f.*, tunic

U

uni, -e [yni], united
unir [yniɪr], to unite
unité [ynite] *f.*, unit
usage [yzaɪʒ] *m.*, use; *faire —
de,* to use
usine [yzin] *f.*, factory
utile[ytil], useful

V

vain, -e [vɛ̃, vɛn], vain; **en —,**
in vain, uselessly
*****vaincre** [vɛ̃ɪkr], to conquer
vallée [vale] *f.*, valley
*****valoir** [valwaɪr], to be worth;
— la peine, to be worth the
trouble
vapeur [vapœɪr] *m.*, steamer; *f.*,
steam
vase [vɑɪz] *m.*, vase; *f.*, mud
vaurien [vorjɛ̃] *m.*, wastrel
veille [vɛɪj] *f.*, the evening before
veiller [vɛje], to watch
venger [vɑ̃ʒe], to avenge
*****venir** [vəniɪr], to come; **— de**
(+ *inf.*), to have just
vent [vɑ̃] *m.*, wind
ver à soie [vɛraswɑ] *m.*, silk-
worm
Verdun [vɛrdœ̃] *m.*, Verdun
vermeil, -le [vɛrmɛɪj], rosy,
bright red
verre [vɛɪr] *m.*, glass; **— à boire,**
drinking glass
vers [vɛɪr], toward
verser [vɛrse], to pour

vert, -e [vɛɪr, vɛrt], green
vertu [vɛrty] *f.*, virtue
veston [vɛstɔ̃] *m.*, jacket
*****vêtir** [vɛtiɪr], to dress, clothe
veuf [vœf] *m.*, widower
veuvage [vœvaɪʒ] *m.*, widow-
hood
veuve [vœɪv] *f.*, widow
viande [vjɑ̃ɪd] *f.*, meat
vice [vis] *m.*, vice
vide [vid], empty
vie [vi] *f.*, life
vieillard [vjɛjaɪr] *m.*, old man
vieillot, -te [vjɛjo, -ɔt], oldish
vieux, vieil, vieille [vjø, vjɛɪj],
old
vif, -ve [vif, viɪv], vivid, lively
vilain, -e [vilɛ̃, -en], ugly
villageois [vilaʒwa] *m.*, villager
ville [vil] *f.*, town, city; **en —,**
in town
vin [vɛ̃] *m.*, wine
vingt [vɛ̃], twenty
visage [vizaɪʒ] *m.*, face
viser [vize], to aim
vite [vit], rapidly, quickly
vitrail [vitraɪj] *m.*, stained-glass
window
*****vivre** [viɪvr], to live, dwell
vœu [vø] *m.*, desire, vow
voici [vwasi], here is, here are
voilà [vwala], there is, there are
voile [vwal] *f.*, sail; *m.*, veil
*****voir** [vwaɪr], to see
voix [vwa] *f.*, voice
vol [vɔl] *m.*, flight, theft
voler [vɔle], to fly; to steal
voleur [vɔlœɪr] *m.*, thief
volonté [vɔlɔ̃te] *f.*, will
voltiger [vɔltiʒe], to fly about

vôtre [voːtr] *pron.*, yours

*vouloir [vulwaːr], to want,
wish; — bien, to be willing

voûte [vut] *f.*, vault, arch

voyage [vwajaːʒ] *m.*, travel, trip

voyager [vwajaʒe], to travel

vrai, -e [vrɛ], true

vue [vy] *f.*, sight, view; à la —
de, at the sight of

W

wagon [vagɔ̃] *m.*, coach, car
(railroad)

Y

y [i] *adv.*, there; *pron.*, to it, by
it, at it, to them, etc.

yacht [jɔt] *m.*, yacht

yeux [jø] *m.*, *pl. of* œil, eyes

Z

zèle [zɛːl] *m.*, zeal

zinc [zɛ̃ːg] *m.*, zinc

zizanie [zizani] *f.*, tare (weed);
quarreling, discord

zone [zoːn] *f.*, zone

A

to abandon, **abandonner**

to abide by, **obéir à**

to be able, ***pouvoir**

about, **de, vers**

to be acquainted with, ***connaître**

to act, **agir**

addition: in —, **de plus**

advice, **le conseil**

affair, **l'affaire** *f.*

after, **après**

afternoon, **l'après-midi** *m.* or *f.*

again, **de nouveau**

against, **contre**

age: for ages, **il y a un (des) siècle(s)**

aid, **l'aide** *f.*, **le secours**

all, **tout, -e,** *pl. m.,* **tous,** *pl. f.,* **toutes;** at —, **du tout**

ally, **l'allié** *m.*

alms, **l'aumône** *f.*

along, **le long de**

also, **aussi**

always, **toujours**

American, **américain, -e**

American, **l'Américain** *m.*

to amuse oneself, **s'amuser**

to be angry, **se fâcher, être fâché, -e**

answer, **la réponse**

anything, **n'importe quoi;** anything better, **ne . . . rien de mieux;** — else, **ne . . . rien d'autre**

appearance, **l'apparence** *f.;* in —, **en apparence**

arm, **le bras;** with open —s, **à bras ouverts**

army, **l'armée** *f.*

as, **comme;** — yet, **pas encore**

as for, **quant à**

to ask for, **demander**

to assure, **assurer**

at, **à;** — once, **tout de suite**

attractive, **attrayant, -e**

audacity, **l'audace** *f.*

B

back: to be —, ***être de retour**

bad, **mauvais, -e**

balloon, **le ballon**

to bathe, **se baigner**

battlefield, **le champ de bataille**

beautiful, **beau, bel, belle**

become, ***devenir**

before, **avant de** (+ *inf.*)

before, **devant** (location), **avant** (time)

believe, ***croire**

to belong to, **être à**

to bend, **plier**

beside, **à côté de**

better, (*adv.*) **mieux,** (*adj.*) **meilleur, -e**

bird, **l'oiseau** *m.*
black, **noir, -e**
to blame, **blâmer**
to blind, **aveugler**
to boast, **se vanter**
body, **le corps**; in —, **de corps**
to boil, ***bouillir**
book, **le livre**
bookshelf, **le rayon**
to be born, ***naître**
to borrow, **emprunter (à)**
bountiful, **bon, -ne, plein, -e**
  de bonté
box, **la boîte**
boy, **le garçon**
Brazil, **le Brésil**
to break, **rompre**
breakfast, **le petit déjeuner**
breeze, **la brise**
bridge, **le pont**
to bring, **apporter**
brother, **le frère**
to build, **bâtir**
but, **mais**
to buy, **acheter**

C

California, **la Californie**
to call on, **faire une visite (à)**
to be called, **s'appeler**
calm, **calme**
cap, **la casquette**
car, **l'automobile** *m.* or *f.*
card, **la carte**; to play —s,
  jouer aux cartes
cat, **le chat**
to catch, **attraper**
Catholic, **catholique**
cautious, **prudent**

celebrated, **célèbre, fameux, -se**
certainly, **certainement**
chair, **la chaise**
to change, **changer**
chap: my old —, **mon vieux**
charming, **charmant, -e**
child, **l'enfant** *m.* and *f.*
China, **la Chine**
to choose, **choisir**
cigar, **le cigare**
city, **la ville**
climate, **le climat**
to climb, **gravir**
to be closed, ***être fermé, -e**
to clothe, ***vêtir**
clothes, **les habits** *m.*, **les vête-**
  ments *m.*
cold: to catch a—, **attraper**
  un rhume
to come, ***venir**; — running,
  ***venir en courant**; — near,
  s'approcher de, approcher
comfortable, **confortable**
to commit, ***commettre**
common, **commun, -e**
companion, **le compagnon**
to complain, ***se plaindre**
comrade, **le** or **la camarade**
to concern, **concerner, regarder**
to conclude, ***conclure**
confidence, **la confiance**; to
  have —, **avoir confiance**
confusion, **la confusion**
to conquer, ***vaincre**
constant, **constant, -e**
to constitute, **constituer, *faire**
to converse about, ***s'entretenir**
  de
to convince, ***convaincre**
cook, **le cuisinier, le chef**
to cook, ***cuire, *faire cuire**

to co-operate, **coopérer**

council, **l'avis** *m.*, **le conseil**

country, **le pays**; in the —, **à la campagne**

courage, **le courage**

of course, **bien entendu**

coward, **lâche**

coward, **le lâche, le poltron, le couard**

cowardly, **en couard**

crime, **le crime**

to criticize, **critiquer**

to cross, **traverser**; — swords, **croiser l'épée**

crowd, **la foule**

cruel, **cruel, -le**

to cry, **pleurer**

to curse, **jurer**

custom, **la coutume**

to die, *****mourir**

direction: in the — of, **du côté de**

disagreeable, **désagréable**

to do, make, *****faire**

dog, **le chien**

dollar, **le dollar**

done, **fait, -e**

door, **la porte**

to doubt, **douter**

doubt, **le doute**; to have one's doubts, **avoir ses doutes**

downpour, **l'averse** *f.*

dozen, **la douzaine**

to dream, **rêver**

dress, **la robe**

to drink, *****boire**

to drive, *****conduire**

dry, **sec, sèche**

duty, **le devoir**

D

danger, **le danger**; in —, **en danger**

to dare, *****se permettre, oser**

dash, **l'élan** *m.*

to dash, **s'élancer**

daughter, **la fille**

day, **le jour, la journée**

deal: a great —, **beaucoup**

debt, **la dette**

defense, **la défense**

delighted, **enchanté, -e**

delightful, **délicieux, -se**

departure, **le départ**

desirable, **désirable**

to desire, **désirer**

desire, **le désir**

to despise, **mépriser**

to deteriorate, **détériorer**

E

each (*adj.*), **chaque**

each one (*pron.*), **chacun, -e**

to earn, **gagner**; — one's living, **gagner sa vie**

easy, **facile**

to eat, **manger**

else: anything —, **n'importe quoi, autre chose**

empty, **vide**

end, **la fin**

to end in, **finir par**

England, **l'Angleterre** *f.*

Englishman, **l'Anglais** *m.*

enough, **assez (de)**

to enter, **entrer (dans)**

enterprise, **l'entreprise** *f.*

envy, **l'envie** *f.*

equal, **égal, -e**

estate, **la propriété**
European, **européen, -ne**
even (*adv.*), **même**
event, **l'événement** *m.*
ever, **jamais**
ever so much, **beaucoup**
everybody, **tout le monde**
evil, **le mal**
to excel (in), **exceller (à)**
expensive, **coûteux, -se, cher, chère**
experience, **l'expérience** *f.*
extreme, **extrême**
eye, **l'œil** *m.*, *pl.* **yeux**

F

face, **la face, le visage, la figure**
to fail, ***faillir**
faithful, **fidèle**
to fall, **tomber**
family, **la famille**
famous, **célèbre, fameux, -se**
father, **le père**
fear, **la peur**
to fear, ***craindre**
to feel, ***sentir**
fellow, **le compagnon, le camarade**
field, **le champ**
to fight, ***se battre**
finally, **enfin, finir par, finalement**
to find, **trouver**
to flee, ***fuir, *s'enfuir**
floor, **l'étage** *m.*
foliage, **le feuillage**
to follow, ***suivre**

fortune, **la fortune**
for, **pour**
friend, **l'ami** *m.*
frontier, **la frontière**
future, **l'avenir** *m.*

G

game, **le jeu**
to gather, pick, ***cueillir, ramasser**
gay, **gai, -e**
general, **le général**
generous, **généreux, -se**
genius, **le génie**
gentle, **doux, douce**
gentleman, **un homme comme il faut, le monsieur**
George, **Georges**
gift, **le don, le présent, le cadeau**
to be glad to, **se réjouir de**
glove, **le gant**
to go, ***aller;** — away, ***s'en aller, *partir;** — on, **continuer;** — out, ***sortir**
to go by (a name), **porter**
God, **Dieu** *m.*
good, **bon, -ne**
gratitude, **la reconnaissance, la gratitude**
green, **vert, -e**
to grind, ***moudre**
to grow, ***croître**
guide, **le guide**

H

hand, **la main**
handsome, **beau, bel, belle**
hanger-on, **le parasite**

happen, **arriver, se passer**

happiness, **le bonheur**

hard, **fort** (*adv.*); to work —,
travailler dur

to hasten, **s'empresser, *accourir**; — to, **s'empresser
auprès de**

hasty, **prompt, -e, précipité, -e**

hat, **le chapeau**

to hate, ***haïr**

haughty, **fier, -ère**

headache, **le mal de tête**; to
have a —, **avoir mal à la tête**

to head for, **se diriger vers**

health, **la santé**

hear, **entendre**

heart, **le cœur**

to help, **aider, *secourir**

to help oneself, ***se servir (de)**

here, **ici**

high, **haut, -e**

hill, **la colline**

home, **à la maison, chez** (+
disj. pron.)

homework, **le devoir**

to honor, **honorer**

horse, **le cheval**

house, **la maison**

to hunt, **chasser**; go hunting,
*aller à la chasse

to hurry, **se hâter, se dépêcher**

I

idleness, **l'oisiveté** *f.*

ignorance, **l'ignorance** *f.*

important, **important, -e**

intelligence, **l'intelligence** *f.*

interest, **l'intérêt** *m.*

interested, **intéressé, -e**

interesting, **intéressant, -e**

to introduce, **présenter (à)**

to invite, **inviter (à)**

isn't it? **n'est-ce-pas?**

J

just, **donc**; — think, **pensez
donc**

just as, **tout comme**

just: to have —, ***venir de**

K

to keep, **garder**; — informed,
*tenir au courant

keeper, **le gardien**

kindness, **la bonté**

knife, **le couteau**

to knock at, **frapper à**

to know, ***savoir, *connaître** (to
be acquainted with)

L

laborious, **appliqué, -e,** (hard-
working); **industrieux, -se**

to be lacking, **manquer**

lady, **la dame**

large, **grand, -e**

last, **dernier, -ère**

late: to be —, ***être en retard**;
too —, **trop tard**

latest, **dernier, -ère**

to laugh, ***rire**

law, **la loi, le droit** (science)

laziness, **la paresse**

lazy, **paresseux, -se**

to lead, ***conduire, mener**

to leave, ***partir, laisser**

to lend, **prêter**

to listen to, **écouter**

to live, ***vivre, demeurer**

long, **longtemps**

to look at, **regarder**; — for, **chercher**; — like a sick man, **avoir l'air malade**; — after, **s'occuper de**

to lose, **perdre**

loser, **le perdant**

lost, **perdu, -e** (*p.p.* cf **perdre**)

M

man, **l'homme** *m.*

mannered: to be well —, **avoir de bonnes manières**

to mean, ***vouloir dire**

to meet, **rencontrer**

memory, **la mémoire**

to mention, **mentionner**

merely, **seulement**

merit, **le mérite**

Mexico, **le Mexique**

midnight, **minuit** *m.*

to milk, ***traire**

mind, **l'esprit** *m.*; in —, **d'esprit**

minute, **la minute**

miserable, **malheureux, misérable**

mistake, **la faute**

to be mistaken, **se tromper**

modesty, **la modestie**

moment, **le moment**

Monday, **le lundi**; by —, **lundi**

money, **l'argent** *m.*

morning, **le matin**

most, **la plupart de** (+ *art.*)

mother, **la mère**

mountain, **la montagne**

to mourn, **pleurer**

mouth, **la bouche**

to move, ***mouvoir**

much: ever so much, **beaucoup**

must, to have to, ***devoir**

N

name, **le nom**

narrow, **étroit, -e**

nasty, **méchant, -e**

nearly, **à peu près**

to be necessary, ***falloir, *être nécessaire**

neck, **le cou**

neither . . . nor, **ni . . . ni**

never, **ne . . . jamais, jamais**

new, **neuf, -ve, nouveau, nouvel, nouvelle**

next, **prochain, -e**

nice, **joli, -e, gentil, -le**

night, **la nuit**; at —, **la nuit**

no, **non, pas de**; — friends at all, **pas d'amis du tout**

not, **non, ne . . . pas, ne . . . point**; isn't it so? **n'est-ce pas?**

nothing, **ne . . . rien**

to notice, **remarquer**

now, **maintenant**; by —, **maintenant**; — . . . —, **tantôt . . . tantôt**

O

object, **l'objet** *m.*

o'clock, **l'heure** *f.*

to offer, ***offrir**

officer, **l'officier** *m.*

often, **souvent**

old, **vieux, vieil, vieille**; to be . . . —, **avoir . . . ans**

once, **une fois**

at once, **tout de suite, de suite**

one (*pron.*), **on**

only, only one, **seul, -e**

only, **seulement, ne . . . que**

to open, ***ouvrir**

opinion, l'opinion *f.*
to order, commander
outside, dehors
to overexert, se surmener
to owe, *devoir
owner, le propriétaire

P

painting, la peinture, le tableau
palace, le palais
paper, le papier
parasite, le parasite
pardon, le pardon
to pardon, pardonner
parents, les parents *m. pl.*
path, le sentier
patience, la patience
to pay, payer; — a visit, *faire
  une visite
peach, la pêche
people, les gens *m. pl.*
people, le monde
perseverance, la persévérance
person, la personne
perturbed, bouleversé, -e
physician, le médecin
picture, le tableau, la peinture,
  la photographie, l'image *f.*
to pity, *plaindre
plate, l'assiette *f.*
platinum, le platine
to play, jouer; — cards, jouer
  aux cartes; — the piano,
  jouer du piano
play, la pièce
to please, *plaire; if you please,
  please, s'il vous plaît
pleasure, le plaisir; to be a —
  to, *se faire un plaisir de

to plough, labourer
polite, poli, -e
poor, pauvre
poor, le pauvre
to possess, posséder
to practice, pratiquer, s'exercer
  à
presumption, la présomption
pretty, joli, -e
to prevent, empêcher
to print, imprimer
professor, le professeur
to promise, *promettre
proposition, la proposition
prosperity, la prospérité
to protect, protéger
Protestant, le protestant
to punish, punir
to put, *mettre

Q

quickly, vite

R

to rage, sévir
rain, la pluie
to rain, pleuvoir
rapidly, rapidement
ray, le rayon
to read, *lire
ready, prêt, -e
real, réel, -le
to receive, *recevoir
red, rouge
reed, le roseau
to require, demander
to resist, résister
to resolve, *résoudre

to rest, **se reposer**
to return, **rendre**
rich, **riche**
rich-looking, **avoir l'air riche**
riches, **la richesse**
river, **la rivière**
roof, **le toit**
room, **la chambre**
rose, **la rose**
rosy, **rose**
round, **rond, -e**
to run, ***courir**
to run through, ***parcourir, traverser**
to rush toward, **s'élancer vers**

S

sale, **la vente**; for —, **à vendre**
same, **même**
satisfied, **content, -e, satisfait, -e**
to say, ***dire**; that is to —, **c'est-à-dire**
school, **l'école** *f.*
secret, **le secret**
to see, ***voir**
to seem, ***paraître, sembler**
to sell, **vendre**
to send, ***envoyer**
to sew, ***coudre**
to shine, **briller, scintiller**
short, **court, -e**; in —, **en somme**
shutter, **le volet**
sick, **malade**
side, **le côté**; at (to) her —, **auprès d'elle**
sister, **la sœur**
to sit, ***s'asseoir**; to — down, ***s'asseoir**; to — up, **veiller**

skill, **le talent, l'habileté** *f.*
to sleep, ***dormir**
sleep, **le sommeil**
to smell, ***sentir**
so, **si, tellement**
society, **la société**
soldier, **le soldat**
someone, **quelqu'un**
something, **quelque chose**; — else, **quelque chose d'autre**
son, **le fils**
song, **le chant**
soon, **bientôt**
soup, **la soupe**
source, **la source**
South America, **l'Amérique du Sud** *f.*
Spaniard, **l'Espagnol** *m.*
to speak, **parler**
spectacle, **le spectacle**
spectator, **le spectateur**
to spend, **dépenser, passer**
spite: in — of, **malgré**
spot, **l'endroit** *m.*, **la place, le lieu**
star, **l'étoile** *f.*
to stay, **rester**
to steal, **voler**
steep, **raide, à pic**
step, **le pas**
story, **l'histoire** *f.*
stout, **gros, -se**
strange, **étrange**
stranger, **étranger, —** **ère**
street, **la rue**
strong, **fort, -e**
student, **l'élève** *m.* and *f.*, **l'étudiant** *m.*
study, **l'étude** *f.*; — hall, **la salle d'étude**

to study, **étudier**
to succeed in, **réussir à**
success, **le succès**
to suffice, ***suffire**
suit of clothes, **l'habit** *m.*, **le co-
stume, le complet**
sum, **la somme**
summer, **l'été** *m.*
sun, **le soleil**
supervisor, **le surveillant**
sure, **sûr, -e**
surprised, **surpris, -e** (*p.p.* of
***surprendre**)
surprising, **surprenant, -e**
to swear, **jurer, certifier sous
serment**
Swiss, **le Suisse**
Switzerland, **la Suisse**

T

to take, ***prendre**
tall, **grand, -e**
to telephone, **téléphoner**
to tell, ***dire**
theater, **le théâtre**
to think, **penser;** — of, **penser
à;** — of, **penser de** (*opinion*)
through, **par**
time, **le temps;** in —, **à temps**
tired, **fatigué, -e**
tobacco, **le tabac**
today, **aujourd'hui**
together, **ensemble**
tomorrow, **demain;** — morning,
demain matin
too many, **trop (de)**
to totter, **chanceler**
to touch, **toucher**
toward, **vers, envers**

tower, **la tour**
town, **la ville;** in —, **en ville**
trade, **le métier**
tragedy, **la tragédie**
train, **le train**
to travel, **voyager**
trip, **le voyage**
true, **vrai, -e**
to trust, **avoir confiance en**
truth, **la vérité**
twice, **deux fois**
tyrant, **le tyran**

U

uncle, **l'oncle** *m.*
to understand, ***comprendre**
to undertake, ***entreprendre**
unfortunate, **malheureux, -se**
ungrateful, **ingrat, -e**
uniform, **l'uniforme** *m.*
The United States, **les États-
Unis** *m. pl.*
to use, **employer, *se servir de**
useful, **utile**

V

valiant, **vaillant, -e**
valor, **la vaillance, le courage,
la valeur**
very, **très**
victory, **la victoire**
virtue, **la vertu**

W

to wait, **attendre**
to walk, **marcher, se promener;**
to take a walk, **se promener**

wall, **le mur**
to want, ***vouloir**
want, **le besoin**
to be wanting, **manquer de**
to warm up, **réchauffer**
to wash, **laver**
weapon, **l'arme** *f.*
weather, **le temps**
well, **bien;** — mannered, **comme il faut**
as well as, **aussi bien que**
what: — about me, **et moi donc**
what, **ce qui, ce que, quoi** (*relat. pron.*); — **que?** (*interrog. pron.*)
when, **quand, lorsque**
where, **où**
wherever, **où que, partout où**
while, **pendant que**
why, **pourquoi**
window, **la fenêtre**

wish, **le souhait, le désir**
to wish, ***vouloir, désirer**
wit, **l'esprit** *m.*
with, **avec, à, de**
without, **sans**
to withstand, **résister à**
work, **le travail**
to work, **travailler**
to worry, **se tourmenter, se tracasser**
to be worth, ***valoir**
to write, ***écrire**
written, **écrit, -e**

Y

year, **l'an** *m.*, **l'année** *f.*
yesterday, **hier**
yet: not —, **pas encore**

INDEX

à: contraction 1; with disjunctive pronouns 56; before infinitive 162-165; meanings 187-188.

a from **avoir** 3.

active voice 89.

adjectival clause: subjunctive in 143.

adjectives: agreement 25; comparative in a sentence 29; comparative and superlative 28-29; demonstrative 38; formation of feminine 25; gender 25-26; indefinite 47; interrogative 38-39; number 27; numeral 45-46; position 27-28; possessive 37-38; qualifying 25-29.

adverbial clauses: subjunctive in 144-145.

adverbs: comparison 181; derivative 178-179; formation 178-180; position 180-181; primitive 178.

agreement (*gender, number, person*): of demonstrative adjectives 38; of demonstrative pronouns 64; of past participles 58, 155-156; of personal pronouns 52; of possessive adjectives 37; of possessive pronouns 62; of qualifying adjectives 25; of verbs 166-168.

-aine 46

aller: idiomatic uses 72-73; with infinitive 126; with past participle 173.

anterior tenses: 20, 117-119, see also Appendix.

articles: definite 1-3, 38; indefinite 8, 39; partitive 9-10.

au, aux 1.

aucun: with **ne** 47, 83, 196.

aussi . . . que 29.

autrui: 81

auxiliary verbs: *see avoir, être*.

avoir: in compound tenses 19-21; conjugation of 3-4, 10, 203-205; replaced by **être** 99; with **sortir** 100.

-ayer: verbs in 57.

ce: contraction 8; demonstrative adjective 38; demonstrative pronoun 64, 65; for indefinite article 8; use in familiar speech 142.

ce dont 72.

ce que, ce qui 72.

ceci 63.

cela 63.

cent 46.

-cer: verbs in 57.

c'est: for **il est** 8, 142.

-ci: with demonstrative adjectives 38; with demonstrative pronouns 63.

combien de temps 182.

comme: 194.

comparison: of adjectives 28-29; of adverbs 181; in a sentence 29.

compound tenses 19-20, 58.

conditional mood: perfect form 21; present form 20; uses 90, 133-135.

conditional sentences 136.

conjugations 89, 208-225.

conjunctions: co-ordinating 191-193; subordinating 145, 193-195.

conjunctive pronouns 52-55.

connaître: idiomatic uses 84-85.

dans 190.

de: for **à** 64; contractions 9-10; before infinitive 161-162, 164; meanings 188-189; with numeral nouns 46; partitive article 9-10.

definite articles 1-3; for possessive adjective 38.

demonstrative adjectives 38.

demonstrative pronouns 63-65.

depuis quand 181-182.

derivative adverbs 178-179.

des: contraction of **de** plus **les** 1; distinguished from **quelque** 47; partitive article 9-10.

descendre: with **avoir**, 100.

deuxième 46.

devoir: idiomatic uses 83-84.

disjunctive pronoun 52, 55-56.

dont 70-71.

douzaine 46.

du: contraction of **de** plus **le** 1; partitive article 9-10.

-eler: verbs in 66.

en: adverb 53; preposition 186, 189-190; pronoun 53-55.

entrer: with **avoir** 100.

-er: verbs in 39 note.
est-ce que 39, 47, 80.
-eter: verbs in 66.
être: in compound tenses 19-21; conjugation 3-4, 10, 205-207; with intransitive verbs of motion (for **avoir**) 99; with pronominal verbs 57-58.
euphonic l, 81-82.
euphonic -t- 40.

faire: idiomatic uses 92-93.
falloir: idiomatic uses 91-92.
feminine, *see agreement:* adjectives 25-26; nouns 15-17.
future: anterior, or perfect, 20, 126-127; irregular stems of present 11; present 11; replaced by **aller** 72; uses of future tenses 97, 125-127.

gender, *see agreement:* adjectives 25-26; definite article 1; interrogative adjectives 38-39; nouns 15-17; numbers 46.
-ger: verbs in 57.

"how long" 182.

idiomatic expressions 6, 13, 22, 32, 42, 49, 58, 67, 75-76, 85, 94, 103, 112, 122, 130, 137, 149-150, 158, 169, 175-176, 183-184, 196: list of 226-233.
-ième 46.
"if" clause 136.
il: with impersonal verbs 48.
il est: distinguished from **c'est** 64.
imperative mood 90: irregular form 66; regular forms 66; replaced by infinitive 166; tonic pronouns with 54-55; uses 171-172.
imperfect indicative: forms 10; uses 98-99.
imperfect subjunctive: forms 147-148; uses 152-153.
impersonal verbs 48.
indefinite adjectives 47.
indefinite article 8; omission 39.
indefinite pronouns 81-83.
infinitive mood 161-165; uses 90, 165-166.
intensive disjunctive pronoun 56.
interrogation: word order 80.
interrogative: adjectives 28-29; form of verbs 39-40, 47-48; pronouns 79-81.
irregular present subjunctive forms 157.

irregular verbs 218-225.

-là, with demonstrative adjectives 38; with demonstrative pronouns 63.
le, la, les: as definite article 1-3; for possessive adjective 38; as pronoun 52, 55.
lequel 71.
l'on 81-82.
lorsque 97.

-même: in intensive disjunctive pronouns 55.
même: adverb 83; pronoun 83.
mettre: idiomatic uses 129.
mil 46.
mille 46.
moi for **me** 54-55.
moins: in comparative 28.
moins . . . que 29.
mon for **ma** 37.
monter: with **avoir** 100.
moods 89-90: conditional 20-21, 90, 133-135; imperative 54-55, 66, 90, 171-172; indicative 90, *see tenses*; infinitive 90, 161-166; participial 90, 172-174, 205 ff.; subjunctive 90, 136, 140-148, 157, 172.

ne: with **aucun** 47; with **nul** 47, 83, 196; with **pas** 47-48; without **pas** 195-196; with **que** 13 note.
negation 192.
negative form of verb 3: -interrogative form of verb 47-48.
noun clause: subjunctive in 141-142.
nouns: common 15; gender 1, 15-17; number 18-19; proper 15.
nul: with **ne** 47, 83, 196.
number, *see agreement:* of adjectives 27, 37-38; of definite article 1; of indefinite article 8; of nouns 1, 18-19; in numerals 46; of past participle 58; of pronouns 52, 62, 64; of verbs 167-168.
numbers, *see numerals.*
numeral: adjectives 45-46; nouns 46.
numerals: cardinal 45-46; ordinal 46.

omission: of indefinite article 39; of **pas** 195-196.
on: with euphonic l, 81; indefinite pronoun 81-82; for passive voice 119.
orthographic peculiarities of verbs 57, 65-66.
ou: conjunction 192.
où: pronoun 71.

par 190.

participial mood 90: forms 205ff.; present 172-173; past 173-174; uses 172-174.

partitive article 9-10.

pas: omission of 195-196; with un 83.

passive voice: agreement of past participle in 155-156; forms of 109-110; substitutions for 119-120; uses of 89.

past anterior tense: forms 20, see also Appendix; uses 117-119.

past definite tense: forms 3, 10-11; uses 108-109.

past indefinite tense, *see perfect tense*.

past participle, *see moods, passive voice:* agreement 58, 155-156; uses 173-174.

penser: idiomatic uses 120-121.

perfect tense: forms: indicative 19-20, see also Appendix, conditional 20-21 subjunctive 148; uses: indicative 107-108, subjunctive 153.

personal pronouns 52-56.

personne 82, 196.

peu: singular verb after le peu 167.

plaire: idiomatic uses 101.

pluperfect tense: forms: indicative 19-20, subjunctive 148; uses: indicative 116-117, subjunctive 136, 153-154.

plural, *see number*.

plus: comparative 28; with de 29; with que 29.

possessive: adjectives 37-38; pronouns 62.

pouvoir: idiomatic uses 73.

premier 46.

prepositions 186-196: past participles as 174.

present indicative of irregular verbs: acquérir 148; aller 31; assaillir 168; asseoir 121; battre 85; boire 85; bouillir 168; conclure 174; conduire 175; connaître 48; coudre 136; courir 74; craindre 93; croire 74; croître 93; cueillir 196; devoir 31, 128; dire 40; dormir 128; écrire 121; envoyer 175; faire 31; falloir 85; fuire 121; haïr 196; lire 111; luire 136; maudire 136; mettre 49; moudre 182; mourir 101; mouvoir 110; naître 101; offrir 128; partir 58, 128; plaire 93; pleuvoir 111; pourvoir 129; pouvoir 40; prendre 58; recevoir 129; résoudre 182; rire 67; savoir 49; suffrire 148; suivre 67; se taire 196; tenir 196; traire 182; vaincre 129; valoir 148; venir 58; vêtir 111; vivre 74; voir 67; vouloir 40.

present participle, *see moods:* uses 172-173.

present tense: forms: conditional 20; indicative 10, subjunctive 147, uses: conditional 133-134, indicative 96-97, 182, subjunctive 152.

primary tenses 91.

primitive adverbs 178.

principal parts: irregular verbs, *see List of Irregular Verbs in Appendix;* regular verbs 29-30.

pronominal voice 89: agreement of past participles in compound tenses 58, 155-156; forms 57.

Pronouns: demonstrative 63-65; indefinite 81-83; interrogative 79-81; personal: conjunctive 52-55, position 54, disjunctive 52, 55-56; possessive 62; relative: compound 71-72, simple 70-71; tonic 54-55.

qualifying adjectives 25-29.

quand 97, 193-194.

que 29, 64, 193.

quel 8, 38-39.

quelque: distinguished from des 47.

qu'est-ce que, qu'est-ce que c'est que 80.

quiconque 82.

reciprocal verbs 58, 89.

reflexive: for passive 120; pronoun 53; verbs 89; voice 89.

regular conjugations 208-218.

relative pronouns 70-72.

rien 82, 196.

savoir: idiomatic uses 73-74.

se: with reciprocal verbs 58; as reflexive pronoun 53.

second 46.

secondary tenses 91.

sequence of tenses: in conditional sentences 136; with subjunctive 154.

si: in comparisons 29; uses 194-195.

son for sa 37.

sortir with avoir 100.

subjunctive mood: tenses: formation 146-148, irregular forms in the present 157, sequence 154; uses 90, 152-154: in adjectival clauses 143, in adverbial clauses 144-146, in commands 172; in conditional sentences 136, in main clauses 146, in noun clauses 141.

subordinating conjunctions 145, 193-195.

superlative: subjunctive in 143.

sur 191.
syntax of past participle 174.

-t-: inserted in interrogative verb.
temps surcomposés 127 note.
tenses 90-91: compound 19-20, 47;
formation from principal parts of
verbs, 29-30; future anterior: forms
20; uses 126-127; future indicative:
forms 11; uses 125-126; imperfect
indicative: forms 10; uses 98-99;
imperfect subjunctive: 147-148;
past anterior: forms 20; uses 117-
119; past definite: forms 3, 10-11;
uses 108-109; perfect conditional:
forms 20-21; uses 134-135; perfect
indicative: forms 19-20; uses 107-
108; perfect subjunctive: 148; pluperfect indicative: forms 19-20;
uses 116-117; pluperfect subjunctive: 148; present conditional:
forms 20; uses 133-134; present
indicative: forms 10; uses 96-97,
182; present subjunctive: forms
147; uses, *see subjunctive mood*.
toi for te 54-55.
ton for ta 37.
tonic pronouns 54-55.
tout, toute, tous, toutes 83.
tout le monde: singular verb after
167.

un: indefinite article 8; indefinite pronoun 81, 83; numeral 46.
unième 46.

valoir: idiomatic uses 120
vas for va 66.
verbal syntax 166-168.
verbs, *see mood, tense, voice:* agreement 166-168; auxiliary 3, 10, 19-
20, 203-207; impersonal 48; interrogative form 39-40, 47-48; intransitive 99, 155-156; irregular: principal parts 218-225; negative form
3, 47-48; orthographic peculiarities
57, 65-66; with prepositions before
infinitive: with à 162-165, with de
161-162, 164; with no preposition
before infinitive 163-164; principal
parts 29-30; pronominal 89; reciprocal 58, 89; reflexive 89; regular
conjugations 208-218.
vingt 46.
voices: active 89; passive 89: agreement 155-156; forms 109-110; pronominal 89: agreement 155-156.
voici 64.
voilà 64.
vouloir: idiomatic uses 100; use in
second person plural 66 note.

y: adverb 53; pronoun 53.
-yer: verbs in 53.

946
877
794
1,676
989